Peter Lucantoni

Cambridge IGCSE®

English as a Second Language

Teacher's Book

Fifth edition

CAMBRIDGE
UNIVERSITY PRESS

University Printing House, Cambridge CB2 8BS, United Kingdom

One Liberty Plaza, 20th Floor, New York, NY 10006, USA

477 Williamstown Road, Port Melbourne, VIC 3207, Australia

314–321, 3rd Floor, Plot 3, Splendor Forum, Jasola District Centre, New Delhi – 110025, India

79 Anson Road, #06–04/06, Singapore 079906

Cambridge University Press is part of the University of Cambridge.

It furthers the University's mission by disseminating knowledge in the pursuit of education, learning and research at the highest international levels of excellence.

www.cambridge.org
Information on this title: www.cambridge.org/9781108566698 (Paperback)

First published 2018

20 19 18 17 16 15 14 13 12 11 10 9 8 7 6 5 4 3 2 1

Printed in Spain by GraphyCems

A catalogue record for this publication is available from the British Library

ISBN 978-1-108-56669-8 Paperback

....

Contents

Introduction

This Teacher's Book supports the *Cambridge IGCSE English as a Second Language Coursebook*, fifth edition.

The Teacher's Book provides the following:

- full guidance on how to approach all the tasks in the Coursebook
- suggestions for differentiated activities to use with mixed-ability classes
- answers to the exercises in the Coursebook
- sample answers to exam-style questions
- marking and grading criteria for Core and Extended writing and speaking

The Coursebook is divided into 20 units, with each one focusing on particular aspects of the Cambridge IGCSE English as a Second Language syllabus. Speaking skills are integrated throughout the book and are practised through discussion work, role play and specific tasks. While it is probably best to follow the units consecutively, there is no reason why teachers should not focus on a particular language skill or exam question. Videos are not representative of exam conditions. Teachers should refer to published material on how to conduct oral tests for precise details. When practising speaking tests it is best if the same person is not the examiner all the time.

The material becomes progressively more demanding, with longer and more advanced reading and listening texts in the second half of the book. The exercises in the 'Further practice' section of each unit are particularly useful for homework, for early finishers or for practice outside the classroom, and the exam-style questions at the end of each unit could be used in class to give students a feel for the examination itself. Note that the word limit for writing activities is 100–150 for the Core curriculum and 150–200 for the Extended curriculum. Throughout this resource, you will find sample answers for most of the exam-style questions, including examples from both the Core and Extended curricula. The author is wholly responsible for the answers to the exam-style questions.

The progressive step-by-step approach of *Cambridge IGCSE English as a Second Language* – including Top Tips that focus on key areas and Language Tips that highlight specific vocabulary and grammar items – will help to build students' confidence in all the main skill areas, while also developing the techniques and additional skills necessary for success.

For each activity, suggestions are made about whether students should work on their own, in pairs, in small groups or as a whole class. These are offered as a guide only – the amount of time available and the number of students in the class will determine the best approach. However, it is a good strategy to include activities with different group sizes within each lesson; this offers variety and gives students the opportunity to interact in different ways. To promote confidence, try not to interfere too much when students are working together (whether in pairs or in small groups), but monitor and provide support if requested. You can, of course, make notes to deliver as feedback once students have completed the activity.

Peter Lucantoni

Assessment criteria
for writing and speaking

Below are the criteria for Cambridge IGCSE English as a Second Language writing and speaking. For full details, go to the Cambridge International Examinations website.

Writing

Marks	Content (maximum 8 marks)	Marks	Language (maximum 8 marks)
7–8	**Relevance** • Instructions are followed. • Consistently appropriate style and tone for the text type. • Excellent sense of purpose and audience. **Development of ideas** • Writing is very well developed, at an appropriate length. • Meaning is communicated skilfully and effectively.	7–8	**Range and accuracy** • A varied range of high and low frequency vocabulary used competently. • A varied level of complex and simple sentence structures used appropriately. • A considerable level of language accuracy throughout. Some errors may remain, but these do not hinder communication of ideas or meaning. • The errors present relate to low frequency vocabulary and more complicated structures. **Organisation** • Consistently well-organised and ordered. • A varied range of connecting words and other cohesive methods, used consistently well.
5–6	**Relevance** • Instructions are followed. • Generally appropriate style and tone for the text type. • Generally good sense of purpose and audience. **Development of ideas** • Writing is developed, at an appropriate length. • Meaning is generally communicated clearly.	5–6	**Range and accuracy** • A good range of high frequency vocabulary used competently. Attempts to use some lower frequency vocabulary. • A good range of simple sentence structures used competently. Attempts to use some more complex sentence structures. • A good accuracy level throughout. Some errors are present, but these usually do not hinder communication. • The errors present usually relate to low frequency vocabulary or more complex sentence structures. **Organisation** • Often well-organised and ordered. • A varied range of connecting words and other cohesive methods, used appropriately.

Marks	Content (maximum 8 marks)	Marks	Language (maximum 8 marks)
3–4	*Relevance* • Instructions are generally followed. • Reasonably appropriate style and tone for the text type, but this may not be consistent. • Some sense of purpose and audience. *Development of ideas* • Some development of writing, but it may be repetitive or insufficient in some areas. • Meaning is communicated, but may lack clarity in places.	3–4	*Range and accuracy* • Mostly uses high frequency vocabulary, reasonably appropriately. • Mostly uses simple sentence structures, usually appropriately. • Reasonable accuracy level throughout. Some errors may hinder communication. • Errors are present when using some high frequency vocabulary or simple sentence structures. *Organisation* • Reasonably organised and sequenced. • Some connecting words and other cohesive methods, used reasonably appropriately.
1–2	*Relevance* • Instructions may only be partially followed. • Style and tone for the text type may be inappropriate. • Inappropriate sense of purpose and audience. *Development of ideas* • Limited attempt to develop writing, there may be gaps, irrelevance and/or repetition. • Limited attempt to communicate meaning, it lacks clarity in places.	1–2	*Range and accuracy* • Limited use of vocabulary. • Limited use of sentence structures. • Lack of control of vocabulary. Meaning is generally unclear. • Errors occur when using common vocabulary and simple sentence structures. *Organisation* • Organisation lacks order. • Limited attempt to use connecting words and other cohesive methods.
0	• No response worthy of credit.	0	• No response worthy of credit.

Speaking

Give a mark out of 10 for each category (structure, vocabulary, development and fluency), and then add these marks to give an overall total out of 30.

Mark	Structure	Vocabulary	Development and fluency
9–10	The student demonstrates their ability to use a range of sentence structures accurately, confidently and consistently.	The student demonstrates enough command of vocabulary to respond to questions with accuracy and understanding. Meaning is conveyed with precision, and some sophisticated ideas are communicated.	The student demonstrates a continued ability to maintain a conversation and to contribute appropriately. The student can respond to changes in the direction of conversation. There is clarity in pronunciation and intonation.
7–8	Sentence structures are usually sound, but are not used entirely accurately or with confidence. There are some errors when more complex sentence structures are attempted.	The student has a sufficient range of vocabulary to convey meaning and ideas with competence.	The student responds relevantly and at length which makes frequent prompting unnecessary. The student can hold a competent conversation, and pronunciation and intonation are generally clear.
5–6	The student can use simple structures efficiently but has some difficulty venturing beyond them.	Vocabulary conveys simple ideas and information with clarity. Errors are somewhat noticeable, and only partial competence is achieved.	The student attempts to respond to questions and prompts. Effort and additional prompting is necessary to develop the conversation. There is some lack of clarity of pronunciation and intonation, but it is unlikely to impede communication.
3–4	Sentence structures will largely be very simple, limited and with some errors, which will hinder communication.	Vocabulary is not particularly varied and there is difficulty in conveying simple ideas. There is hesitation and repetition.	Responses are short and widely spaced. The student has to be encouraged to develop brief responses and continue the conversation. Pronunciation and intonation cause some difficulties in communication.
1–2	Some attempt at a response will be made during the conversation. Attempts at structured sentences will rarely achieve satisfactory communication.	Vocabulary will generally be insufficient to convey simple ideas.	Responses are so brief that little is communicated. The student hardly engages in conversation. Pronunciation and intonation patterns cause difficulty for the listener.
0	Completely limited/no attempt at a response.	Completely limited/no attempt at a response.	Completely limited/no attempt at a response.

Focus on reading: skimming and scanning

NOTE on Assessment Objectives (AOs) for Reading and Writing Exercise 1: In reading activities which assess *skimming* and *scanning* skills, students read a text (for example: an article, blog or web page) and answer a series of questions with short/single-word answers. This type of activity requires students to identify and select relevant information (R1).

Learning objectives (LOs)

There are **five** LOs in every unit. The first LO always focuses on the video which students watch and respond to at the start of the unit, while the other four LOs highlight the particular skills which students will use and develop throughout the unit. It is essential for students to understand the purpose of the unit, so the LOs box is important.

Suggested activity: Start every unit by focusing for a few minutes on the LOs box, making sure that students understand what they are going to be doing. Using the first LO as an example, ask students to identify where in the unit they can find the activities for the other four LOs. Get students to say which of the activities appeal to them the most, and ask them for their reasons.

A Watch, listen and talk

Note: In this new fifth edition, **Section A** in every unit is called **Watch, listen and talk**. Students will watch and listen to some IGCSE students talking about the unit's main topic, and carry out a task. These tasks will be quite broad in scope, asking students to make notes rather than answer comprehension questions. Then, after watching and listening, students have the chance to talk to each other about the task they completed, and to introduce their own ideas about the topic. This section provides an important introduction to the unit, and links directly to **Section B Speaking and vocabulary**.

1a Whole class then alone

Explain that your students are going to watch and listen to some IGCSE students talking about their **free time**. The videos are unscripted, i.e. the students were asked to respond to some prompts and to speak freely, without any help. As your students watch and listen, they should make notes about **three** things that the speakers enjoy doing, and **three** things that they do not enjoy doing in their free time. Play the video a second time so that students can check or add to their notes.

Differentiated activities

Note: Use differentiated activities to both support and challenge your students. Apply differentiated activities from the earlier units as you progress through the book. Just because an activity appears in Unit 1 does not mean that you cannot use it somewhere else.

Support

Provide a list of five or six possible answers. Students listen for the ones which the speakers actually mention (or do not mention).

Challenge

i   Allow stronger students to listen to but **not** watch the video during the first playing. This will increase the challenge and encourage students to listen more carefully. Make sure these students are allowed to watch the video during the second playing.

ii Students expand on their notes, adding one or two extra details for each speaker.

Answers

a   Things that the students enjoy doing (any **three** from): drawing, painting, engraving, arts and crafts, creative writing, lying on the beach, lying on the grass, reading books (includes comic books and reading novels), swimming, playing tennis, watching a band perform.

Three things that the students do not enjoy doing: going on the computer, playing video games, shopping.

1b Pairs or small groups

Depending on the size of your class, put students into pairs or small groups. They can discuss their notes and then talk to each other about the things that **they** like and do not like doing in **their** free time. Do not interfere too much, but make sure you get feedback from the class so that they know their efforts have been worthwhile. If time permits, you could write their ideas on the board and rank them according to your students' preferences.

B Speaking and vocabulary

Note: In this new fifth edition, **Section B** in every unit is called **Speaking and vocabulary**. There is a specific link to **Section A**, and the unit topic is expanded further. Students are introduced to key vocabulary, and are given the opportunity to not only talk more about the topic, but also move into other areas of discussion relating to the topic. Very often, there are no right or wrong answers and it is worth pointing this out to students. Encourage them to speculate, to discuss their ideas and to give reasons for their choices.

1 Pairs or small groups

With this type of question, when students write down their words or phrases, do not worry too much about language accuracy, as this may create a barrier to creativity. Use the question: *What do these pictures show?* to promote discussion in English. You could offer help to students with derivatives of words, for example: *relaxing – relax, relaxed, relaxation.*

When students have finished, gather class feedback. Again, remember that there are no right or wrong answers, so encourage all your students to participate – even the ones who need more support.

Possible answers

shopping, having fun, playing sport, meeting up with friends, surfing the internet and so on

> **LANGUAGE TIP**
> Throughout the Coursebook, you will find **Language Tip** boxes. The aim of these is to draw students' attention to areas of language that may cause them problems. The tip in Unit 1 – **B Speaking and vocabulary** will help students with Activity B2, so make sure you focus on it immediately after students have finished Activity B1.
>
> In this new fifth edition, at the end of some **Language Tips**, there is a note directing students to an accompanying activity in their **Workbook**. You could use the **Workbook** for early-finishers to keep them busy, or for any student who needs extra support, or for whole class homework.

2 Alone, then pairs or small groups

Again there are no right or wrong answers here. Students work alone and add their own ideas to the table, using the previous activities for help if necessary.

When students have written down their ideas, get them to compare their lists in pairs, identifying similarities and differences.

In class feedback, encourage students to talk not only about their own ideas, but also their partner's, to give them some practice in using the third person singular.

Differentiated activities

Support

i   Reduce the number of ideas they need to write – perhaps ask for just two or three.

ii   Get them to copy any ideas from Activity B1.

Challenge

Ask them to write complete sentences as in the **Language Tip**, rather than just notes.

C Reading

> **TOP TIP**
> Throughout the Coursebook, you will find **Top Tip** boxes. The aim of these is to draw students' attention to areas of the examination, or particular examination-taking skills, that are especially important. **Top Tip** boxes can be useful for revision nearer to the examination and can be used by students to test each other on key areas. The first one in Unit 1 – **C Reading** will provide more guidance and feedback to Activity C1.

1 Pairs

These pre-reading discussion questions are designed to get students thinking about how they read a text, and there are no right or wrong answers. The purpose is to encourage students to discuss in English (as much as possible), and they should not be corrected if they make mistakes. During feedback, establish that when we read for pleasure, we often read in a different way from when we are trying to find something quickly in a text (for example in an examination situation).

2 Alone

This activity gives students an example of how important skim reading is. Give students 10 seconds to answer questions **a** and **b**.

Answers

a   six   b   Datasource NewsFeed

3 Whole class

Get students to tell you how they found the answers in the previous activity. Encourage them to be specific about the reading skill/s they used.

4 Alone

Make sure students understand what the question is asking for, so they know what they should be looking for in the text (the % sign). They do not need to write anything yet.

Answer

Datasource Trainer

5 Alone

The purpose of this activity is to show students that they do not need to write long answers for this type of question. While all the options **a–e** are correct, the best answer here is probably **d** (Datasource Trainer), because it is short and concise. No time would be wasted in writing a long answer. Make sure students understand that they simply need to include all the necessary information – which may only be one or two words. Full sentences are not normally necessary.

TOP TIP

The second **Top Tip** in Unit 1 – **C Reading** reinforces the point about students not having to write long answers for this type of question. It also draws students' attention to the importance of including symbols or units of measurement in their answers, if required.

6 Pairs

Before they begin this activity, remind students not to write anything yet. Give them time to work through the questions **a–g**, asking and answering.

7 Pairs

Working together, students write the answers to the questions in Activity C6. Then they exchange their answers with a different pair and check for similarities and differences. During class feedback, you can provide the answers if students have missed anything.

Answers

a   three (Puzzle Finder, Trainer, Comic Fun)

b   by signing up to the Datasource loyalty scheme

c   Datasource Puzzle Finder

d   a million

e   three from: get a voucher for $5; 21-day money-back, no-questions asked guarantee; monthly newsletter; membership card and number

f   NewsFeed

g   Comic Fun

Differentiated activities

Support

Tell/Show students in which part of the text they can find the answers to the questions.

Challenge

Get them to work alone when they write their answers to Activity C6. If they finish quickly, ask them to write two or three more questions about the Datasource text, then give them to a partner to answer.

8 Alone

Knowing where a text comes from can help students to understand more about its layout and content. Students quickly look at the text and then choose one of the options in the box. There is no right or wrong answer – the important thing is to encourage students to give a *reason* for their choice. However, because of the internet address at the top of the text, hopefully students will identify this text as coming from a website.

9 Pairs

Students need to have an effective strategy for approaching all types of examination exercises and reading the question carefully before doing anything else saves a lot of time.

Answer

b, **d**, **c**, **a**

10 Alone

You can follow a similar approach to Activities C6 and C7, but this time students work alone. They do not need to write the answers to the questions yet, but should identify and note down the key word/s in each question.

Suggested answers

Different students may choose different key words. They can check their choices when they come to write their answers in Activity C11.

3

a Who

b When / next publication

c How many / sections

d maximum number / creative story

e angry / which section

f Which section / how many words

g finished / what / do

h How long / title

i final box / not receive

> **TOP TIP**
> The **Top Tip** next to Activity C10 introduces students to the idea of key words in questions.

11 Alone, then pairs

Students write their answers in their notebooks. Remind them to keep their answers brief, but to include all the information that the questions ask for. When they have finished, students discuss and check their answers. Words in brackets below are optional; words separated by / are alternative answers.

Answers

a teenagers (who want to share their writing)

b 31st July

c four / 4

d 275

e My Opinion

f My Poem

g complete and submit the form (electronically)

h (maximum) five / 5 words

i information about other products

D Language focus: adjective + noun

1a Alone

Focus on the position of the adjective before the noun in the examples. Point out that other languages may use a different word order. Also mention that it is possible – and quite common – to have more than one adjective. Then students complete the short definition about adjectives in part **a**.

Answer

Adjectives are used to provide **more information/details** about **nouns**. In English, adjectives usually come **before** the noun.

1b Pairs

Highlighting or comparing with L1 can help students to remember things in L2, so use this activity to do exactly that.

2 Alone, then pairs

The purpose of this activity is to encourage students to notice language in context, so that they can focus on both form and meaning. Allocate two to three minutes for students to skim the two texts (Datasource and You Write!) to find at least three more examples from each. Then they can compare their answers with a partner.

Answers

Datasource text: new + apps, special + discount + price, normal + download + price, amazing + app, up-to-date + app, online + puzzles, discount + price, amazing + images, amazing + price, incredible + app, fantastic + app, free + minutes, favourite + movies, new + releases, delightful (but) + simple + app, huge + number, next + purchase, monthly + digital + newsletter

You Write! text: amazing + online + webzine, next + issue, funny (or) + serious + original + creative + stories, interesting + person, unusual + place, funny + pet, extreme + weather, inspired + writing, new + cinema, local + team, recent + match, First + name, last + birthday, other + products, such + information

Differentiated activities

Support

i Tell them to look at only one of the two texts.

ii Provide students with a list of the answers and ask them to find these in the two texts.

Challenge

i Get them to find more than three examples.

ii Students work in pairs, with each student looking at only one text. They then tell each other an adjective (without the noun) from their text, to see if their partner can remember the noun. Then they change roles.

3 Alone, then pairs

Tell students to copy the table into their notebooks, then to fill in as many gaps as possible. Make sure they understand that not all the gaps can be filled, and that more than one answer may be possible in some cases. When they have done as much as they can, pair them up to check their answers. Allow them to use different reference sources for help.

Adjective	Noun	Adverb	Verb
amazing	amazement	amazingly	amaze
special	speciality, specialisation, specialist	specially	specialise
incredible	incredulity	incredibly	
delightful	delight	delightfully	delight
funny	fun	funnily	
serious	seriousness	seriously	
original	origin, originator	originally	originate
creative	creation, creator	creatively	create

4 Alone, then pairs

Students choose at least five more adjectives from the texts they have read and add them to their table. Then they add the corresponding noun, adverb and verb for each one. They can use different reference sources for help, then check their answers with a partner.

5 Alone, then pairs

There are many possible adjective endings. From the previous activities, students should be able to identify the following: -ing, -al, -ible, -ful, -y, -ious, -ive, -ent, -ed, but there are others too. Students then write three words for each adjective ending.

6 Alone

This activity gives students the opportunity to use adjective + noun combinations in their own writing.

Differentiated activities

Support

i   Reduce the number of sentences students need to write.

ii Tell students to use the adjective + noun combinations from the text in their own sentences.

Challenge

Ask students to write more complex sentences – perhaps with adjective + adjective + noun combinations.

> **WORD TIP**
>
> This is a new feature in the fifth edition, which focuses on commonly confused pairs of words which students will have come across in the unit's listening or reading texts. The **Word Tip** box includes contextualised examples for the words, and a request for students to complete an exercise in their **Workbook**.

E Speaking: Showing preferences and making suggestions

Speaking is an important part of many English as a Second Language examinations. In this section, students have the opportunity to listen to and use language to express preferences and make suggestions.

1 Alone

Tell students they are going to listen to a short exchange between two teenagers, which includes expressions showing a preference or making a suggestion. Ask students to give you some examples of both, and write these on the board. Then students listen to Maria and Christos, and count how many expressions they use that show a preference or make a suggestion. They can also check if any of their suggestions were used by the two teenagers.

CD1, Track 2

Maria:	Hi Christos, how are you?
Christos:	Hey Maria, I'm really great, what about you?
M:	Everything's fine! Why don't we go to the shopping centre later? I want to see if I can get some new trainers.
C:	Yes, we could do that, but I'd rather go at the weekend. Can you wait until then?
M:	I suppose so, but why?
C:	Well, I get paid for my part-time job tomorrow, so I'll have some money to spend.
M:	Fair enough! So let's go at the weekend instead. But what are we going to do today?

Answer
three (underlined)

2/3 Alone, then pairs

After listening, students look at Appendix 3 in their Coursebook and identify the three underlined phrases. Then, with their partner, they think of more ways to show a preference and make a suggestion, and add them to a copy of the table in Activity E3. Do not worry about corrections at this stage.

4 Alone

Make sure students understand that giving a reason is an important part of showing a preference or making a suggestion. In this activity, they need to identify the reasons given by Maria and Christos.

Answers

Maria – she wants to get some new trainers; Christos – he'll have some money to spend

> **LANGUAGE TIP**
> This is an important tip, because it highlights the structures used after showing a preference or making a suggestion. Show students that there are three possibilities: phrase + infinitive, phrase + *to* infinitive, phrase + *-ing*.
>
> After students have looked at the information in the box, you could get them to close their books and try to remember which phrases are followed by which ending. Stronger students could work with all three endings, while for weaker students, you could allocate just one phrase + ending.

5 Pairs

Before students do Activity E5, make sure they read carefully the information in the **Top Tip** box in the Coursebook. This gives some general advice on how to approach a speaking assessment. You can pair students in various ways for this activity. To give support to students, you could pair them with someone stronger, but make sure the more confident student does not dominate the conversation. You could also give the role of the person suggesting to a weaker student and the person responding to a stronger student. There are no 'right' answers, so allow students to speak freely without interruptions and corrections. You can gather class feedback once students have finished.

6 Alone, then whole class

This is quite a demanding activity, but it is extremely useful. The purpose is for students to prepare a short speech, which they can then deliver to their class, then respond to any questions the class may have about the content of the speech. Allow sufficient planning and preparation time, and provide plenty of guidance where needed – particularly for students who need more support.

Differentiated activities

Support

Students work in small groups (maximum three students), made up of one stronger and two other students. They could all be involved in the preparation – writing down ideas, making a mind map, thinking of reasons for suggestions and preferences, and so on. The speech itself could be delivered by all members of the group, with different students taking on more or less, depending on their abilities. If there are visuals to support the content, students could be involved by displaying and/or explaining these. During the questions at the end, one student could field (but not answer) the questions.

F Reading

1 Alone, then pairs

Students work alone, looking at the headings for the six sections and deciding in which section they think they will read the information (**a–f**). Encourage them to have reasons ready for their answers, which they can then share with a partner.

2 Pairs

In pairs, students think about other information they might read in each of the six sections. There are no right or wrong answers, but students should be encouraged to give reasons for their choices.

3 Alone

Students read the text quickly and check their answers to Activities F1 and F2.

4 Whole class, then alone

Go through questions **a–j** with the class, checking that students understand what information each question is asking for. Then students write their answers.

Answers

a monthly, **b** 20.00, **c** $600, **d** two (Olympic pool and children's starter pool), **e** The Achileas Sports Shop and the Achileas Restaurant, **f** four (lose weight, tone up, increase your strength or improve your health), **g** have an initial consultation, **h** regular reviews, **i** to motivate you to reach your potential, **j** state-of-the-art machines and user-friendly equipment

5 Alone or pairs/small groups

This activity could be done individually or with support, depending on the level of your students and the time you have available. Students are going to design their own information leaflet, loosely based on the one they have just looked at.

a Give students a few minutes to decide what type of information leaflet they are going to design. There are some suggestions in the Coursebook.

b Next they need to decide what information sections the leaflet will contain. These could be the same as or similar to the ones in the Achileas Sports Centre leaflet, or completely different.

c Students write about 50 words (depending on their level) for each section.

d Finally, they write eight questions, two for each section, and exchange these and their information leaflet with another student (or group). Students then read the information leaflet and answer the questions they have been given.

Reflection

This is a new feature in the fifth edition, which reinforces the LOs given at the start of the unit by reminding students of what they have achieved.

They are then asked to self-assess by giving themselves a score from 1 to 5 for each of the five LOs. Students will no doubt treat this quite light-heartedly, which is fine, but make sure they complete the task. At the end of the Reflection, students are asked to set themselves a personal goal, based on the scores. As they progress through the book, setting these goals will become easier, but in the early units you may want to offer guidance and even set their goals, after discussing with them.

A typical personal goal might be: *I need to do more speaking practice so that I can make suggestions more confidently*, or *One area I should improve in is reading texts more quickly.*

Exam focus

Each unit contains at least one exam-style question (some contain more than one), which helps students to practise and develop specific exam-taking skills. In this unit, the focus is on answering questions through skim reading.

Reading, Exercise 1, skimming and scanning

1 a in the main Market Square opposite the City Hall

b stalls change on a daily basis

c mending

d Sunday

e the arts, crafts and local produce market

f street traders' market

g gives them somewhere to sell things

h trees and purpose-built covers

i reputation for quality, affordable prices, improved public transport and people can talk to the makers of the products

NOTE on Assessment Objectives (AOs) for Reading and Writing Exercise 2: In a *multiple matching* activity, students read a continuous text divided into sections, or a number of shorter texts, and answer a series of questions that test more detailed comprehension. Candidates match the correct answer to the question. This type of activity requires more intensive reading, and students will need to understand things which are implied but not directly stated (for example: gist, speaker's purpose, intentions and feelings) (R4). Students also need to identify and select relevant information (R1), understand ideas, opinions and attitudes (R2) and show understanding of the connections between them (R3).

Learning objectives (LOs)

Suggested activity: Start the unit by focusing for a few minutes on the LOs box, making sure that students understand what they are going to be doing. Using the first LO as an example, ask students to identify where in the unit they can find the activities for the other four LOs. Get students to say which of the activities appeal to them the most, and ask them for their reasons.

A Watch, listen and talk

1 Whole class then alone

Explain that your students are going to watch and listen to some IGCSE students talking about **television programmes**. As your students watch and listen, they should make notes about **three** different types of programme that the speakers like, and the programmes that they **never** watch. Play the video a second time so that students can check or add to their notes.

Answers

a   Types of programme that the students like (any **three** from): documentaries, history documentaries, biology documentaries, dramas, dance shows.

Types of programme that the students **never** watch: soap operas, sports news.

2 Pairs or small groups

Depending on the size of your class, put students into pairs or small groups. They can discuss their notes and then talk to each other about the television programmes that **they** like and do not like watching. Do not interfere too much,

but make sure you get feedback from the class so that they know their efforts have been worthwhile. If time permits, you could write their ideas on the board and rank them according to your students' preferences.

B Speaking and vocabulary

1 Pairs or small groups

Students should look carefully at the pictures and discuss what type of programme each one shows, and say if the students they watched in the video mentioned any of the programme types. If you think your students may struggle with the types of programme, supply a list of possible answers for them to choose from. Remember that some will have been mentioned in the video.

Answers

1   cartoon   **2**   sports news

3   chat show   **4**   game show   **5**   dance show

2 Pairs or small groups

If students have already thought of plenty of different types of television programme, you could skip this stage.

Possible answers

drama, soap, sport, news, quiz, talent, lifestyle (e.g. cooking, gardening), documentary, travel, cartoon

LANGUAGE TIP
Make sure you focus students' attention on the **Language Tip** *before* they attempt Activity B3.

3 Pairs

In pairs, students discuss questions **a–c**. You could give students a time limit for each question, to make sure they do not spend too long on a single question.

Differentiated activities

Support

It is important to make sure that students understand exactly what you want them to do in speaking activities. However, it is even more important to provide them with the vocabulary and structures they need to complete the activity successfully. This is particularly important for those students who may struggle to find the required language resources independently. In order to support students, do a couple of whole class examples, reinforcing the key structures that students could use, for example *It depends on … , It varies … , I usually/sometimes/rarely … , My friends watch the same … , I like/dislike/hate …* . Write these structures and vocabulary on the board so that students can refer to them.

Challenge

For stronger students, get them to think of additional questions to use in the activity, for example: *Do you think we watch too much TV nowadays?; How do you think television programmes will change in the future?; What would your life be like without television?*

4/5 Pairs, then class feedback

Show students a sample TV schedule, either something online or from a newspaper, so that they understand what they are going to create. Go through each of the stages so that students are aware of what they have to do, and remind students to look back at the previous activities for ideas about what to include. Give a clear time limit based on your knowledge of your students' abilities. Try not to allow this to overrun.

When each pair has created their TV schedule, get them to share with other students and decide which TV programmes they are going to watch next weekend.

6 Alone, then pairs or small groups

Refer students back to Unit 1, Activity B2 of the Coursebook, in which they made a list of activities they enjoy and don't enjoy doing. Now for this activity, they need to copy the table into their notebooks and complete the first two columns for themselves. They should then complete the third column by interviewing their partner and making a note of their responses. Make sure students are confident about asking the question: *How many minutes each week do you spend (doing something)?*

7 Pairs – Optional

Working with a partner, students look at the graph and answer questions **a–e**. In some IGCSE exam exercises, students may be asked to show their understanding of information represented in a graph or chart, so this type of analytical activity is useful preparation.

Answers

a   time spent by young people on activities,

b   minutes per week,

c   activities,

d   left-hand is vertical, bottom is horizontal,

e   the exact number of minutes

> **LANGUAGE TIP**
> This **Language Tip** includes an activity for students to complete, focusing on adjectives ending in *-al* and *-ar*, which describe shape or position.

Answers

a   cylindrical,

b   triangular,

c   diagonal,

d   hexagonal,

e   symmetrical,

f   three-dimensional,

g   spherical,

h   angular

8 Pairs

Students work in pairs and decide which of the activities are represented in the graph in Activity B7. Give an example and/or double-check that students understand what all the data means (although everything should be clear from the previous activity). Make sure students appreciate that there are four extra activities that they do not need to use.

Suggested answers

A   doing voluntary work,

B   reading books and magazines,

C   doing homework,

D   doing sport,

E   playing computer games,

F   using social media

9 Whole class

Give students the answers and hold a class discussion. Check if they were surprised by anything. Ask if they think the same data would be true for their country. Find out which four activities they did not choose and ask them why.

10 Alone or pairs

The final activity in this section requires students to collect information and then display it in a graph or chart. Students can work alone or in pairs if they need support, but whatever the case, you will need to guide students, particularly at the start. Make sure that they understand exactly what the outcome of the activity is (i.e. a graph or chart showing how much time students spend on various activities), and explain how they are going to reach that outcome (i.e. by collecting and recording the necessary information, then deciding on how to represent it). Different students will produce different variations of the outcome. If possible, display students' work on the classroom wall, or even on a webpage, so that they can look at each other's work and give feedback.

C Reading

1 Whole class, then pairs

Go through the statements **a**–**e** checking that students understand everything. Check the meaning of: *focal point* (question a), *transformed* (b), *provide an experience* (c), *predicted* (d), *here to stay* (d) *multitask* (e). Students then work in pairs to decide if they agree or disagree. They should not look at the text yet, and they can ignore the paragraph references for the moment. Encourage students to give reasons for their choices during class feedback.

2 Alone, then pairs

Students quickly read the text to check if the writer has the same ideas. The paragraph number is provided so explain to students that this will help them to read quickly and efficiently. They should also start to realise that they do not need to read and understand everything in the text to find the information they need.

Answers

a the writer disagrees: '*But nowadays, every screen in the house …*',

b agrees,

c agrees,

d agrees,

e agrees

3 Alone, then pairs

Your students' written and spoken language will become more fluent if they can confidently combine adjectives and nouns. This activity focuses on the adjective + noun combinations from the text they have just read. Get students to work alone at first, matching the adjectives and nouns, and thinking about whether or not there are multiple possibilities.

Answers

a + 7, b + 1, c + 5, d + 8, e + 3, f + 2, g + 6, h + 4. These answers are from the text, but there are countless other acceptable combinations, for example: daily + programmes, high-quality + televisions/programmes/viewing/wireless internet, high-quality/high-speed/top-quality/widespread + wireless internet and so on. Encourage students to give you some examples of these combinations in sentences.

4 Alone

Students read the text again to check their answers to Activity C3.

5 Alone, then pairs

Students will need to read the text in more detail for this activity, and you may wish to use differentiated activities for support and challenge.

Differentiated activities

Support

i   Allocate the four paragraphs to different students to reduce their reading load;

ii Tell students in which paragraphs they can find the information.

Challenge

i   Allow students to read the text again, but then ask them to cover it while they answer the true/false questions;

ii Ask students to correct any false information.

Answers

a   true [paragraph 1],

b   true [2],

c   false [2] – *usually attached*,

d   true [2],

e   true [3],

f   true [4],

g   true [4]

D Language focus: adverbs

> **LANGUAGE TIP**
> Spend some time going through the content of the **Language Tip**, but reassure students that they will also be doing practice activities in the **Coursebook** and the **Workbook**. Make sure students are clear about the different ways in which adverbs are used.

1 Alone

In this activity students need to apply their understanding of how adverbs are used. Do a couple of examples and then ask students to work alone to decide on the role of the adverbs in italics in each phrase from the text. Make sure they feed back which word the adverb is describing.

Answers

a   to describe the verb *transformed*,

b   to describe the verb *makes*,

c   to describe the adjective *large*,

d   to describe the adjective *attached*,

e   to describe the verbs *looks* and *sounds*,

f   to describe the adverb *openly*,

g   to describe the adjective *widespread*

2/3 Pairs, then whole class

This activity works well as a competition, so you might like to set a time limit. If you have time, students could check their answers online or in a dictionary.

Differentiated activities

Support

i   Allow students to choose fewer letters.

ii Students think of ten adjectives, but not using consecutive letters of the alphabet.

iii Give students a bank of the first few letters of adverbs for them to complete, for example: *com… = completely; fri … = friendly.*

Challenge

i   Students write two words for each alphabet letter.

ii When pairs have completed their ten adverbs, each pair passes its words to a second pair, who have to add other adverbs for each letter. When they finish, once again the words are passed on and the next pair tries to add more adverbs.

iii Students have to write adverb + adjective combinations.

4/5 Alone, then pairs

In these activities students need to use adverb phrases to complete (Activity D4) and then make sentences (Activity D5). Ask them to work alone to start with, but make sure you go through the examples first, and perhaps do one or two further examples if necessary. Explain that there are many possible answers. In Activity D5, students have the chance to create their own sentences, using adverb phrases.

Differentiated activities

Support

i   Supply (some of the) possible endings for students to match to the sentence stems.

ii Give students some *adverb + verb, adverb + adverb,* or *adverb + adjective* phrases, which they then use to help them to complete the sentences.

Challenge

i   Ask students to change the linking word that appears in most of the sentences. For example: in **a**, change *but* to *and*, and immediately a different ending is required. Students will need to use more of their own adverb choices in order to do this successfully.

Possible answers Activity D4

a   it was incredibly expensive,

b   playing really badly,

c   very dirty,

d   absolutely stunning,

e   all completely different colours,

f   totally unexpectedly,

g   really very boring,

h   completely disagreed,

i   usually prefer to visit smaller shops,

j   really didn't care.

E Speaking: Would/wouldn't do

1 Whole class, then alone

Write the paragraph title on the board and get students' reaction to it. Find out what their daily expenses are. However, try not to talk too much about the points in Activity E2. Then give students a few minutes to read the paragraph and to check any unknown words or phrases. If you prefer, you could deal with these **before** the students read.

2 Small groups

The paragraph should motivate students to discuss exercises (**a–d**). As always, do not allow too much time for students to ask and answer; give them a minute or so for each exercise before asking them to move on to the next one. If you plan on doing whole class feedback (not essential) you might ask students to take some written notes during their discussions.

3 Pairs

This activity focuses on useful language for saying *would* or *wouldn't do something*. Do a couple of examples and then get students working with their partner to distinguish between *would* and *wouldn't* phrases.

Answers

Would	Wouldn't
I would be prepared to clean the car	Cleaning the car is something I'd never do
I wouldn't have a problem with cleaning the car	Cleaning the car is the last thing I'd do
Cleaning the car is fine by me	I certainly wouldn't ever clean the car
I wouldn't mind cleaning the car	I can't imagine myself ever cleaning the car
I would enjoy cleaning the car	There's no way I'd ever clean the car
I'd be quite happy to clean the car	

LANGUAGE TIP

Highlight the expressions to request something in a polite manner, and in particular the different verb forms (e.g. modal + *have*, *to have*, *if I had* and so on).

4 Pairs

Students have now seen plenty of language in order to complete this speaking activity successfully, so remind them to refer back to the previous activities and to use the expressions there. Do whole class feedback and get students to compare their ideas.

F Reading

1 Whole class, then pairs

Check students understand what a blog is, and what style a blog is usually written in: *A blog is a frequently updated online personal journal or diary. Really, it's anything you want it to be. Blog is a short form of the word weblog and the two words are used interchangeably* (http://blogbasics.com/what-is-a-blog). Then go through the three statements **A–C** and quickly check if students agree or disagree with any of them. In the box there are six phrases, which students need to look at and predict in which of the three blogs they would expect to read them. It does not matter if students are not 100% sure, but encourage them to give reasons for their answers – this is important. Remind them that there are two phrases from each of the three blogs. Do not supply any answers as students will find out for themselves when they read the text in Activity F3.

2 Pairs

Students need to carefully read the three conclusions (**a–c**) and decide in which blog they would expect to read them, once again giving reasons for their choices. It does not matter if they are unsure. Do not supply any answers as students will find out for themselves when they read the text in Activity F3.

3 Alone, then pairs

Students now read the three blogs and check their predictions from Activities F1 and F2. As this is a 'look and find' activity, i.e. they need to find words and phrases they have already seen, keep the time brief.

Differentiated activities

Support

i   You could provide support by asking some students to work in pairs, rather than alone. Then allocate two blogs to each student, in order to reduce their reading load.

ii   Again in pairs, but this time reduce the number of phrases and/or conclusions that students need to find.

Challenge

Working alone, see if students can look and find without referring back again to Activities F1 and F2.

TOP TIP

Multiple-matching activities require students to identify relevant information in one or a number of texts. Often the texts may say similar things, so students need to look for key words to correctly identify the information that is being asked for.

4 Alone, then pairs

This is a multiple-matching activity, similar to the type found in examinations. There are three texts (the three blogs students have already seen) on the same topic or theme, written by three different people. Then there is a list of exercises **a–h**, all of which begin with: '*Which person …?*' Students need to decide which blog writer is the answer to each of the exercises. The people may be chosen more than once.

Students should do this on their own and then work with a partner to check their responses and to discuss where they found the relevant information to make their choices.

Answers

a	C,	**e**	B,
b	C,	**f**	C,
c	B,	**g**	B,
d	A,	**h**	A

WORD TIP

These words (*obviously, apparently*) are sometimes confused or misused, so go through the information and then direct students to Unit 2 of their **Workbook** to do the practice exercise.

Reflection

Use the **Reflection** to remind students of what they have achieved in the unit. Students should set themselves a **personal goal** based on their scores for Unit 2.

Exam focus

Reading: Exercise 2, multiple matching

This is another multiple-matching activity, in the style of an examination exercise.

Answers

a	D,
b	C,
c	A,
d	B,
e	D,
f	C,
g	A,
h	C,
i	A,
j	B

Unit 3: Food
Focus on writing

NOTE on Assessment Objectives (AOs) for Reading and Writing Exercise 5: Students write approximately 100–150 (Core) or 150–200 (Extended) words of continuous prose, in response to a short stimulus which may take the form of pictures and/or short prompts printed on the paper.

The question includes information on the purpose, format and audience, as well as the word count and how the marks are allocated. Specifically, students need to show that they can communicate information/ideas/opinions clearly, accurately and effectively (W1), organise ideas into coherent paragraphs using a range of appropriate linking devices (W2), use a range of grammatical structures and vocabulary accurately and effectively (W3), show control of punctuation and spelling (W4), and use appropriate register and style/format for the given purpose and audience (W5).

Learning objectives (LOs)

Suggested activity: Start the unit by focusing for a few minutes on the LOs box, making sure that students understand what they are going to be doing. Using the first LO as an example, ask students to identify where in the unit they can find the activities for the other four LOs. Get students to say which of the activities appeal to them the most, and ask them for their reasons.

A Watch, listen and talk

1 Whole class, then alone

Explain that your students are going to watch and listen to some IGCSE students talking about **food**. As your students watch and listen, they should make notes about **three** different types of food that the speakers like, and the **reasons** they give. Play the video a second time so that students can check or add to their notes.

Answers

a Different types of food that the students like (any **three** from): fish balls, spicy food, cake, moon cakes, pasta, traditional food from Kazakhstan, sweets.

The **reasons** they give: it's mostly made of flour, you can choose different sauces [fish balls]; because the student is Indian [spicy food]; the food is special to the student [moon cakes].

2 Pairs or small groups

Depending on the size of your class, put students into pairs or small groups. They can discuss their notes and then talk

to each other about the food and their reasons. Do not interfere too much, but make sure you get feedback from the class so that they know their efforts have been worthwhile. If time permits, you could write their ideas on the board and rank them according to your students' preferences.

B Speaking and vocabulary

1 Whole class, then small groups

Students look at the food pictures and say what the foods are, and which (if any) they like/dislike. Then put students into small groups to talk about Questions **a** and **b**. Remember that with this type of question, there are no right or wrong answers and it is worth pointing this out (again) to students. Encourage them to speculate, discuss their ideas and give reasons, without fear of being corrected if they make language mistakes. This is particularly important for those students who may be reluctant to participate because they are worried about being 'wrong' or making a mistake. Your role here is to monitor the discussion and to guide the feedback when students have made their choices. For **c**, check that students know what all the different foods are, and then get them to put the foods into two groups: 'fast' and 'slow/traditional' food. When they are ready, they can think of more examples of food for each group (**d**).

2/3 Small groups, then pairs

Explain to students that they are going to read an internet article called *Eight things your fast-food worker won't tell you*. In small groups they should discuss what they think these eight things might be. Ask students if they think these things will be positive or negative, and to give their reasons. There is an example in the Coursebook, but you can provide an extra one or two if necessary. When they are ready, students work in pairs (Activity B3) and look at statements **a–h**, and decide if they are true or false. Encourage them to speculate and to give reasons. Do not give any answers at this point as students will find out when they read the text.

4 Alone

Students look quickly at the text and check their answers to Activity B3. They should be ready to say in which paragraphs they found the information.

Answers

a	true [8],	e	false [6],
b	true [1],	f	true [2],
c	false [5],	g	true [7],
d	true [4],	h	true [3]

5/6 Alone, then pairs

Put students into A/B pairs. Each student has four words or phrases from the text to check. When they are ready, students share their ideas and check that their partner has the right meanings.

7 Alone

Students work on their own and choose six of the eight words and phrases from the previous activities to use in sentences of their own. Give students time to share their sentences and compare how they have used the words and phrases.

Differentiated activities

Support

i   Reduce the number of sentences, or choose words that you think students will find easier to use in their own writing.

ii   You could also give students some vocabulary to help them write their sentences, for example: *cabinet + place, food, stored*.

Challenge

Ask students to use all the eight words and phrases, and/or ask them to choose two or three more words from the text and to write them in sentences of their own.

WORD TIP

These two words (*insist*, *persist*) are commonly confused and/or misused. Go through the explanations and then direct students to the practice exercise in the **Workbook**.

LANGUAGE TIP

The text includes examples of different ways to express *if: providing, as soon as, supposing*. Ask students to replace the highlighted words with *if* to notice that the meaning is similar; however, also point out that the highlighted phrases are not always interchangeable. For example, you cannot replace *supposing* with *providing* and vice versa, but both could be replaced by *if*. Go through the examples and then direct students to the practice exercise in the **Workbook**.

C Reading

1 Alone, then pairs

Tell students that they are going to read a newspaper article about fast food in Italy and to write down three things that they consider to be Italian fast food. Then, for questions **a–f** in this activity, students work alone, although they can use reference sources for help. Once they have completed all the questions, they can join up with a partner and compare answers. The activity requires students to look in close detail at the text.

Answers

a   **i** decade, **ii** arm, **iii** boost, **iv** potential, **v** exploit

b   set foot = arrive, suspicion = doubt/uncertainty, offensive = campaign/attack, playing to = relying on, commercial = advertisement

c   a = workforce, b = worldwide, c = market share, d = sector, e = target

d

Noun	Verb	Adjective	Adverb	Noun translation/s
finance	finance	financial	financially	
investment *(thing)* investor *(person)*	invest	invested		
culture		cultural	culturally	Depends on students
provision *(thing)* provider *(person)*	provide			
dinner *(thing)* diner *(person)*	dine	dining		

e   f = supplier/seller/producer, g = close/shut down, h = metres, i = branch/outlet, j = burgers/food/sandwiches

f   **i**   30% = decrease in foreign investment in Italy since 2007; €350 million = the amount McDonald's plans to spend in Italy in the coming years; 3,000 = the number of new jobs to be created

    ii   450 = McDonald's restaurants in Italy; €1 billion = estimated annual sales in Italy; 10% = McDonald's market share in Spain and France; 2% = share of 'informal eating out' in Italy; 3% = target in coming years for 'informal eating out' in Italy

    iii   5,000 = number of people who visited McDonald's on its final day

2/3 Alone, then pairs

Students begin by working on their own to do two things: (1) identify the key word/s in questions **a–g**, and (2) look at the text again and identify where the answers to the questions are. They do not need to write the answers yet. For Activity C3, students compare their answers, then together write the answers to the questions.

Differentiated activities

Support

Show students in which paragraph to look for the answers, and also reduce the number of questions they need to do.

Challenge

Encourage students not to look back at the text and instead answer the questions from memory.

Answers

a   pizza-lovers,

b   open more than 100 new restaurants; spend €350 million; hire 3,000 people,

c   they were suspicious,

d   Italy,

e   made sandwiches with crusty bread filled with Parmesan cheese and sliced ham,

f   a theme park,

g   to make way for a new fashion shop

D Language focus: *to*-infinitive

1 Whole class, then alone

The *to*-infinitive (ie, *to* + base form of the verb) is used in many different sentence constructions, often expressing the purpose of something or someone's opinion about something. The text in the previous section includes several examples: *… is opening more than 100 new restaurants* **to convert** *pizza-lovers to its burgers; This is our way* **to show** *we believe …; … which strives* **to preserve** *traditional ….*

Working alone, students need to match the four common uses (**a–d**) of the *to*-infinitive with the eight examples (**1–8**) given. Before they do this, go through the four uses, checking that students can understand the differences.

Answers

a   4 and 8,   **c**   3 and 6,

b   1 and 7,   **d**   2 and 5

2 Alone, then pairs

Do an example and then students work alone to unjumble the letters and make complete sentences which include a *to*-infinitive form. Allow students to check their answers together before doing class feedback.

Answers

a   She appears to have hurt her head.

b   My instructions are to write 150 words.

c   We need to leave immediately.

d   Would you like to eat anything / anything to eat?

e   I'm calling to find out about your father.

f   He asked me not to come with him.

3/4 Alone, then pairs

Once again students work alone and then pair up to check their answers. All the sentences come from the two texts the students have read, and they can refer back to these in Activity D4.

Answers

a + 6, b + 1, c + 2, d + 7, e + 4, f + 3, g + 5

5 Alone

In this final activity students can make their own sentences containing a *to*-infinitive form.

Possible answers

a   He arrived too late to see the performance.

b   Do you understand where to go?

c   The students need a library to study in.

d   Your brother has gone to see about the meal.

e   I'd like you to tell me where it is.

E Writing: Informal letters

Students are going to write a letter to a friend about a fast-food restaurant they have recently visited. Before they actually write their letters, there is a series of activities which involve planning and preparing for the writing. Depending on the time you have available, and the level of your students, you may decide not to ask students to complete all the activities.

1 Pairs, then whole class

Students discuss questions **a–c** together. You may consider limiting the time for each question so that this first activity does not take up too much time. When students are ready, take whole class feedback, but remember there are no right or wrong answers to the questions.

2 Pairs

Working in pairs, students complete a copy of the table, adding their ideas about the advantages and disadvantages of fast-food and traditional restaurants.

Possible answers

Fast-food restaurants	
Advantages	**Disadvantages**
quick service price availability	limited choice nutritional value packaging

Traditional restaurants	
Advantages	**Disadvantages**
choice atmosphere health value	more expensive slow service availability

3/4 Pairs

We often tell students to 'read the question carefully' before writing their answers. We do this because we know that some students may miss the point of the question – or fail to fully grasp what the question is asking them to do – if they haven't spent a minute or two checking it. Questions often use the words *explain*, *describe*, *write*, *say*, and these two activities ask students to consider what these words mean, then to use them to complete the gaps in an exam-style question.

Answers

a   Write,

b   explain,

c   describe,

d   say

> **TOP TIP**
>
> The **Top Tip** next to Activity E4 in the Coursebook helps students understand the way in which exam questions may be written, and the things they should look out for.

5 Pairs, then whole class

In pairs, students think of expressions they could use to open and close an informal letter. You could divide the class into groups: one half thinking of expressions to open an informal letter and the other half thinking of expressions to close one. During feedback, put all the expressions on the board for students to copy into their notebooks.

Possible answers

Opening phrases	Closing phrases
Hi Satish!	Best wishes
Dear Satish	All the best
Hello Satish	See you soon
Thanks for your letter.	Take care
Lovely to hear from you.	Yours
How are you?	Love
How are things?	Lots of love
Hope you're well.	Speak to you soon

6 Pairs

In this activity, students compare two letters written in response to the previous exam-style question. They do not need to correct the letters, nor rewrite them; the point here is for students to recognise a good answer and a not-so-good answer, and to say why.

Answers

Letter B is the better of the two because: the layout is easier to follow, the writer has fully responded to all the points in the question, there is no unnecessary content, the level of accuracy is good with a wide range of vocabulary.

Letter A is not as effective because: the writer has not used any paragraphs and therefore the content is more difficult to follow, not all the points in the question have been dealt with, there is a lot of unnecessary information, there is a higher level of inaccuracy and a limited range of vocabulary.

7 Pairs

This activity asks students to identify specific elements within each letter.

Answers

a	B,	d	neither,
b	A,	e	A
c	B,		

8 Pairs

Having looked at and practised using adjectives and adverbs in earlier units, students should now be reasonably confident about improving Letter A. There is no single correct answer; allow your students to play around with the language, to be creative, to try out different word combinations, and to share their ideas. If time permits, you could do feedback by putting ideas on the board and getting students to decide which are the best improvements. They can then use some of these ideas when they write their own answers in the next activity.

9 Small groups

Divide students into small groups to discuss and plan their own responses to the exam-style question in Activity E4. While they will be writing their letters on their own, discussing the content in groups will give students support if needed. Encourage them to use a copy of the mind map supplied in order to make their notes.

> **TOP TIP**
> Before students do Activity E10, focus on the **Top Tip** next to Activity E7 in the Coursebook, which gives important information about how to approach this type of question.

10 Alone, then pairs

Set a reasonable time limit for students to write their answers. Remember that this is not a test! The whole purpose of this section is to guide and support students in writing an informal letter, so even at this stage, you should be available to help them. Also, allow students to ask each other for help. If you have Core and Extended students in the same class, remember that they have different word counts (Core 100–150, Extended 150–200). Encourage students to look back through the section and make use of some of the opening/closing phrases from Activity E5, as well as their ideas from Activities E8 and E9. They could also refer to Maroulla's letter (B) as a good model of what is required. When students have finished, they can look at each other's answers and provide feedback.

> **TOP TIP**
> This **Top Tip** highlights the fact that students will receive marks in two broad areas: **content** and **language**. There is a copy of the marking scheme for assessing extended writing in the **Assessment criteria for writing and speaking** section in this book.

F Speaking: Expressing opinions

1 Alone

Students listen to a short exchange. As they listen, they need to decide in how many different ways the two speakers express their opinion. There are **four** examples, underlined in the audioscript here.

CD1, Track 3

Anna: To my mind, fast-food restaurants are here to stay.

Terry: If you ask me, people are starting to realise how unhealthy fast food is.

Anna: But it's so convenient! In my opinion, people are not going to give that up.

Terry: Know what I think? People are lazy and will always take the easy option!

2 Small groups

Refer students to the audioscript in Appendix 3 of their Coursebook to focus on the four underlined phrases. Then they should work together to think of more phrases to express opinions. Use the **Language Tip** for feedback and to provide students with more phrases.

LANGUAGE TIP

Point out which expressions are more common in spoken and written English, and encourage students to start using other expressions, to introduce more variety into their spoken and written language. Remember that assessment is on **variety** and **breadth** of language, just as much as on **accuracy**.

3 Pairs, then whole class

Throughout the unit, students have been talking and writing about fast food and traditional food. For this activity, they are going to be involved in a class discussion (led by either the teacher or one or two students) about the advantages and disadvantages of the two types of food. Give students time to plan their ideas before the discussion begins, referring them back to previous activities in the unit for help.

TOP TIP

The **Top Tip** gives some advice on considering both content and language. At the end of the **Top Tip** there is a suggestion for students to look at the speaking-test cards in Appendix 1 of the Coursebook. In doing so, they will understand that the phrases they have practised in this unit will help them to discuss more or less any topic.

Reflection

Use the **Reflection** to remind students of what they have achieved in the unit. Students should set themselves a **personal goal** based on their scores for Unit 3.

Exam focus

Writing, Exercise 5

There are **two** extended writing questions which reflect the type of questions students may see in an IGCSE examination. Both require students to write in an informal style (1 = letter to a friend, 2 = email to a cousin), and both could be used with either Extended or Core candidates. When marking your students' writing, refer to the assessment criteria in the **Assessment criteria for writing and speaking** section in this book.

1 Here are two sample answers written by (i) an **IGCSE Core** student and (ii) an **IGCSE Extended** student. Both these attempts would probably score in the top mark band for both content and language.

i Core

Dear Sebastian,

How are you? I haven't seen you in a very long time! Last night was my dad's birthday and I made him that pizza recipe that we saw together on television. With my mum's

help we managed to make three different pizzas, but one of them was a bit burnt. My dad, mum and my sister ate our pizzas outside in our garden and we all agreed that they tasted very nice. My mum and dad liked the Margherita pizza most, but my sister and I liked the one with the tuna and olives. I think our dog enjoyed the pizza most of all, he stole half of the burnt Pepperoni!

Lots of love,

Martha [*117 words*]

ii Extended

Dear Anna,

Hi and how are you? It's been such a long time since we last spoke! I'm so glad that I will get to see you in a few weeks' time. As soon as we meet up I will cook for you the meal I made for my brother yesterday, moussaka!

As you know, it was Alex's birthday yesterday and instead of giving him a present he asked me to make his favourite meal for him instead. He loves moussaka more than any other food on this planet! Unfortunately, it takes around two whole days to make; it is such a long process! After two long days of preparation and cooking, my whole family, mother, father, brother, aunts, uncles and grandparents, sat in the garden together under the olive tree and enjoyed the deliciously home-made moussaka. I was really proud of myself!

Just in case you don't know, moussaka is made from aubergines, courgettes, meat and potatoes all placed on top of each other like a tower. It's really yummy and everyone said I made it perfectly! I hope you will enjoy it as much as they did!

See you soon,

Katerina [*193 words*]

2 Here are two sample answers written by (i) an **IGCSE Core** student and (ii) an **IGCSE Extended** student. Both these attempts would probably score in the top mark band for both content and language.

i   Core

Hi Andrew,

How are you? You will not believe what happened to me a few days ago! We went with a few friends of mine to this new fast-food restaurant that has opened in town. My cousin visited it a few days ago and he told me to try one of their burgers, he thought they were awesome!

So we decided on Saturday to go and have dinner there and I ordered a burger. The restaurant was really cool, there was loud music playing and the waiters were really great! Our food came quickly but as I opened my burger to take out the lettuce (because I hate lettuce), I saw two dead flies! I couldn't believe it and I refused to eat the burger! Thankfully the restaurant didn't make us pay for our dinner but I will not be going back there again!

Speak to you soon,

Anya [*149 words*]

ii   Extended

Dear Adiba,

Last Friday night I went with a large group of friends to our favourite Lebanese restaurant. We were celebrating our graduation from school. What we thought was going to be a normal evening out with friends, turned out to be a very unusual and exciting experience!

We arrived at the restaurant and were seated at my favourite table outside in the garden. The food was soon brought to us, but as we were eating, a very large bird landed on our table and started stealing large pieces of bread. Some of my friends got scared of the bird and ran away, but I thought it was very funny! The waiters eventually managed to get rid of the bird and were very apologetic.

Not long after we were all happily enjoying our meal again and laughing about our unusual experience at the restaurant. In the end we had a great meal!

I hope to hear from you very soon.

Lots of love,

Leila [*164 words*]

Reading, Exercise 1, skimming and scanning

There are **two** reading exercises which reflect the type of Exercise 1 students may see in an IGCSE examination.

1 Hospitality with dates

Answers

    a   coffee and dates

    b   1.1 million metric tonnes

    c   shops, markets, oases, sides of every major street, every garden and yard

    d   medicinal properties

    e   they are one of the best sources of food and are easy to grow

    f   cancer

    g   they contain anti-inflammatory properties

    h   it is lost

    i   shade from the sun, thatching/roofing on huts, support pillars in buildings, furniture

2 Shellfish in Oman

Answers

    a   research into marine life is growing stronger

    b   because of the pearls they contain

    c   the shores of Dhofar

    d   produces omega-3 fatty acids

    e   it has only one shell

    f   young ones live in small groups underneath medium-sized rocks; adults live in groups of up to 12, in cracks in rocks

    g   to avoid overfishing

    h   because of its environmental requirements for cool water conditions

    i   face mask and knife (not fins)

    j   shallow, cold, nutritious, brightly lit water

NOTE on Assessment Objectives (AOs) for Listening **Exercise 1:** Students need to demonstrate that they can listen to four short extracts and answer questions on each. Questions require short answers, no longer than three words. Text types are recorded phone messages or brief dialogues (formal or informal). Specifically, students need to show that they can listen and select relevant information (L1).

Learning objectives (LOs)

Suggested activity: Start the unit by focusing for a few minutes on the LOs box, making sure that students understand what they are going to be doing. Using the first LO as an example, ask students to identify where in the unit they can find the activities for the other four LOs. Get students to say which of the activities appeal to them the most, and ask them for their reasons.

A Watch, listen and talk

1 Whole class, then alone

Explain that your students are going to watch and listen to some IGCSE students talking about **methods of transport**. As your students watch and listen, they should make notes about **three** methods of transport that the speakers mention, and the **reasons** they give. Play the video a second time so that students can check or add to their notes.

Answers

a   Methods of transport that the students mention (any **three** from): walking, bicycles, cars, planes, taxis, buses, trains.

   The **reasons** they give: because it's faster, you are treated well, you get food [planes]; there are a lot, it's free [buses]; they are fast, they are efficient [trains].

2 Pairs or small groups

Depending on the size of your class, put students into pairs or small groups. They can discuss their notes and then talk to each other about the methods of transport that **they** prefer and their reasons. Do not interfere too much, but make sure you get feedback from the class so that they know their efforts have been worthwhile. If time permits, you could write their ideas on the board and rank them according to your students' preferences.

B Speaking and vocabulary
1 Pairs

Focus on the four pictures in the Coursebook and quickly check that students can tell you what the types of transport are (1 to 4: train, balloon, camper van, plane). Then give students a few minutes to confirm their favourite method of transport and their reasons.

2 Alone, then pairs

Students work alone to identify ten different methods of transport in the word snake. This activity is good for checking spelling and for recognising word boundaries. After finding the ten words, students check with their partner and then see how many of the methods of transport in the word snake they thought of in Activity B1.

3 Pairs

Students discuss with their partner which of the methods of transport they would prefer for going on holiday – and give reasons. They should also discuss if their choice depends on the type of holiday. You may need to prompt them: *skiing holiday*, *sightseeing holiday*, *shopping holiday* and so on. Allow students plenty of freedom to do this activity – monitor them, but do not interfere in their discussions. Take a note of anything particularly interesting you hear. Also note down any errors that you feel need to be dealt with in feedback.

4 Alone, then pairs

Students copy and complete the table with their own ideas. They should choose **five** or **six** methods from the previous activities, but this will depend on how much time you have available. To challenge students, they could make notes about more methods. There are no right or wrong answers. Try to get students to write **two** or **three** ideas for each method of transport, then compare their answers.

5 Pairs

Students decide together which method of transport is the most expensive, then make a ranked list. They need to consider all the factors that could make a method of transport more or less expensive. For flying by plane, for example, they might also consider the cost of getting to the airport. If going by car, they should consider the cost of petrol and parking fees.

C Listening 1

1 Pairs

Students discuss which of the methods they think they will hear about and try to give reasons for their choices. There are no right or wrong answers.

2a–c Alone, then pairs

This activity requires students to answer **three** questions, which are designed to give them a reason for listening and to test basic comprehension. Make sure students understand what they have to do and that they are ready to listen before you start the CD. Allow students to check their answers together before you give feedback.

CD1, Track 4

Speaker 1

Well, of course, we had booked everything well in advance, because in Britain these services get full very early, and we didn't want to be disappointed. Anyway, we got to the terminus in central London in plenty of time and we stood on platform 13E for Edinburgh. It was a beautiful summer's day. There was me, my wife Julia and the three children. They were still quite young then: three, six and eight, I think. We were supposed to leave at 8.30 in the morning and, as it got closer to our departure time, we all began to get quite excited. By 8.30, we had started to get a little bit anxious because the platform was completely empty, apart from us five with all our luggage. At 9.00, Julia told me to go and find out what was happening, so off I went to the booking office to make enquiries. And yes, you can guess what was wrong – we were 12 hours early! Our departure time was 8.30 p.m., not a.m. I had misread the time on the tickets.

Speaker 2

They call it an airport, but it's really just a field. My sister had booked me a flight as a treat for my 13th birthday, which was May 20th, three years ago, and I must admit that I was absolutely dreading it! I've never really enjoyed flying, and the thought of going up in the air for 30 minutes in a basket really didn't appeal to me. I couldn't understand how the thing was driven and steered, and I think that's what put me off. But once we got up in the air, at 9 o'clock in the morning, it was spectacular – the most beautiful views of the hills, fields and villages below, with the sun sparkling on the river. We didn't want to come down!

Speaker 3

I had investigated all the different options available to me and, in the end, this was by far the cheapest, at only $275. Of course, it wouldn't be nearly as fast as going by plane, but the cost was far less and I would be able to see something of the countryside. Some friends had travelled the same route the previous year and had said how brilliant it had been, so I wasn't really worried. What they hadn't told me was how uncomfortable these vehicles are when you've been in one for almost two days. It's very difficult to sleep, and there are no toilets or washing facilities, so you've got to hang on until the scheduled stops, usually every four to five hours. When I finally arrived in the south of Spain, after nearly 48 hours on the road, I slept for over 19 hours!

Speaker 4

We set off in the afternoon, as the sun was starting to drop, and with it the temperature, although it was still incredibly hot and humid. We knew the journey would take about two hours, so we had time to reach the oasis before dark, and before the temperature plummeted. With me was my twin sister, Amelia. She was used to riding horses, so this wasn't as difficult for her as it was for me. Even so, she said that riding without a saddle was very uncomfortable, and I had to agree with her! She also complained about not having a riding hat, but I told her she'd look pretty silly if she did! We moved at a leisurely pace – these wonderful animals won't be rushed – and we had time to be amazed by the beautiful scenery all around us and, as dusk fell, in the sky as well. We arrived, made camp, ate and fell into a deep sleep under the stars.

Answers

a   1 = train, 2 = balloon, 3 = coach, 4 = camel

b   2 and 4

c   2 and 4

2d Alone, then pairs

This activity encourages students to think about **how** they identified the answers to the three questions by asking them what information they focused on. There are no right or wrong answers, but it is important for students to think about their methods for being successful when they do a task.

3 Alone, then pairs

Students listen a second time and answer the questions for each of the four speakers. Allow them to check with their partner before you provide feedback. If you think that students may struggle, you could split the listening into smaller sections, letting them hear just one or two speakers, then checking answers before they listen to the next one/s.

Answers

Speaker 1
a   platform 13E
b   four
c   (quite) excited
d   the platform was empty
e   went to the booking office to make enquiries
f   misread the time on the tickets

Speaker 2
a   birthday present
b   16
c   because he had never enjoyed flying
d   30 minutes
e   exhilarated, delighted (not given – students need to infer)

Speaker 3
a   cheaper, able to see countryside
b   four (slow, uncomfortable, difficult to sleep, no toilets or washing facilities)
c   every 4–5 hours
d   nearly 48 hours

Speaker 4
a   afternoon
b   hot and humid
c   twin sister
d   slowly (at a leisurely pace)
e   beautiful scenery and the sky

Differentiated activities

Support
Let students look at the audioscript **before** they listen (but not while they listen). This will provide support by giving students an idea of what to expect. Set a time limit so they do not spend too long on this – the idea is for them to skim the audioscript to get an idea of the content and to build up their confidence before they listen. Students who need more support could read as they listen. Another option is to give them the chance to look at the audioscript after they have listened (but before they answer the questions) to check what they have understood.

Challenge
Ask students to write two or three extra pieces of information about each speaker (in addition to answering the questions in the Coursebook).

4 Pairs
Students copy the table, then work together to complete it. Not all the gaps can be filled.

Answers

	Speaker 1	Speaker 2	Speaker 3	Speaker 4
Departure time	8.30 a.m.	9.00 a.m.		afternoon
Length of journey		30 minutes	48 hours	2 hours
Arrival time				before dark
Weather / time of year	beautiful summer day	sunny, May		hot and humid
Speaker's feelings	excited, then anxious	worried, then happy	not worried, tired and uncomfortable	amazed
Speaker with who?	wife and three children			twin sister
Cost		free (a gift)	$275	

5 Alone

Students can refer to the audioscript in Appendix 3 of the Coursebook for extra support and to check their answers to Activities C3 and C4.

6 Alone, then pairs

There are several stages for this final activity in Section C1. Firstly, students need to choose a method of transport (not one of the four they have just been hearing about). They should not tell their partner their choice. Next, each student writes a paragraph of around 80 words about their method of transport, including the information listed in the Coursebook, but not giving away the method of transport (the same as in the listening activity C2). Next, students write four or five questions about the content of their paragraph for their partner to answer. Finally, students exchange their writing and the questions, then answer the questions and try to guess the method of transport.

Differentiated activities

Support

Reduce the number of words and/or get them to write five or six individual sentences, rather than a complete paragraph.

Challenge

Increase the number of words students have to write and get them to include more details, for example, in which country the journey took place, the arrival time, people who travelled with the speaker, etc.

Listening 2

7a Whole class, then pairs/small groups

Focus on the picture of the motorbike near to Activity C7 of the Coursebook and ask students what they can see and what they think might have happened. Then refer them to Activity C7 and go through the information about the *boda-boda* motorbike taxi. Next, working with a partner, students discuss questions **a i–iv**. Make sure students understand that there are no right or wrong answers.

7b Different pairs

Put students with a different partner for this next activity, then get them to read the information **b i–v** and the numbers in the box, and ask them to complete the gaps. Once again, it does not matter at this stage if they are right or wrong. The point is to provide them with some information and key vocabulary relating to the information they are about to hear – and to engage their interest in the subject. Do not provide any answers yet.

7c Alone, then same pairs

If you can supply dictionaries, or if your school has digital resources, then this activity will work well. The idea is for students to work alone, researching the meaning of the words in either column A or B. Once they have an idea about their words, students should work together and discuss what they have found out. All the words appear in the next listening text.

8 Alone

Students listen for the first time and check if their answers for Activity C7b were correct. If you want to make this less challenging, you could tell the students to call out when they hear the part of the text that confirms the information in Activity C7b. As all the information in the activity contains a number you could tell students to listen out for these particular numbers.

Answers

i	40%,	**iv**	3343,
ii	62%,	**v**	1800
iii	twice,		

CD1, Track 5

For many years, *boda-bodas* have been called Uganda's silent killers. *Boda-bodas*, our country's ubiquitous motorbike taxis, snake through traffic jams, navigate potholed roads and provide much-needed employment for young people. They are also injuring and killing thousands every year, monopolising hospital budgets and destroying livelihoods. Since they appeared on the streets of Uganda in the 1960s, the number of *boda-bodas* has swelled. One recent news report estimated that there were more than 300 000 bikes operating in the capital, Kampala.

As a result, the number of motorbike accidents has increased dramatically. According to the Injury Control Centre, there are up to 20 *boda-boda*-related cases at Mulago National Referral Hospital in Kampala every day and the strain on the country's limited health budget is growing. About 40% of trauma cases at the hospital are from *boda-boda* accidents. The treatment of injured passengers and pedestrians accounts for almost two-thirds of the hospital's annual surgery budget.

While *boda-bodas* are helping to reduce youth unemployment – one recent study estimated that 62% of young people in Uganda are jobless – the impact of a serious injury can be catastrophic for riders and their families. Ali Niwamanya, 25, a *boda-boda* driver, spent three months in Mulago hospital and another five at home recovering after a collision with a car in the capital in September. Niwamanya is now in debt after taking out a 3 million Ugandan shilling loan (that's about 1200 US dollars) for a new bike.

While the human impact of the *boda-boda* craze is evident in the packed hospital wards, the strain that road fatalities could have on the economy is worrying politicians. The death toll on Uganda's roads is twice the average across the rest of Africa. There were 3343 road deaths in 2011, but the World Health Organization believes the figure could be more than double that. Some people are warning that, in the very near future, the death toll from Uganda's roads will be higher than that from diseases such as malaria.

Some measures are being taken to try to halt the problem. Last month, the government announced that more money would be available to improve and maintain roads. Even though road safety measures were not specifically included within the budget, the government is establishing a national agency to run campaigns and manage roads. In Kampala, the Capital City Authority is introducing regulations, including registration of drivers, first-aid training, reflector jackets and helmets, and a monthly fee of 20 000 Ugandan shillings paid by the city's 250 000 motorbike taxis.

Other initiatives are also springing up. The Global Helmet Vaccine Initiative is holding a one-day workshop for 100 riders, part of a national scheme under which it has trained 1800 *boda-boda* riders in basic road safety. On completion, each participant receives a yellow helmet bearing the slogan: 'Your life is your wealth.'

Adapted from www.theguardian.com

WORD TIP
At IGCSE level, we should be helping students to become more selective about the words they use. The words *catastrophe* and *disaster* are quite similar in meaning, but the former is stronger and more extreme, and is more descriptive. There is an exercise in Unit 4 of the **Workbook** for students to complete.

9 Pairs

Using the numbers in the box, students work together and complete the gaps in **a–f**. Then they listen again to check their answers. If students need practice in saying numbers and dates in English, get them to try saying aloud the completed sentences in Activity C9.

Answers

a	**i** 1960s,	d	**iv** 25,
b	**ii** 300 000,	e	**v** 20 000, **vi** 250 000,
c	**iii** 20,	f	**vii** 100

LANGUAGE TIP
Recognising suffixes can help students in decoding unknown words. Point out the different verbs which are formed from *-ion* nouns. There is an exercise in the **Workbook** for students to complete.

D Language focus: tenses

1 Alone, then pairs

Getting students to recognise aspects of grammar in context is an effective learning strategy. Activity D1 asks students to look at four sentences from the audioscript and decide which verb time (tense) is referred to by the verbs in bold. Let them work alone and then check their answers with a partner.

Answers

a	present perfect,	c	present continuous,
b	past simple,	d	'will' future

2 Pairs

With a partner, students complete the rules for the three remaining tenses and decide what the function is for each one, as they are used in the listening text. Remember that structures/tenses can have more than one function – for example, one function of the present continuous is to describe actions happening at the moment of speaking, but in **c**, the function is different.

Answers

b past simple *regular verbs add -ed, many irregular forms*

Function = *to talk about a complete action in the past*

c present continuous *am/is/are + verb -ing*

Function = *something happening around this time, a trend*

d 'will' future *will + infinitive*

Function = *making a prediction based on evidence*

3 Alone, then pairs

In this activity, students decide which is the most suitable tense for the verbs in brackets, in order to complete sentences **a–g**. In some cases, there might be more than one possible answer, so make sure students are able to give reasons for their choices. Let them work alone and then share their answers with their partner.

Answers

a   will get,

b   have seen,

c   are thinking,

d   told, caught,

e   is trying,

f   will be,

g   has had

E Speaking

1/2 Alone

These two activities focus on giving students some clear models of structures to show surprise. Get students to listen once, then to listen again and write down the four phrases that show surprise:

The thing that surprised me more than anything was …

What surprised me most was …

I couldn't believe …

I had no idea about …

CD1, Track 6

i Male teenager:	The thing that surprised me more than anything was the number of *boda-bodas* on the roads.
ii Female teenager:	What surprised me most was the number of injuries and deaths.
iii Male teenager:	I couldn't believe how long Ali Niwamanya was in hospital for.
iv Female teenager:	I had no idea about the rate of unemployment.

3 Small groups

Students discuss the three questions **a–c**. Encourage them to use the phrases from the previous activities during their discussions. As with all speaking activities, make sure you provide feedback and do not just focus on students' errors. Give them positive feedback about their ideas and the way in which they practised the key phrases.

4 Alone, then small groups

Many exams require students to look at information given in a table or other graphic format and to show that they have understood certain elements. This is also an important life skill, as we often need to look at graphs and interpret the data shown. The table in this activity contains a lot of information, in both words and numbers. Before students attempt the questions, give them a few minutes to just

look at the table and check they understand what it shows. Then, in small groups, they can answer the questions. There is no need for any writing – this is a speaking activity.

For the final question (**g**), students need to create a graph based on some information from the table. This could be a bar graph, a pie chart, a line graph or similar. Help students to select information from the table (e.g. the statistics for dangerous driving from January to November, or all the statistics for one particular month such as June), then create a graph or chart that displays the information.

Answers

a   the information is still being checked and is not final

b   **i** deaths; **ii** everyone has to pay the same amount

c   RTA = Road Traffic Act and detention is when the police take charge of a vehicle

d   an offence is something done against the law, so this refers to illegal actions by road users (drivers)

e   'Careers'

f   leaflets, papers, books, articles

5 Pairs

Students now discuss the information in the table by asking each other five questions. Go through the example in the Coursebook first, making sure students understand that they need to ask a follow-up question (*What surprises you most … ?*) in order to practise the key phrases from earlier in this section. Monitor and give feedback.

6 Small groups

This activity extends the speaking practice for this section. If time permits, you could turn this into a class debate, with students offering different responses to the question: *If you were in charge of solving traffic problems and reducing the accident rate, what would you do?*

F Listening

TOP TIP

The **Top Tip** near Activity F1 of the Coursebook advises students to read the questions and underline key words in listening activities, and it is worth reinforcing this. Give students plenty of opportunities to practise thinking about the type of answer that a question requires – for example: a number, a nationality, a street name, and so on.

1 Pairs

After focusing on the **Top Tip**, students should practise identifying what information questions **a–d** require in their answers.

Answers

a i an article, something
 ii a number
b i type of weather
 ii a number of degrees
c i location, somewhere
 ii activity
d i name of sport
 ii price

2 Alone

Students work alone and decide which of the answers given could match the questions in Activity F1.

Answers

a d **ii** price
b c **i** location
c b **i** type of weather
d a **ii** a number

e a **i** something
f b **ii** a number of degrees
g d **i** sport
h c **ii** activity

3 Alone

Prepare students for listening and answering the questions in Activity F1. Remember that they have already decided what type of answer is required and seen some possible answers for all the questions.

CD1, Track 7

A

Woman: Good morning, Mega Music Store, how can I help you?

Gregory: Hi, I'd like to know if I can order something from you.

W: Yes, of course – we can help you with DVDs and MP3 downloads, as well as other software and tablets, and so on.

G: Actually, I don't want any of those; I just want to order a power cable. The product number is CD39 dash 2BK. Can you do that?

W: Certainly. Let me take your details …

B

Here is the weather forecast for tomorrow for your local area. There will be some light rain overnight, turning to sunny spells in the early morning and there will be high clouds by the end of the morning. Heavy showers are forecast for the late afternoon and evening. The top temperature is expected to be 18° Celsius.

C

Marina: Hello, could I have some information about your evening classes, please?

College secretary: Of course. Are you interested in anything in particular, or do you want details of everything we offer?

M: I'm interested in learning a new language. I want to learn Italian!

CS: If you look over there, behind those bookshelves, you'll find leaflets about all our evening classes, or you could use one of the computers to check online.

D

Thank you for calling the Health and Fitness Sports Centre, the home of tennis, squash, badminton, futsal and swimming. The Sports Centre management has just introduced new prices for using the tennis facilities, so for non-members a weekend court will now cost €12 an hour, while during the week, the daytime price is €8 and €10 after 6 p.m. For members, the price is €9 at any time during the week, and €11 at the weekend.

Answers

a **i** power cable, **ii** CD39-2BK
b **i** high clouds, **ii** 18 °C
c **i** information office/library, **ii** learn Italian
d **i** tennis, **ii** €9

4 Pairs

Students compare their answers and then look at the audioscript in Appendix 3 in the Coursebook to check.

LANGUAGE TIP

This **Language Tip** highlights the importance of linking words and phrases in listening activities. Make sure students understand that linking words and phrases can provide important clues about what the speaker is saying, as well as what the speaker is going to say. There is an exercise for students to complete in Unit 4 of the **Workbook**.

27

Reflection

Use the **Reflection** to remind students of what they have achieved in the unit. Students should set themselves a **personal goal** based on their scores for Unit 4.

Exam focus

Reading, Exercise 1, skimming and scanning

Answers

a   because they are more vulnerable

b   need to concentrate on the road and other traffic

c   identifies you to other road users

d   after dark and in poor conditions

e   keep clear of the kerb and do not ride in the gutter; don't hug the kerb if a car behind you gets impatient; don't weave between lanes or change direction suddenly; show drivers what you plan to do in plenty of time; always look and signal before you start, stop or turn

f   make eye contact with drivers

g   on the tyre itself

h   all road users

i   jump red lights at pedestrian crossings; cycle on pavements; cycle the wrong way up a one-way street; ride across a pedestrian crossing

Listening, Exercise 1, Part A, short extracts

CD 1, Track 8

Question 1

And now for the prices and opening times at the Star Cinema. All tickets are priced at $10 for adults and $6.50 for students and children. Our weekend opening time is two o'clock in the afternoon and on weekdays we open one hour later, at three.

Question 2

Daniela: Do you sell street maps?

Shopkeeper: Well, yes, we do, but I'm afraid we've sold out.

D: Do you know where I can get one?

S: Try the newsagent's on the other side of the park. Or the shop at the bus station will have plenty.

D: Isn't there anywhere closer than the bus station?

S: Let me think … Oh yes, the supermarket across the road from here.

Question 3

Jason: Excuse me! Sorry to trouble you but I'm completely lost! This is my first day working here and I can't find where I need to go!

Woman: You must be the new part-time helper, right? Don't worry, you'll soon find your way around. This is the staff room. But where do you want to go?

J: I'm trying to find the supervisor's office. I need to give him my contact details.

W: Well, you're not too far away. Look, you see the lift over there? Go up to the second floor and when you get out of the lift, turn left and left again at the end of the corridor. The supervisor's office is the first door on the right.

J: Thanks so much.

Question 4

Welcome aboard our city sightseeing bus. First, let me tell you about the tour. We're going to travel through the most historic parts of the city for about an hour, with lots of opportunities for you to take photos, or just admire the wonderful buildings and scenery. Then we'll drop you off near the market place. You can visit the museum, which is very interesting, or why not buy some fruit and cheese from the market and have a snack in the park next to the museum? But please please please come back promptly to the bus after one hour – we can't wait for any latecomers!

Now for some safety information … .

Answers

1 a   Star Cinema

  b   3.00 p.m.

2 a   street map

  b   supermarket, nearby

3 a   part-time helper

  b   supervisor

4 a   get a snack

  b   one hour

Listening, Exercise 1, Part B, short extracts

CD 1, Track 9

Question 1

Adult man: Everything half price before we close today. Fruit, vegetables, lovely flowers, you can get everything you need here, in your local market. Come to the front and take a good look. You won't believe my prices today. Potatoes and carrots for lunch tomorrow, apples and melons, everything 100% fresh and half prices. Yes, madam, what can I get for you?

Adult female: Just some fruit please … hmmm I'll take a kilo of oranges please.

Adult man: Certainly madam, no problem. How about some strawberries? They were grown locally, just down the road. Or some lovely pears?

Adult female: Yes, they look delicious, but not today thanks. But on second thoughts, I'll take 5 kilos of potatoes.

Question 2

Hi Fatma, this is Muna. How are you? I don't know if you remember me, but we were in sociology class together during summer school. We were so pleased to see each other in the classroom after meeting at the registration day in April. Anyway, I'll be working in Bahrain next month and I'd love to see you and go for a coffee. I was supposed to be coming in September, but my trip was postponed. So, I'll be coming in November instead. Can you let me know if you have any free time? Hopefully, we'll meet again soon.

Question 3

Teenage girl: Hi, Ali, how are you? Last time I spoke to Uncle Fahad he said you were going away with your school basketball team.

Teenage boy: Yeah, we were supposed to go for two weeks but it was cut short.

TG: So when did you get back?

TB: In the end the trip was just one week, which was kind of disappointing.

TG: I suppose so, but did you win your matches?

TB: We played two warm-up matches, which we lost, and six competitive matches. We won four of those, which wasn't bad I suppose. We didn't win the competition cup, but we all got a medal for taking part.

TG: Excellent! Well done!

Question 4

Adult male: Hello, do you have a table for three, please? I have a young baby so perhaps somewhere not too noisy? We didn't make a reservation.

Adult female: No reservation? For three, let me just check …. Unfortunately, we are fully booked but I think I might have a table for two somewhere. We can add a highchair for the baby, if that's OK?

AM: It depends where the table is …

AF: Just there, by the window.

AM: Hmmm it might be a bit too cold there for the baby. Do you have anywhere else?

AF: As I said, sir, we are fully booked, so that's all I can offer you at the moment, unless you can wait until after eight o'clock.

Answers

1 a in the market
  b oranges, potatoes
2 a summer school
  b September
3 a a week
  b four
4 a somewhere quiet
  b (bit) too cold

NOTE on Assessment Objectives (AOs) for Listening Exercise 2 and Speaking: Students need to demonstrate that they can listen to a formal talk and complete gaps in notes/sentences based on what they hear. Specifically, students need to identify and select relevant information (L1) and understand ideas, opinions and attitudes (L2).

Furthermore, for speaking, students need to communicate ideas/opinions clearly, accurately and effectively (S1), develop responses and link ideas using a range of appropriate linking devices (S2), use a range of grammatical structures and vocabulary accurately and effectively (S3), show control of pronunciation and intonation patterns (S4) and engage in a conversation and contribute effectively to help move the conversation forward (S5).

Learning objectives (LOs)

Suggested activity: Start the unit by focusing for a few minutes on the LOs box, making sure that students understand what they are going to be doing. Using the first LO as an example, ask students to identify where in the unit they can find the activities for the other four LOs. Get students to say which of the activities appeal to them the most, and ask them for their reasons.

A Watch, listen and talk

1 Whole class, then alone

Explain that your students are going to watch and listen to some IGCSE students talking about **holidays**. As your students watch and listen, they should make a note of the **three** favourite types of holiday that the speakers mention, and the **reasons** they give. Play the video a second time so that students can check or add to their notes.

Answers

a Favourite types of holiday that the students mention (any **three** from): beach holidays, shopping holidays, self-tour holidays, lone holidays, inactive holidays, Edinburgh, Spain (Madrid), France (Paris) [cities].

The **reasons** they give: it's a tradition, the student discovered famous destinations, the student tried famous cuisines, the student bought traditional clothing, the student got to explore the city, the city had an appealing culture, the student is studying the language, to broaden knowledge about the culture, to improve language skills.

2 Pairs or small groups

Depending on the size of your class, put students into pairs or small groups. They can discuss their notes and then talk to each other about the types of holiday that **they** prefer and their reasons. Do not interfere too much, but make sure you get feedback from the class so that they know their efforts have been worthwhile. If time permits, you could write their ideas on the board and rank them according to your students' preferences.

B Speaking and vocabulary

1 Pairs

Students focus on the seven pictures of different types of holiday, and discuss what they think each holiday involves. This is a speaking activity so do not worry too much about language errors – allow students to discuss freely and without correction to help them build up their confidence. There are no right or wrong answers. Encourage students to say two things about each holiday.

2 Pairs

There are many possibilities with this matching activity, so make sure students are not too worried about getting things 'right'. The aim is for them to think and discuss possible combinations to create the names of seven holidays, and finally to match them to the pictures in B1.

Answers

a	6,		e	7,
b	1,		f	3,
c	5,		g	4
d	2,			

3 Pairs, then whole class

For **a–e**, students work in pairs, discussing each question. You may decide to limit the time available for each question, so that the activity does not take longer than is necessary. Once again, there are no right or wrong answers, to encourage fluency. Challenge students by encouraging them to give reasons for their answers. Provide some time for whole class feedback and to reveal to students that all the holidays are 'real' except for 'Chocolate cake baking in Hawaii'. Finally, focus on question **f**, which asks students to think of another unusual type of holiday and agree on a name for it. Anything goes! Display all of their answers and allow some time for students to choose which of these holidays they would like to go on.

C Listening

1 Whole class
Tell students who they are going to listen to, and what the speaker is going to be talking about. Then get them to answer questions **a** and **b** with you, all the while referring them to the map, which will provide them with some clues.

2 Alone
Students listen once to Wang Yanghua being interviewed about aerial tourism, and check their answers to C1 **a** and **b**.

CD1, Track 10

Chen Wen: Hello everyone, my name's Chen Wen, and today we are very lucky to be talking to someone who has an amazing job! Please welcome Wang Yanghua, an aerial tourism helicopter pilot based in Guilin, Southern China.

Wang Yanghua: Hello, Chen, thank you for inviting me.

CW: So, aerial tourism? What on earth is that?!

WY: Well, it's basically holiday sightseeing, but from a helicopter. Instead of seeing things from the ground, I take tourists and holidaymakers up in a helicopter, and we look at things from above.

CW: That's certainly a different way of doing things. Tell us how you became interested in flying. Is it something that you've always wanted to do?

WY: Well, actually, no. As a teenager I wanted to be a doctor.

CW: So how did you become a pilot?

WY: Well, I was at the cinema and watching a film, and at some point there was a dramatic scene with helicopters flying over cities and forests …

CW: … and that made you want to become a pilot?

WY: To be honest, it just suddenly hit me that flying helicopters was what I wanted to do. Strange, but true! I got my full licence seven years ago.

CW: What is a normal workday for you?

WY: Well, it depends very much on the time of year, because obviously the weather impacts greatly on when I can fly, and to which sights. But on a summer's day I need to be at the airfield a couple of hours before that day's sightseers are ready to board the helicopter, so usually I'm there around seven in the morning.

CW: Where exactly do you take the tourists?

WY: We are very lucky in this part of China to have such stunning scenery. Guilin offers breath-taking lakes and rivers, as well as rolling hills, and spectacular views.

CW: Do sightseers ever want to avoid nature and look down on cities instead?

WY: Certainly they do. I have a colleague, who flies in Beijing, and she only does city sightseeing tours. She tells me that the most popular attractions are the Beijing National Stadium, known as the Bird's Nest, and, of course, the Great Wall of China.

CW: Describe how different it is to see something from a helicopter.

WY: Well, firstly, ground-level sightseeing is usually static. It's **stationary***. People get off the coach or out of the car and stand in front of something and take a photo or two, or a couple of selfies. Often people sit and admire something and really only see a building or a statue from one static angle. But when you're in a helicopter, sightseeing becomes more dynamic …

CW: Which means?

WY: Well, the angle of view and speed are constantly changing because, obviously, the helicopter is constantly moving. What you see is a panorama, from east to west and from north to south, and if you close your eyes for a few seconds, when you open them again the view will be completely different.

CW: So if you blink you may miss something?!

WY: Yes! Secondly, how high or low the helicopter is flying …

CW: … its altitude?

WY: Exactly. Altitude impacts hugely on how we see something.

CW: What else is different?

WY: Well, at ground level, it's usually very difficult to know what other things are around the sight you are looking at. But from the air, you can see

31

the building or lake or whatever it might be, in a context. And that of course helps us to appreciate its size and shape in relation to other things.

CW: Finally, Wang, what's the most interesting thing you've ever seen from a helicopter?

WY: You know something? Every time I fly, I see things differently, so something which may not have struck me as being very interesting on one day could look completely different on another. So, every day is fascinating in some way or another. Every day I see something which amazes me.

CW: As I said at the start, you really do have an amazing job! I definitely know what my next holiday activity is going to be! Wang Yanghua, aerial tourism helicopter pilot, thank you so much, and fly safely!

WY: Thank you!

LANGUAGE TIP

These two words (*stationary**, *stationery*) are easily confused, not least how to spell them. Talk through the information and then direct students to complete the exercise in Unit 5 of the **Workbook**.

---

3 Alone

Tell students they are going to listen again. As they listen, they need to check in which order they hear the eight adjectives (**a–h**) in the box, and also make a note of what each adjective is describing. One example has been done.

Differentiated activities

Support

Provide students with a list of the nouns that each adjective describes in the listening, and give them a few minutes to think of possible combinations before they listen.

Challenge

Ask students to note down any other adjective + noun combinations that they hear (e.g. breath-taking lakes, rolling hills, sightseeing tours, interesting thing) and then ask them to think of other nouns that could combine with each adjective, e.g. breath-taking views.

Answers

1 amazing + job, 2 dramatic + scene, 3 normal + workday, 4 stunning + scenery, 5 spectacular + views, 6 popular + attractions, 7 ground-level + sightseeing, 8 static + angle

4 Pairs

Completing gaps in notes while listening to someone talking is a complex and challenging skill, and students need plenty of practice in order to build up their confidence. Before they listen to the interview again, they should look at the incomplete notes and together discuss what information is missing.

5 Alone, then pairs

When students are ready, play the interview and tell them to check their answers.

Answers

Full name: *Wang Yanghua*
Work location: *Guilin, Southern China*
Licence obtained: *seven years ago*
Normal day starts at: *around seven in the morning*
Takes tourists in Guilin to see: *scenery: lakes, rivers, hills, views*
Popular attractions in Beijing: *National Stadium, Great Wall of China*
Advantages of aerial sightseeing: *more dynamic, panoramic, gives everything a context*

6 Pairs

For the final activity in this section, students look at the audioscript in Appendix 3 of the Coursebook and find more examples of adjective + noun combinations.

Answers

breath-taking lakes, rolling hills, sightseeing tours, interesting thing

D Language focus: compound (multi-word) adjectives

> **LANGUAGE TIP**
>
> While in the previous section compound adjectives were not specifically focused on, this **Language Tip** highlights the use of two or more adjectives to modify a noun. Usually these adjectives are hyphenated to avoid confusion. There is an exercise for students to complete in Unit 5 of the **Workbook**.

1 Pairs (A and B)

In **Section D**, students are going to read about two of the holidays mentioned previously. Before they do so, they are going to focus on a number of adjectives which appear in the texts.

a   **i** Students discuss what the adjectives 1–12 mean. If time is limited, you could divide up the 12 adjectives and distribute to different pairs (or small groups) of students, and then allow them to share their ideas.

   ii Remind students what the titles of the two texts are: *Hiking with huskies in Finland* and *Swimming with dolphins at the Mediterraneo Marine Park*, and ask them which adjectives they think will appear in the texts, and for their reasons. For example, 'sturdy' in *Hiking with huskies* because the term is often associated with boots, which hikers wear and 'Abundant' in *Swimming with dolphins* because the term is often associated with areas with lots of wildlife and animals, such as underwater. Do not supply any answers as students will find out for themselves when they read the texts in **Section E**.

b   There are plenty of possible combinations here and it is worth reminding students that it is not important to 'get things right'. The essential thing is for them to think about which adjectives (1–12) could combine with the nouns and noun and verb phrases (**a–l**). Encourage them to give reasons for their choices. Do not supply any answers as students will find out for themselves when they read the texts in **Section E**.

c   You could use this activity to challenge any students who finish 1a and 1b early. There are endless possibilities.

E Reading and speaking

1 Pairs (A and B)

Students are each going to read a different text: **Student A** is going to read **Text 5A** in Appendix 2 of the Coursebook:

Hiking with huskies in Finland and **Student B** is going to read **Text 5B** in Appendix 2: *Swimming with dolphins at the Mediterraneo Marine Park*. Note that the texts are on different pages so that Student A cannot see Student B's text, and vice versa. Students read their allocated text and check their answers to D1a (ii) and D1b. Encourage them to give reasons for their answers whenever possible.

Answers

D1a (ii) and D1b

1 abundant **Text 5 B + c**	7 memorable **B + e**
2 advisable **A + i**	8 more intensive **A + f**
3 comprehensive **B + b**	9 paramount **B + d**
4 customised **B + a**	10 shock-absorbing **A + g**
5 husky-trekking **A + j**	11 more strenuous **A + h**
6 innovative **B + l**	12 sturdy **A + k**

2 Same A/B pairs

Under the texts which students have read in Appendix 2 is a set of questions. These questions refer to the **other** text, i.e. the text which the students have **not** read. Taking turns, students ask and answer the questions, making a note of their partner's answers.

3 Same A/B pairs

Without referring to either of the texts or any notes, students now tell each other as much as they can remember about their partner's text. They can ask questions for clarification.

F Listening

1 Pairs

This activity gives students more practice in seeing how adjectives and nouns combine. Try to encourage your students to learn 'chunks' of language for immediate productive use in either their writing or speaking. Do not supply any answers as students will find out for themselves when they listen in F2.

2 Alone, then pairs

Students listen to the man talking about winter holidays in Dali and **a** check their answers to F1, and **b** say in which order they hear the noun + adjective chunks (1–9). Then they can compare their ideas in pairs.

33

Answers

1 snow-white seabirds, 2 snow-capped mountains,
3 freshwater lake, 4 lush green leaves, 5 natural attraction,
6 complex landscape, 7 professional guide, 8 thrilling
experience, 9 spectacular event

CD1, Track 11

For anyone wanting a winter holiday, the area around
Dali, in the province of Yunnan in southern China,
offers many attractions, such as beautiful islands and
delightful mountain scenery, as well as wonderful
wildlife. One example of this can be found near Xiao
Putuo island in Erhai Lake, where thousands of snow-
white seabirds take to the air whenever food is thrown
at them. As you know, birds often fear humans, but this
event really happens. Some of the birds even fly toward
the food held out by visitors and take it from their hands.
The whole scene is breath-taking, with blue water and
sky, white clouds, and snow-capped mountains in the
distance.

Erhai (meaning *ear-shaped*) Lake is the second-largest
freshwater lake in the region, covers an area of 257 square
kilometres and has an average depth of 11 metres. The
lake is an important food source for the local people, who
are famous for their amazing method of fishing. They train
cormorant birds to catch fish who then return them to the
fishmongers!

Xiao Putou island, where Erhai Lake is found, is covered
with lush green leaves and flowers, and the recent building
of several hotels along the lake's shores makes this an
increasingly popular place for tourists to visit. Locals can
rent you a small boat to visit both the island and the lake.
Nearby Cangshan Mountain is another natural attraction,
with almost 95% of it covered by forest. Along with the
complex landscape of the mountain, the forest makes
walking difficult for novices. Up to 200 people lose their
way each year, and have to be rescued, so a professional
guide is essential if you want to go walking in the area. If
you insist and really want to explore the mountain, but are
looking for an easier option, a 45-minute cable-car ride will
transport you to the top, which is 4,000 metres above sea
level.

This ride is a thrilling experience during the winter time.
You will be amazed by the green mountain landscape at
lower levels, which gradually changes to a white blanket of
snow as you slowly travel upwards. Then, as the cable-car
reaches higher levels, it can get quite shaky if the weather's
windy.

Another attraction near the lake are the hot springs at
Eryuan, which is in fact the original source of the water
in Erhai Lake. There are 200–300 hot springs open to
the public, attracting many winter visitors from Taiwan,
Thailand, Myanmar, Hong Kong and Japan, as well as
South Korea. Improved transport links are planned to
increase tourism, and there are currently 15 domestic air
links connecting the region with major cities.

Major events, such as the six-day shopping festival,
encourage locals and tourists to buy herbal medicine,
agricultural products and clothes, as well as food and gift
items. As many as 30 000 people visit the festival every
year. Another spectacular event is the annual singing fair,
which attracts nearly 100 000 people.

3 Alone, then pairs

Give students a few minutes to look at the incomplete
notes and to make some guesses about the missing
information in each gap. They do not need to write
anything yet. Go through their answers orally, without
correcting anything. Then play the audio again and
students write their answers. Point out that they should
write only one or two words in each gap. Students
compare their answers in pairs.

Answers

a   delightful mountain,

b   ear-shaped,

c   257/two hundred and fifty-seven,

d   (cormorant) birds,

e   island,

f   95%,

g   each year,

h   sea level,

i   white,

j   windy,

k   transport,

l   6-/six-day,

m   singing

4 Alone

Students can read the audioscript after Activity F3 to check their answers.

G Speaking

TOP TIP

Go through the **Top Tip** and explain that the rest of this unit will give students practice in preparing for part of an exam, which is designed to put students at their ease by asking them questions of a personal nature, and which should not be too demanding.

1 Alone

Students write five questions which they think they might be asked in the first part of the exam.

TOP TIP

Point out that questions do not always start with a *Wh-* question word. Sometimes the other person may say: *Tell me about …, Talk about …, Describe …,* etc.

2 Pairs

Students ask and answer their questions from Activity G1.

3 Pairs

Students work together to unjumble the words to make ten questions (**a–j**). Point out that some do not begin with a question word (**c, g** and **j**). Students can also see if any of the questions are similar to the ones they thought of in G1. Do not supply any answers as students will find out for themselves when they listen in G5.

4 Pairs

Ask students to think about the order in which the questions might be asked, and to give reasons. There are no right answers here, but probably questions about the student's name and family would come first, followed by travel, school and career plans, and finally the weekend.

5 Alone

Students listen to Stefanos and the other person and check their answers to G3.

Answers

1 d What's your name?

2 e How do you spell your family name?

3 a Which town do you live in?

4 g Describe how you travelled here today.

5 f How many brothers and sisters do you have?

6 j Tell me what you enjoy doing in your free time.

7 c Talk to me about your favourite subjects at school.

8 h What career would you like to follow?

9 i What did you do last weekend?

10b What are your plans for next weekend?

CD1, Track 12

Interviewer: Hello. What's your name?

Stefanos: Stefanos.

I: How do you spell your family name?

S: ALEXANDROU.

I: Which town do you live in, Stefanos?

S: Nicosia.

I: Thank you. Describe how you travelled here today.

S: Car.

I: How many brothers and sisters do you have?

S: None.

I: Tell me what you enjoy doing in your free time.

S: Playing on my computer.

I: Thanks, Stefanos. Talk to me about your favourite subjects at school.

S: Science.

I: OK. And what career would you like to follow?

S: I want to be a doctor.

I: Thank you. What did you do last weekend?

S: I visited my grandparents.

I: And what are your plans for next weekend?

S: I don't know.

I: Thank you very much, Stefanos.

6 Alone

Before students listen a second time, ask them if they can remember how Stefanos answered questions **a–f**. Then play the interview again and students check their ideas.

Answers

a   Car.

b   Playing on my computer.

c   Science.

d   I want to be a doctor.

e   I visited my grandparents.

f   I don't know.

7 Pairs

Students discuss which of the answers they think could be better, and give reasons. Students should avoid giving single-word answers whenever possible, so answers **a** and **c** are not particularly strong. We also need to encourage students to add information to statements they give, so answers **b**, **d**, **e** and **f** could also be better.

Possible answers

a   My mum drove me here in her car.

b   I enjoy playing on my computer.

c   I like science subjects, especially physics and chemistry.

d   I want to be a doctor, but I'm not really sure yet.

e   I visited my grandparents. They live in a village in the mountains.

f   I don't know yet. It depends on the weather.

8 Alone, then pairs

Students listen to Maria and decide if she performs better or worse than Stefanos. Encourage students to discuss their reasons with their partner.

CD1, Track 13

Interviewer:	Hello. What's your name?
Maria:	Hi. I'm Maria.
I:	How do you spell your family name?
M:	**Actually** it's quite easy: CHRISTOU.
I:	Which town do you live in, Maria?
M:	I live here in Nicosia, well, just outside actually.

I:	Thank you. Describe how you travelled here today.
M:	**Well**, my mum drove me.
I:	How many brothers and sisters do you have?
M:	I don't have any.
I:	Tell me what you enjoy doing in your free time.
M:	**To be honest**, I don't have much free time but I like watching TV.
I:	Thanks, Maria. Talk to me about your favourite subjects at school.
M:	**Hmm**, I like everything but my favourite subject is English.
I:	OK. And what career would you like to follow?
M:	**So far**, I have no idea but maybe teaching.
I:	Thank you. What did you do last weekend?
M:	**Let me think**. OK, I had an exam at school so I did some studying.
I:	And what are your plans for next weekend?
M:	**Next weekend?** I don't know. Maybe I'll go shopping with some friends.
I:	Thank you very much.

9 Alone, then pairs

Before students listen again to Maria, get them to give you some examples of 'fillers'. Maria uses quite a few, which help to improve her responses to the other person's questions.

Answers

Actually, Well, To be honest, Hmm, So far, Let me think, Next weekend?

10 Alone

Refer students to the audioscript in Appendix 3 of the Coursebook to check their answers.

11 Whole class

Ask students in what way 'Next weekend?' is different from the other fillers.

Answer

Maria repeats some key words from the question, to give herself time to think.

H Watch, listen and talk

1/2 Alone, then pairs

Students are going to watch two students answering an examiner's questions. As they watch, students should check which of the questions already discussed in this section the examiner asks, and then discuss with their partner which of the two students performs better, and give their reasons.

3 Pairs

This activity gives students an opportunity to practise the language introduced in this unit. They can take the roles of examiner and student, and then change roles to get practice in both asking and answering questions. Allow this activity to run freely without too much intervention from you, but encourage students to use the language from the unit.

Reflection

Use the **Reflection** to remind students of what they have achieved in the unit. Students should set themselves a **personal goal** based on their scores for Unit 5.

Exam focus

Listening, Exercise 2, note-making

Answers
Global Volcanoes
[marks given in square brackets for guidance]

a   Volcanoes are powerful, prized, beautiful, **exciting** [1 mark]

Talk is about five volcanoes in Asia, USA, Indonesia, **Africa**, Europe [½]

b   Mount Fuji **3776** metres high [½]

Many Japanese hope to reach the top during lifetime

c   Shape of top of Mt Fuji is like a **cone** [½] and possible to see it from **Tokyo's skyscrapers** [½]

Distance to volcano is **133 km** [½]

d   Mt Semeru is the **highest** [½] volcano in Indonesia

Mt Bromo: wonderful **sunrise** [½] views

e   Virunga is Africa's first **national park** [½]

Possible to see **gorillas** [½] and the world's largest **lava lake** [½] at Mt Nyiragongo

f   Near Naples, Mt Vesuvius, famous for devastating eruption almost **two thousand / 2,000** [½] years ago

Volcanology research information from visit to **observatory** [½]

g   Crater Lake landscape not seen until you reach edge of crater, and lake is different shades of **blue** [½]

h   Lake surrounded by cliffs and **pine forests** [½]

Visitors can drive or hike.

Focus on reading and writing: note-making

NOTE on Assessment Objectives (AOs) for Reading and Writing Exercise 3 (note-making): Students need to demonstrate that they can make brief notes under a supplied heading or headings relating to an article/text (for example: from a newspaper or magazine) printed in the question paper. Specifically, students need to identify and select relevant information (R1), understand ideas, opinions and attitudes (R2) and show understanding of the connections between ideas, opinions and attitudes (R3).

Learning objectives (LOs)

Suggested activity: Start the unit by focusing for a few minutes on the LOs box, making sure that students understand what they are going to be doing. Using the first LO as an example, ask students to identify where in the unit they can find the activities for the other four LOs. Get students to say which of the activities appeal to them the most, and ask them for their reasons.

A Watch, listen and talk

1 Whole class, then alone

Explain that your students are going to watch and listen to some IGCSE students talking about **school facilities**. As your students watch and listen, they should **a** make a note of the **three** most important facilities that the speakers mention, and **b** make a note of the facilities that the speakers would like to have. Play the video a second time so that students can check or add to their notes.

Answers

a The most important facilities that a school should offer: a library, an outdoor area, a big hall.

b **Extra** facilities the students would like to have: an outdoor area, a big hall.

2 Pairs or small groups

Depending on the size of your class, put students into pairs or small groups. They can discuss their notes and then talk to each other about the facilities that **they** think are the most important in a school, and the extra facilities they would like to have in their school. Do not interfere too much, but make sure you get feedback from the class so that they know their efforts have been

worthwhile. If time permits, you could write their ideas on the board and rank them according to your students' preferences.

B Speaking and vocabulary

1 Small groups

Ask students to think about schools and make sure they understand what *facilities* means. In small groups, they look at and discuss the pictures, then answer the questions. You may like to limit the time available for each question.

a They need to discuss if any of the facilities are the same as the ones from **Section A**, and talk about which ones (if any) they have and would like to have in their own school. Encourage them to give reasons for their ideas. Monitor, but do not interfere with the discussions. Provide feedback afterwards.

b Leading on from question **a**, students talk about what facilities they would expect a school to have but which are missing from the pictures.

c For the final question, students need to think about the differences between primary and secondary schools, and universities and colleges, and to give reasons why different places of learning need different facilities.

2 Alone

If you have access to the internet, you could get students to search for 'schools', either in their own country or somewhere else, and check the facilities that they offer. If you can't use the internet, prompt students with some questions – for example: *Where could you borrow a book from?* Students should make a list of facilities and then put them into rank order.

Next, get your students to convert their list into a graph or chart. Each student needs to prepare their own graph or chart for the next activity.

3 Small groups

Using their own graph or chart, students now say three things about it to the others in their group, then answer any questions. Use the example in the Coursebook to check that students understand what they have to do. Monitor, but do not interfere. Provide positive, encouraging feedback once students have finished talking about their graphs and charts.

C Reading

1 Pairs

The first activity in this section focuses on vocabulary. Students work in pairs to find out the meaning of the ten words and phrases. During feedback, make sure that there is general agreement on the meanings.

Differentiated activities

Support

i   Reduce the number of words and phrases that students should look up.

ii   Supply students with the correct definitions for a matching activity.

Challenge

Once students have agreed on the definitions, ask them to do some word building, for example: *extensive* (adjective) – *extend* (verb) – *extensively* (adverb) – *extension* (noun).

2 Alone, then pairs

The headings in the box are all services and facilities that a language school might offer. Students skim the text and decide which heading goes with each of the five paragraphs, then check with their partner. There are three extra headings that students do not need to use.

Answers

1 IT centre,

2 Library and Multimedia Resource Centre (LMRC),

3 Counselling service,

4 Cafeteria,

5 Accommodation and welfare

Differentiated activities

Support

You could point out which headings are not needed (Banking facilities, Social and leisure programme and Sports centre), to reduce what students have to think about.

Challenge

Tell students to cover up the box in Activity C2 and think of their own headings for the five paragraphs.

WORD TIP

The spellings of these two words (*practice, practise*) are commonly confused. Refer students to the practice exercise in Unit 6 of the **Workbook**.

3 Alone, then pairs

Students skim the text again and identify which facilities and services the school offers, then check if these are the same as the ones they listed in Activity B2. Working with a partner, they can add more facilities and give reasons for choosing them.

4 Pairs

For this activity, students find the words in the text from Activity C1 and check if the meanings they agreed on were correct and make sense.

5 Alone, then pairs

This is an information-transfer activity, similar to the type of question found in many examinations. Students need to read the text carefully in order to complete their copy of the table. All the missing information relates to the opening and closing times of three facilities.

Differentiated activities

Support

i   Ask students to complete the information for only two (or even one) of the facilities, rather than all three.

ii   Highlight which specific time slots they need to complete.

Challenge

When students have completed the table, ask them to use the information to write one or two sentences about each of the facilities.

Answers

Facility	Time	0600	0700	0900	1600	1700	1900	2100	2200
Cafeteria		Opens M–F		Opens weekend	Closes weekend			Closes M–F	
IT facilities			Opens M–F	Opens weekend		Closes weekend			Closes M–F
LMRC				Opens M–F			Closes M–F		

> **! TOP TIP**
>
> Point out what is required in a note-making question, and highlight the importance of careful text reading to select the correct information.

6 Pairs

Note-making questions require students to identify relevant information and to select correct details, and they may also need to identify facts, opinions and attitudes. The information students find should be rewritten under the headings provided. Activity 6 asks students to look at some notes based on the text they have read, and then to write some additional notes.

a Put students into A/B pairs, with A looking at paragraph 1 and B looking at paragraph 2. Each student needs to write four or five notes based on the content of their paragraph.

b In pairs, students exchange their notes and decide if they agree and if anything is missing or should be added.

c Without referring back to the paragraphs, students use the notes they have been given to write a paragraph.

d Students exchange their paragraphs and compare the content with the original texts in the Coursebook.

7/8 Alone, then pairs

This is quite a challenging activity, so if necessary consider reducing the load and/or supplying prompts to help students to complete the questions. Forming questions in English is a challenge for many learners, due to the sometimes complex word order used and the use of auxiliary verbs, so this activity provides useful practice. Do a couple of examples first, then get students to work alone to write the questions. Once they have finished, let them work in pairs to see if they have written the same

questions. Let them ask and answer, as this is an effective way to check how logical their questions are.

Suggested answers

a How often do students get IT lessons?

b When is the IT centre/are the IT facilities open at weekends?

c What does the special software help you practise? / What can you practise in the IT centre?

d How many volumes/books/titles are there in the LMRC/library?

e What do many books have so that you can listen to the story?

f Where can you purchase/buy books and audio files?

g What does the counselling service use to help you choose a career?

h What can you use to access English-language magazines and newspapers in the cafeteria?

i How many people can help you with accommodation and welfare?

j Why is staying with an English-speaking family a popular option?

D Language focus: prefixes and suffixes

> **LANGUAGE TIP**
>
> Spend some time reviewing the two **Language Tips** near **D Language focus: prefixes and suffixes** in the Coursebook, as it is an important area for students to understand and they will need to refer to it for the activities that follow. Note that we use the term *affix* to describe both prefixes and suffixes. Refer students to the exercise in Unit 6 of the **Workbook**.

1 Pairs

All the phrases are taken from the article students read in the previous section, so they will have already seen them in context. Students need to decide if they change the grammar or the meaning of the words. Refer them to the **Language Tips** near **D Language focus: prefixes and suffixes** for help if they need it.

Answers

... _self_-study lessons prefix – meaning

... facilities including _inter_net prefix – meaning

... lactose _in_tolerant prefix – meaning

... one week_ly_ timetabled lesson suffix – grammar

... from begin_ner_ to advanc_ed_ suffix – meaning

... suit_able_ for suffix – grammar

2 Pairs

With a partner, students look at the prefixes and decide what each one means. Then they match each prefix with a word or word base to create new words, and tell each other what the words mean.

Note – the prefix _self-_ is always followed by a hyphen (-), as is _ex-_ (for example, _ex-president_) and the prefix _multi-_ is often, but not always, followed by a hyphen.

Answers

auto + matic = automatic = without human control

hyper + market = hypermarket = large shopping centre

sub + marine = submarine = underwater boat

trans + continental = transcontinental = across large areas of land/continents

equi + distant = equidistant = equally far or close to something

bi + annual = biannual = every two years

mono + lingual = monolingual = using only one language

anti + dote = antidote = a substance that stops another substance from damaging your body

ex + president = ex-president = former president

contra + diction = contradiction = a big difference between two statements about the same subject

3 Pairs

Split the pairs into A/B. Student A looks at prefixes **a–d** and Student B looks at **e–h**. Each student decides what their prefixes mean and then thinks of more words that contain each one.

Answers

a   by yourself, alone (self-portrait, self-employed)

b   having many (multi-storey, multi-purpose)

c   between/among (international, intercom)

d   with/together (conversation, contact)

e   relating to hearing/sound (audio-visual, audio-lingual)

f   opposite (disapprove, disrespect)

g   for/support/approve (proactive)

h   three (triangle, triathlon)

4 Alone, then pairs

Now that students have practised prefixes, we move on to suffixes. Go through the information in Activity D4, making sure students understand the role of a suffix, then get them to complete the task. In some cases, there is more than one possible answer. Point out the importance of checking spelling very carefully (e.g. _happy_ + _ness_ = _happ**i**ness_). Give students some time to check their answers with a partner before you give feedback.

Answers

accidental = adjective, accidentally = adverb

availability = noun

cheaply = adverb

exciting = adjective, excitement = noun

guidance = noun

happiness = noun, happily = adverb

imagination = noun, imagining = verb

lovely = adjective, lover = noun, loving = adjective

luxurious = adjective, luxuriously = adverb

saying = noun

5 Alone

Make sure students clearly understand what they have to do in this activity. Firstly, they must create ten words using the suffixes in the box (there are two examples), then they should choose five words to use in complete sentences. There are multiple possible answers here so make sure you spend time giving students feedback on their efforts.

Differentiated activities

Support

i Reduce the number of words students need to create by giving them some of the answers.

ii Give your students gapped sentences, which they need to complete once they have created the words.

Challenge

Increase the challenge of this activity by telling students that they still have to write five sentences, but that each sentence must contain **two** words from the ten, thereby using all the words that they have created.

E Speaking: Giving advice and making suggestions

1 Small groups

Students are going to read a newspaper article called *Why can't teenagers get up in the morning?* Put students into small groups to discuss questions **a–d** and tell them that they should be prepared to present their ideas to the class. Monitor, but do not interfere, then offer positive feedback on their discussions. You could limit the time available for each question to keep the discussions focused and moving forwards.

2 Alone, then pairs

Tell students that they are going to listen to ten different people giving advice about how to wake up in the morning. Before they listen, give students a few minutes to look through the phrases in columns A and B. Play the audio and students match the phrases to make complete sentences.

Answers

1	h,	6	b,
2	d,	7	f,
3	i,	8	c,
4	e,	9	a,
5	j,	10	g

3 Alone, then pairs

This is a **noticing** activity. While listening a second time, students notice which <u>advice expressions</u> are followed by *to* + verb? Which ones are followed by *-ing*? Which ones are

followed by infinitive without *to*? Do a couple of examples using the phrases in Activity E2. Notice that 'If I were you …' does not use any of these patterns, and is followed by 'I would / I'd do something'.

Answers

1   I reckon you should … **+ infinitive without** *to*

2   Why don't you … **+ infinitive without** *to*

3   How about … **+** *-ing*

4   If I were you, …

5   I suggest … **+ infinitive without** *to*

6   You'd really better … **+ infinitive without** *to*

7   I would strongly advise you … *to* **+ verb**

8   My advice would be … *to* **+ verb**

9   It might be a good idea … *to* **+ verb**

10   You might try … **+** *-ing*

4/5 Pairs

Students are going to think about the advice they would give to someone who finds it difficult to concentrate while studying. Focus on the example in the Coursebook first, then students work with a partner, using the advice phrases from the previous activity. Afterwards, they can join up with different pairs and share their advice, using reporting verbs if possible (as in the example). Get the class to choose the best piece of advice.

> **LANGUAGE TIP**
> The **Language Tip** near Activity E2 of the Coursebook focuses on two words that are commonly confused: *advice* (noun) and *advise* (verb). Spend some time going through the information, checking that students fully understand the difference between the two words in spelling and meaning. Refer students to the exercise in Unit 6 of the **Workbook**.

F Reading

1 Small groups

Students are going to read the text about why teenagers can't get up in the morning. First, in small groups, students look at statements **a–e** and discuss if they think they are true or false, giving reasons for their answers. Do not supply any answers yet as students will find out when they read the text.

2 Pairs

Students should be used to these vocabulary activities by now. Make sure they have access to reference sources. Remember that for some students you may want to reduce the number of words and phrases they need to check.

3 Pairs

The phrases all appear in the text, but students need to discuss what information they think they will read about each one, and give reasons. If time is short, or to differentiate, you could divide up the phrases between different pairs of students.

4 Alone, then pairs

Go through the three things that students need to know when they read the text for the first time. Firstly **a** they need to find out what Dr Ralph advises: (*Schools and universities should ideally not start before 11 a.m.*), then **b** check if the statements in Activity F1 are true or false and (c) check if their ideas from Activity F3 appear. Set a time limit for this activity and encourage students to read the text quickly. When they have their answers, get them to compare with a partner.

Answers to 4b

a   false: ***most*** children [paragraph 1],

b   true [2],

c   false: ***more*** likely to smoke [6],

d   false: *very few teenagers* [7],

e   true [8]

Differentiated activities

Support

i   Point out the paragraphs in which they will find the answers to the questions.

ii   Ask students to answer just **a** and **b**, or just **a** and **c**.

Challenge

i   After students have answered questions **a–c**, get them to cover the text and discuss where in the text they found the words and phrases from Activity F3.

ii   Tell students to continue to Activity F5 and fill in the gaps. When they have finished, they can share their answers with the class.

5 Alone, then pairs

Students use the eight words and phrases from Activity F2 to complete the gaps in the text, and then check with their partner. If some students have already done this activity, team them up in groups with other students and let them 'teach' each other.

Answers

i	**d** moan,	v	**b** jeopardises,
ii	**e** out of sync,	vi	**a** bleak,
iii	**h** trivial matter,	vii	**c** metabolism,
iv	**f** sleep deprivation,	viii	**g** succumb to sleep

TOP TIP

Make sure your students recognise that questions which use words such as *According to the chart/graph/picture …* will require them to refer to information not necessarily contained in the text itself.

6 Alone, then pairs

The comprehension questions include one that requires students to interpret data in a pie chart. Get students to read through the questions and find this one. Then get them to underline the key words before they attempt to answer. When they have finished, allow time for them to check their answers with each other before you give feedback. For some students, you could omit question **i**.

Answers

a   refuse to go to bed at a decent hour, moan about getting up for school, lie in bed for hours at weekends

b   body clock is out of sync

c   future prospects, health and lives

d   because teenagers perform very poorly in the mornings

e   changing sleep cycle had shocking consequences

f   50%

g   in the morning at school, in class

h   6–7 hours

i   how the human sleep cycle works: hormones stimulated by light stop us falling asleep during the day; in the evenings, the human body produces melatonin which makes us sleepy; also body temperature drops; metabolism slows down how teenagers are different: pressure to fall asleep is more gradual; easier for teens to stay awake later; melatonin produced an hour later than usual.

7 Various

This final activity gives students some further practice in note-making, based on the content of the text they have read. To save time and/or to differentiate you could give one heading to different students or pairs of students, and then bring everyone together to share their ideas. Note that there may be more possible answers than are required for each heading.

Possible answers
Teenagers and their sleep problems

'Terrible teens' behaviour

refuse to go to bed at decent hour

moan about getting up for school

lie in bed for hours at weekends

develop a lazy streak

Health problems faced by sleep-deprived teens

more likely to smoke

prone to depression and stress

cardiovascular system destroyed

kidney disease

Natural body cycle

desire to sleep reduced by light

at dusk it encourages sleepiness

out of sync with everyone else

Differences in teenagers

pressure to fall asleep is more gradual

easier for them to stay awake longer

bodies produce melatonin around an hour later than usual

Reflection

Use the **Reflection** to remind students of what they have achieved in the unit. Students should set themselves a **personal goal** based on their scores for Unit 6.

Exam focus

Reading and writing, Exercise 3, note-making

Answers
Note that there may be more possible answers than are required for each heading.

Tablets versus books before bedtime

Participants:

16 non-smokers	[1]
… aged 22–33	[1]
… familiar with tablets	[1]
no sleep, medical or psychiatric disorders	[1]

Data obtained from recordings:

… brain electrical activity	[1]
total sleep time	[1]
sleep efficiency [Extended]	[1]
percentage of time spent in each sleep stage	[1]
time before first period of REM sleep	[1]

Possible impacts from blue light:

sleepiness	[1]
delayed and reduced brain wave activity	[1]
deeper sleep [Extended]	[1]

[Total: 7 Core, 9 Extended]

NOTE on Assessment Objectives (AOs) for Reading and Writing Exercise 4 (summary writing): Students need to write an 80 (Core) or 100 (Extended) word summary about an aspect or aspects of a text printed in the question paper. To do this effectively, students need to identify and select relevant information (R1), understand ideas, opinions and attitudes (R2) and show understanding of the connections between ideas, opinions and attitudes (R3).

Students need to communicate information/ideas/opinions clearly, accurately and effectively (W1), organise ideas into coherent paragraphs using a range of appropriate linking devices (W2), use a range of grammatical structures and vocabulary accurately and effectively (W3) and show control of punctuation and spelling (W4).

Learning objectives (LOs)

Suggested activity: Start the unit by focusing for a few minutes on the LOs box, making sure that students understand what they are going to be doing. Using the first LO as an example, ask students to identify where in the unit they can find the activities for the other four LOs. Get students to say which of the activities appeal to them the most, and ask them for their reasons.

A Watch, listen and talk

1 Whole class, then alone

Explain that your students are going to watch and listen to some IGCSE students talking about **jobs**. As your students watch and listen, they should **a** make a note about the jobs that the speakers want to do in the future, and **b** make a note about the things that appeal to the speakers about the jobs. Play the video a second time so that students can check or add to their notes.

Answers

a Jobs the students want to do in the future: a lawyer, a doctor, an ambassador (international relations), a business woman.

b What appeals to the students about the jobs: the student is good at debating, the student enjoys learning about law and the legal system [a lawyer]; it is meaningful, you can have the ability and knowledge

to save people's lives and improve their quality of life [a doctor]; the student wants to help the world and improve their country/make contributions to their country [an ambassador]; because the student can wear formal clothes, the student would like to go into a big company, the student wants to be successful, it has been a childhood dream [a business woman].

2 Pairs or small groups

Depending on the size of your class, put students into pairs or small groups. They can discuss their notes and then talk to each other about the jobs that **they** would like to do when they finish school, and what in particular appeals to them about the job. Do not interfere too much, but make sure you get feedback from the class so that they know their efforts have been worthwhile. If time permits, you could write their ideas on the board and rank them according to your students' preferences.

B Speaking and vocabulary

1/2 Whole class

Get students to look at the pictures, and to name at least two things that they can see in each one. Provide any vocabulary that students may ask for. Ask them to describe what is happening in each picture and what job each one shows. For example, the first picture shows a soldier and the second picture shows a teacher teaching a class of students. Allow students freedom to express themselves and do not worry about language errors. Afterwards, ask students if they would like to do any of these jobs and why.

3 Pairs

In pairs, students discuss questions **a**–**c**. Some teenagers have no idea about their future career, so be prepared to prompt them. Monitor the discussions, but do not interfere; be ready to give positive feedback at the end of the activity.

4 Alone, then pairs

Working on their own, students unjumble the letters to identify the seven jobs, then match them with the pictures. When they are ready, students can check their answers with a partner.

Answers

a	comedian,	**e**	gardener,
b	driver,	**f**	astronaut,
c	pharmacist,	**g**	accountant
d	footballer,		

5 Alone, then pairs

Students work alone and write a short definition or description for each job. Look at the example first (comedian). Students can compare their sentences when they have finished. If time permits, you could turn this into a competition by asking students to write their definitions with gaps for the jobs (e.g. *A ... is someone who tells jokes and makes people laugh*). They then exchange their writing and fill in the gaps in their partner's sentences.

6 Whole class

Finish off this section by asking students which of the jobs in the previous activity they would most or least like to do. Get them to give reasons. Once again, allow students the freedom to express themselves without interfering; provide feedback at the end.

C Reading

1 Pairs

Give students a few minutes to decide what a cosmetic scientist does (or might do). There are no right or wrong answers at this stage, so encourage students to speculate without correcting them. This will not only increase their confidence when speaking, but also improve their fluency. Feedback and corrections can be given at the end of the activity.

2 Pairs

Make sure students understand what a cosmetic scientist does (they make perfumes and fragrances, and also find scents that work well together), then get them to look at statements **a–g** and decide if they are true or false. Allow students to use reference sources to check any unknown words. Do not supply any answers as students will find out for themselves when they read the text.

3 Alone, then pairs

Go through the seven headings (**a–g**) to check any unknown words. Then students have a quick look at the text and decide which heading goes with each paragraph. Set a time limit here to encourage fast, skim reading. When they have finished, they can check their choices with a partner.

Answers

a	6,	**e**	7,
b	5,	**f**	4,
c	1,	**g**	3
d	2,		

4 Pairs

Students need to refer back to the true/false information in Activity C2 and guess in which of the seven paragraphs they would expect to find each piece of information, giving their reasons.

5 Alone, then pairs

This text is quite long so you may decide to use a differentiated activity to help students. If the whole class is a similar level, set a time limit for students to skim the text and check if the information in Activity C2 is true or false. They should then give reasons and correct any incorrect information.

Answers

a	true,
b	false (larger companies tend to favour students who have Master's or PhD degrees in Cosmetic Science),
c	false (thousands of scientists and chemists working, the number of jobs continues to grow),
d	true,
e	true,
f	true,
g	false (get involved with social networking sites)

Differentiated activities

Support

i   You could point out in which paragraphs they will find the information from Activity C2.

ii Make the task shorter by distributing the seven pieces of information among several students.

Challenge

When students have finished, tell them to find three or more pieces of information in the text and write them down, with an error in each one. They then exchange their writing with a partner, who has to identify and correct the errors.

6 Pairs

For this activity, students look at the underlined phrases in the text and check that they understand them. Make sure all students understand them before moving on.

D Language focus: modals for advice and suggestions

1 Whole class

Modal verbs have many different functions in English. In this section, the focus is on using modals to offer advice and to give suggestions. Get students to look at the two examples and point out the underlined modals *could* and *should*, and their position before the main verb in bold.

2/3 Pairs

Ask students to work in pairs and write a list of any other modal verbs they know. The modals do not have to be for advice and suggestions. Then students can look at the text to see if any of the modal verbs from their list appear. If they find any, they should decide what their function is (as used in the text).

Point out that modal verbs can have different degrees of strength, so *could* and *should* are not as strong as *must*. Students could add: *need to*, *might*, *have to*, to the continuum.

4 Whole class

Give an oral example of a modal verb followed by *have* + past participle (e.g. *He should have studied harder*) and write it on the board. Concept check to make sure students appreciate that the sentence refers to the past. Then ask them what the form is for present/future time (i.e. modal + infinitive without *to*).

5 Alone, then pairs

a   Ask students to go back to D1 and to rewrite the two examples there in the past.

b   Now students go back to the text and rewrite in the past four examples of modal verbs. Check that they use the correct structure: modal + **have** + past participle.

Answers

You <u>could have</u> *started* your own company

You <u>should have</u> *got* a four-year degree

6 Alone, then pairs

For the final activity, students use four modals of their choice in sentences of their own. Get them to share their answers as a way of checking.

E Writing: Note-making and summary writing

1 Alone

This activity helps students to identify key information in a text and to write that information in note form. Some students may find these skills challenging, so begin by looking at the example and get students to show you where the information is in paragraph 1. Make sure they realise that the notes paraphrase the text – in other words, the information from the text is written in a different way when making notes. Get students to read the text again and write two notes for each paragraph.

Differentiated activities

Support

i   Ask students to write just one note for each paragraph, or allocate two or three paragraphs to each student, thereby reducing how much they have to do.

ii   You could also identify the important information in each paragraph that students need to write in note form.

Challenge

i   Ask students to try to write three notes for each paragraph.

ii   Another option is to put students into pairs: Student A reads one paragraph aloud and Student B writes notes. Then they swap roles. Finally, they look at their notes and compare them with the original text.

2 Pairs, then whole class

Students should now compare their notes to see if they wrote the same or different things (there are many possible answers). They should also try to agree on the most important information contained within each paragraph. When each pair has made its decisions, have a whole-class discussion on each paragraph and agree which pieces of information are the most important.

TOP TIP

Before moving on to Activity E3, go through the **Top Tip** near Activity E3 of the Coursebook with the class, highlighting the key things for students to remember. For note-making tasks, students need to find the information required and transfer it in note form under the correct headings. However, even with notes, it is important that what students write is intelligible.

47

3 Alone, then pairs

Using their notes from the previous activities, students work alone to complete a copy of the notes. They can look back at the text if necessary. Give them time to check with a partner when they have finished.

Answers

1   Get your science degree

    Science degree essential, usually four-year from (**a**) **college or university**

    Many science degrees are common, but (**b**) **physics** also acceptable

2   Maybe get an advanced degree

    Large companies prefer students with (**c**) **Master's or PhD**

    But on-the-job training often (**d**) **more valuable** than qualifications

3   Research cosmetic companies

    Plenty of (**e**) **job** opportunities and number is (**f**) **growing**

    Industry continues to grow despite economic (**g**) **uncertainty**

4   Pick a job

    (**h**) **College/Education** does not usually tell you what job you will get

    Plenty of different jobs available, so best to choose one which (**i**) **fits your interests**

5   Get a job

    Important to start preparing résumé or CV (**j**) **at university** and then send it to (**k**) **HR departments**

    Jobs advertised in (**l**) **newspapers** as well as (**m**) **university careers offices**

6   A temporary assignment

    Having a (**n**) **temporary job** can help find something more permanent in the future

    Use a (**o**) **temp agency with science focus** to help you get your first assignment

7   Network with other cosmetic chemists

    Create your own social network pages because professionals post (**p**) **career information**

    Also best place to begin (**q**) **relationships** with other people in the industry

> **LANGUAGE TIP**
> Focus on the **Language Tip** before students work on Activity E4 in the Coursebook. There is a Workbook exercise which you can direct students to after they have finished Activity E5.

4 Whole class, then pairs

This activity highlights the importance for students of using linking words and phrases in their writing. These will help guide the reader through the writing, and to link sentences, paragraphs and sections both forwards and backwards. Good use of linkers not only makes what has been written easier to follow, but also demonstrates confidence and fluency in writing skills. Focus on the table and the examples and point out that linkers can be used for different purposes, and in this activity students are going to focus on three of the most common uses: adding information, sequencing, and contrasting. Then students work with a partner and decide in which category the words and phrases in the box can be placed.

Answers

Adding information	Sequencing	Contrasting
In addition (to)	Firstly, Secondly, etc.	But
And		However
Also	Finally	Although / even though
As well as	Lastly	Apart from
Furthermore		Besides
Moreover		Despite the fact that
		In spite of
		Nevertheless
		Whereas

5 Pairs

Working together, students think of at least one more linking word or phrase for each category. Make sure students have an opportunity to share their answers so that everyone in the class can build up a list of useful linkers.

6 Whole class, then pairs

Ask students to underline the linkers in the expanded notes for Paragraph 1. Don't forget that *and* is a linking word.

Firstly, the most important thing is to get your science degree, and this is usually a four-year course from a college or university. There are many common degrees, such as Chemistry, Chemical Engineering, Biology and Microbiology. However, Physics is also acceptable in the cosmetics industry.

Put students into A/B pairs, but explain that first they will work alone. Student A combines their notes for Paragraphs 2–4 and Student B combines their notes for Paragraphs 5–7, using linking words and phrases where appropriate. They should underline the linkers they use. There are various possible answers, and not every paragraph will require students to use the same number of linkers. In some cases, linkers may not be necessary. It is a good idea to do the summary orally first, so ask students to tell you about the text, using their notes. Give them a short introductory sentence to get them started, for example: *There are many things you can do to become a cosmetic scientist. Firstly, ...*

Differentiated activities

Support

i   Get students to expand just one of their sets of notes, rather than attempting three. You could allocate different headings to different students to write, then get them to join all the writing together to make one summary. This will give these students a sense of achievement.

ii Allow students to refer back to the text.

Challenge

i   Tell students that they are not allowed to refer to the text, so their summary will be based solely on their notes.

ii Students have to expand notes for six rather than three paragraphs.

Possible answers

[2] Maybe get an advanced degree

A four-year degree is fine, <u>but</u> some large companies prefer to employ students with a Master's degree <u>or</u> a PhD. <u>However</u>, on-the-job training is often more valuable than qualifications.

[3] Research cosmetic companies

There are plenty of job opportunities for cosmetic scientists <u>and</u> the number is growing. <u>Furthermore</u>, the industry continues to grow <u>despite</u> economic uncertainty.

[4] Pick a job

A student's college <u>or</u> university education does not usually tell you what job you will get in the future. <u>But</u> there are plenty of different jobs available <u>so</u> the best action is to choose one which fits your interests.

[5] Get a job

It's important for students to start preparing their résumé <u>or</u> CV while still at university, <u>and</u> then send it

to company HR departments. Jobs are advertised in newspapers <u>as well as</u> in university careers offices.

[6] A temporary assignment

Having a temporary job can help students to find something more permanent in the future, <u>and</u> using a temp agency with a focus on science jobs can help students to get their first assignment.

[7] Network with other cosmetic chemists

It's a good idea to create your own social network pages <u>because</u> professionals post information about their careers online. This is <u>also</u> the best place to begin relationships with other people in the industry.

7 Pairs

Students look at each other's paragraphs and combine them to make one longer piece of writing.

F Listening and speaking

1 Pairs

Make sure students have some idea about what NASA is and does before they start this activity. In pairs, they should discuss the two questions. Tell them not to worry if they do not know very much – they will find out more during the listening activity.

2 Whole class, then pairs

Quickly go through the questions orally to check that students understand what is being asked and to clarify the type of answer required. Then, in pairs, students discuss each question and try to predict the answers. Give them plenty of freedom to speculate – they will find out the real answers when they listen.

3 Alone

Prepare students for the listening activity. They do not need to find the answers to the questions in Activity F2 on the first listening, but should focus on questions **a** and **b**.

CD1, Track 16

Baruti Ngwani: Welcome to this week's show. Today we're going to talk about careers and, in particular, one career which some of you may believe is only for men: working for NASA, the National Aeronautics and Space Administration in the USA! My guest is Kagiso Abaka, a careers adviser for NASA, based here in Joburg. Welcome!

49

Kagiso Abaka: Hi, Baruti.

BN: So, what does a young woman need to do in order to work for NASA?

KA: The same as a young man, of course! For anyone who likes finding out how things work, solving puzzles and problems, or creating and building things, then why not consider a career in science, technology, engineering or maths? Within NASA, women work in all of these areas, and there is information available on careers and how you can prepare for them.

BN: Interesting …. But what is an engineer? What does an engineer actually do?

KA: Good question! Engineers are the people who make things work, using power and materials. Engineers have moved the world into skyscrapers, high-speed cars, jets and, of course, space vehicles. They make our lives interesting, comfortable and fun. Everything in our daily lives relies heavily on the work of engineers: computers, television, satellites ….

BN: Is there just one type of engineer, then?

KA: No, there are many types, including aerospace, chemical, civil, computer, electrical, industrial, mechanical, and so on. Obviously each type specialises in a particular area.

BN: Hmmm, I see. So is an engineer a scientist?

KA: Not really. Scientists are knowledge seekers, who are always searching out why things happen. They are inquisitive, which means that they are always asking questions. Nature, Earth and the Universe are what fascinate the scientist. The scientist questions, seeks answers and expands knowledge.

BN: What career options are available for people like this?

KA: There's an amazing variety. Careers are available in both the life and physical sciences.

BN: For example?

KA: For example … becoming a biologist, medical doctor or nutritionist would all require studies in life sciences, whereas a job as an astronomer, chemist, geologist, meteorologist or physicist would all involve studying the physical sciences.

BN: OK, I see. I've also heard about technicians. What do they do? Is it different from engineers and scientists?

KA: Technicians are an important part of the NASA team. They work closely with scientists and engineers in support of their research. Their skills are used to operate wind tunnels, work in laboratories, construct test equipment, build models and support many types of research.

BN: Most of our listeners are still at school, studying hard, so what should their focus be, if these types of careers are interesting to them?

KA: Well, obviously, education is a critical requirement. Mathematics and science are the basis for most NASA careers and the decisions you make in school can affect your future career possibilities.

BN: And after high school?

KA: It can seem like a long journey, but a career as a scientist or engineer requires four to seven years of college study after high school. A Bachelor's degree requiring four years of study is the minimum necessary. Colleges and universities also offer graduate programmes where students can obtain Master's and doctoral degrees. The Master's programme usually takes two years. An additional two to four years is needed to earn a doctorate.

BN: And for anyone who likes the idea of a career as a technician?

KA: Well, technicians typically earn a two-year Associate of Science degree. Some may continue for two additional years and obtain a Bachelor's degree in engineering technology. Others may earn a Bachelor's degree in engineering or one of the physical sciences.

BN: So for those of you who want to think about a career with NASA, it may seem a long way off, but study hard and who knows? One day one of you might be walking on the moon!

Adapted from http://spaceflightsystems.grc.nasa.gov

Answers

a three (engineer, scientist, technician)

b walking on the moon

4 Alone, then pairs

The second time they listen, students should make notes about the interviewer's questions in Activity F2.

Answers

a same as a young man

b make things work, using power and materials, everything in our daily lives relies on the work of engineers

c no, many types – aerospace, chemical, civil, computer, electrical, industrial, mechanical

d   no – a scientist is a knowledge seeker, finding out why things happen, asking questions

e   support scientists and engineers – they operate machines, work in labs, construct equipment, build models, support research

f   education – maths and science are important at school, then college or university for a degree and Master's

5/6 Pairs

Using the questions and answers from Activities F2 and F4, students take on the roles of the interviewer and the careers adviser and interview each other. When they have finished, they can check the audioscript in Appendix 3 of the Coursebook to see how much they remembered.

Reflection

Use the **Reflection** to remind students of what they have achieved in the unit. Students should set themselves a **personal goal** based on their scores for Unit 7.

Exam focus

Reading, Exercise 3, note-making, Exercise 4, summary writing

1   **Summary answer**

Athletic trainers are important in sports. Although about half are female, they have many difficulties. The job of a CAT is to help athletes with injuries in different work environments. For 20 years after being founded, the National Athletic Trainers' Association had only men, but more women have become members. Furthermore, recently there are more female CATs than male. Female CATs are not represented like men and struggle in professional sport. [74 words]

2 a

Answers

Official figures for the Pushkar fair

Fewer than 5,000 camels for sale	[1]
Dropped from 8,000 in 2011	[1]
Camels sold for around $230 each [Extended only]	[1]

Raikas' relationship with their camels

Most prominent camel herders	[1]
Believe it is religious responsibility to rear camels	[1]
Consider relationship with camels as sacred / only herders not to slaughter camels [Extended only]	[1]

Impact of modernisation on camel trading

Camel population has dropped by 50% in last 30 years	[1]
1982 – 1 million camels nationwide	[1]
2007 – dropped by 50% / over 80% live in Rajasthan / value of camels is less with spread of technology	[1]

[Total: 9 Extended, 7 Core]

2b   **Summary answer**

Traders travel great distances to Pushkar fair, the world's largest livestock market, but fewer camels and buyers means it could soon close. It is the only time of year when breeders earn cash, but because of falling figures for this tourist attraction, many traditions are vanishing and breeders are finding other ways to earn money, like selling camels for slaughter. Also, due to the economic boom in India, camel numbers have dropped because they are no longer needed for agriculture, and young Indians are seeking work in cities, leaving the older generations to seek help from the government to invest in camel milk dairies. [104 words]

51

NOTE on Assessment Objectives (AOs) for Reading and Writing Exercise 6: Students need to demonstrate that they can write a report, a review or an article in response to a short stimulus. This may take the form of pictures and/or short prompts. The question includes information on the purpose, format and audience, in addition to the word count and how the marks are allocated.

Specifically, students need to show that they can communicate information/ideas/opinions clearly, accurately and effectively (W1), organise ideas into coherent paragraphs using a range of appropriate linking devices (W2), use a range of grammatical structures and vocabulary accurately and effectively (W3), show control of punctuation and spelling (W4) and use appropriate register and style/format for the given purpose and audience (W5).

Learning objectives (LOs)

Suggested activity: Start the unit by focusing for a few minutes on the LOs box, making sure that students understand what they are going to be doing. Using the first LO as an example, ask students to identify where in the unit they can find the activities for the other four LOs. Get students to say which of the activities appeal to them the most, and ask them for their reasons.

A Watch, listen and talk

1 Whole class, then alone

Explain that your students are going to watch and listen to some IGCSE students talking about **communication**. As your students watch and listen, they should make a note of **a** three different ways of communicating that the speakers mention, **b** three different ways of communicating that the speakers use with their families and friends, and **c** how important the speakers think spelling is. Play the video a second time so that students can check or add to their notes.

Answers

a Different ways of communicating the students mention (any **three** from): texting, mail, the internet, a letter.

b **Three** different ways of communicating that the students use with their families and friends: the internet, mail, texting.

c How important do the students think spelling is: Not that important (some applications now have auto-checking) **and/or** important for communication

(because if you spell something wrong, it could mean something different).

2 Pairs or small groups

Depending on the size of your class, put students into pairs or small groups. They can discuss their notes and then talk to each other about how important they think spelling is in communication. Do not interfere too much, but make sure you get feedback from the class so that they know their efforts have been worthwhile. If time permits, you could write their ideas on the board and rank them according to your students' preferences.

B Speaking and vocabulary

1 Whole class, then pairs

Students are often confused about the differences between British English (BrE) and American English (AmE). While the first two activities in this section highlight some of those differences, it is also worth pointing out to students that there are far more similarities than differences.

Get students to look at the seven pictures and make some guesses about what they show. The first letter for each word is given. Try to elicit the following words and write them on the board. Use BrE spelling (as given here):

1	colour/s,	5	litre,
2	theatre,	6	licence,
3	traveller,	7	analyse
4	centimetre,		

Then get students to work with a partner to copy and complete the table in Activity B1 by writing the AmE spellings of the seven words.

Answers

1	color,	4	centimeter,
2	theater,	5	liter,
3	traveler,	6	license,
		7	analyze

2 Pairs

Students discuss the words in the box and decide if they have BrE or AmE spellings, using their table from Activity B1 as a guide, where possible. Ask students if they can add any other words.

Answers

fiber = AmE (AmE spelling often favours -*er* endings rather than BrE -*re*)

favour = BrE (-*our* endings are more common in BrE than AmE)

labor = AmE (-*or* endings are more common in AmE than BrE)

paralyze = AmE (AmE prefers -*ze* to BrE -*se*)

fueled = AmE (AmE tends to use single l, whereas BrE uses double ll)

defense = AmE (some AmE endings are -*se* but in BrE they are -*ce*)

dialogue = BrE (BrE uses -*logue* whereas AmE prefers -*log*)

> **LANGUAGE TIP**
> Apart from spelling, students should be aware that in some cases, completely different words are used in BrE and AmE for the same thing: *pavement* and *sidewalk*, for example. There are also some differences in tense usage. It does not matter which system students use (nor which one you teach), as long as you and they are consistent. Refer students to the exercise in Unit 8 of the **Workbook**.

3 Pairs

Students may struggle with the correct spelling of English words. You do not need to be overly concerned about misspellings, but it is worthwhile drawing students' attention to words that often cause difficulties. In this activity, get students to work together and correct the spelling of the words **a–j**. There is no need to provide answers at this point as they will see all the words in the text they are going to read in the Coursebook.

4/5 Alone, then small groups

Working on their own, students think and make notes about questions **a–c**. Then, put students into small groups to discuss their ideas.

> **TOP TIP**
> We all use mnemonic devices, often without even realising it. In simple terms, they are 'tricks' we employ in order to remember things, whether it's how to spell a word, to remember someone's address or phone number, or even where to find something in the supermarket. Encourage students to go online if possible and search for different types of mnemonic devices, to see how helpful they can be.

6 Small groups

Students continue their discussions by deciding which of the strategies in the list is the best method for recording vocabulary. There are no right or wrong answers, because everyone has their own preferences – all the methods can be useful. However, you can advise students that the following are some of the most effective:

- having a separate book for recording vocabulary
- putting words into thematic groups
- recording words in a sentence

These are also useful:

- writing the part of speech and how to pronounce the words
- writing the translation of words
- writing words in alphabetical order
- using mnemonic devices

C Reading and vocabulary

Reading 1

1 Pairs

Students work together to check the meaning of the words (**a–h**) by matching them with an appropriate definition (**1–8**).

Answers

a	8,	d	6,	g	1,
b	2,	e	3,	h	4
c	7,	f	5,		

2 Pairs

The paragraphs in the text *Why is learning to spell important?* are in the wrong order. Students work in pairs and use the tips **a–e** to reorder the paragraphs. Remind them that they do not need to worry about the gaps for the moment.

Answers

3, 2, 5, 4, 1

3 Whole class

Check with students how they decided on the correct order, apart from the clues given in Activity C2.

4 Alone, then pairs

There are **three** parts to this activity:

- Students work alone, focusing on gaps **a–h** and deciding what type of word or phrase (and information) is needed to complete them.
- Students refer back to Activity C1 and use those words and phrases to complete the gaps.
- They can compare their answers with a partner.

Differentiated activities

Support

i   Allow students to work with a partner for all three parts

ii Provide the answers for the first part and tell students to go immediately to the second.

Challenge

Instead of referring back to the words in C1, students have to remember the words and/or think of a suitable alternative.

Answers

Part of speech needed		Answer
a	adjective	crucial
b	verb	correspond
c	adjective	effective
d	adjective	fundamental
e	noun	impression
f	noun	majority
g	noun	abbreviations
h	noun	concern

5 Pairs

Now students can check if they spelt the words in Activity B3 correctly by finding them in the text.

Answers

a	because,	**f**	especially,
b	completing,	**g**	university,
c	decent,	**h**	achieve,
d	reasonable,	**i**	surprising,
e	literacy,	**j**	extremely

6 Alone, then pairs

As this is quite a challenging vocabulary activity, you may want to differentiate by allocating words to different students, or allowing students to work with a partner for the whole activity.

Answers

a	grasp	**e**	proven
b	reasonable	**f**	overall
c	decent	**g**	struggle
d	impression		

Reading 2

1 Whole class, then pairs

Explain that students are going to read a newspaper article about postal services and how they are changing. Before they read, students work together and discuss questions **a–d**. As always, limit the time for each question so that students focus and do not waste time. You could allocate one or two questions to different pairs of students and then they share ideas.

2 Alone, then pairs

This is a guided reading activity, which encourages students to pause after each paragraph to check their understanding by answering two questions.

Answers

a   Seven (people, aeroplanes, bicycles, trains, trucks, animals, birds)

b   19th century / 1 May 1840

c   nearly three decades

d   Various possible answers, for example: people no longer handwrite letters, social media most popular way to communicate nowadays

e   mobile phones and internet-based messaging have taken over

f   weighing a small parcel or buying a stamp (to put on a handwritten letter)

g   sent abroad/internationally

h   because purchases need to be delivered by a postal service

i   competition and sensible financial investments

j   much wider service/more efficient list of services/choice

54

3 Alone, then pairs

If you have access to the internet, students can use it to find out the meaning of the words and phrases. If not, provide dictionaries. Students can of course refer back to the text as well.

Differentiated activities

Support

i   Reduce the number of words and phrases per student to four rather than eight, and then students work together to share their ideas.

ii   Provide definitions for the words and phrases, so the activity becomes a matching task.

iii Rather than working on their own, allow students to work with a partner.

Challenge

i   Increase the number of words and phrases per student.

ii   Students should try to use the context rather than the internet or a dictionary to find the meanings of the words and phrases.

Answers

a   adhesive (adjective) = used for sticking things together

b   strap (verb, but also noun) = to fasten things together

c   remote (adjective) = far away from other places

d   secure (adjective, but also verb) = safe

e   weighed down (phrasal verb) = carried or held too much

f   vanishing (adjective) = disappearing

g   century (noun) = 100 years

h   trend (noun, but also verb) = change or development

i   phenomenon (noun) = something that exists or happens

j   feel the heat (idiom) = face a difficult situation

k   revenue (noun) = financial income

l   held steady (verb + adverb) = remained the same

m   financial investments (adjective + noun) = money used to make a profit

n   innovation (noun) = something new and original

o   embracing technology (gerund + noun) = accepting new ideas and systems

p   injects (verb) = introduces

4 Alone, then pairs

This activity gives students practice in recognising and writing numbers written as words and figures.

Answers

Text numbers	Figure numbers
thousands	*1,000s*
four thousand five hundred	4,500
nineteenth	19th
two to three	*2–3*
three hundred and fifty	350
three point five per cent	3.5%
five million	*5 000 000*

> **WORD TIP**
>
> These two words (*fashion*, *trend*) are not commonly confused, but learners may wonder about the difference in meaning and when to use them. Refer students to the practice exercise in the **Workbook**.

D Language focus: passive voice

1 Whole class

A passive construction occurs when the object of an action is made into the subject of a sentence. In other words, whoever or whatever is performing the action is not the grammatical subject of the sentence. Look at the two examples with the class and ask them to tell you how the passive is formed.

Answer

verb *to be* + past participle (*would not be + completed*, *is + documented*)

2 Alone, then pairs

Students work alone to create full sentences, using the correct tense of the verb *to be* and the past participle of the underlined verb. When they have finished, students share their answers.

Answers

a   It was reported recently …

b   Although it isn't proved …

c   Postal services as we know them today were not really established

d   The address has been written by hand.

e   All mail items nowadays are mostly printed.

f   Worldwide letter-post traffic was estimated …

3 Pairs

Students look back at the text to check their answers to Activity D2.

4 Whole class, then alone

Point out the use of the modal verb *would + be* in the example. Then students look again at the second text and find three more examples of passive forms which include a modal verb.

Answers

would have been weighed down (paragraph 3), *may still be needed* (5), *should be seen positively* (5)

E Writing: formal letters (optional)

NOTE: Writing formal letters is not assessed in Writing and Reading, Exercise 6 on the Cambridge International Examinations IGCSE® syllabus. However, the ability to write a formal letter is an important and useful English language skill.

1 Pairs, then whole class

In Unit 3, students wrote an informal letter, so a good way to start this section is to briefly review what they can remember about the format. Then, working in pairs, students discuss the questions in Activity E1. Follow this with a brief class discussion to check that everyone agrees.

2 Pairs

Students think about how to start a formal letter. Refer them to Activity E5 in Unit 3, in which they wrote a list of possible closing phrases, then get them to decide which endings would be suitable for a formal letter.

3 Alone, then pairs

Students read the email in the Coursebook and decide if the layout is similar to the one they discussed in Activity E1. Guide students if they are struggling to detail the similarities and differences.

4/5 Alone, then pairs

Students need to look at the information (**a–f**) and decide which section of the email (1–6) it refers to.

Answers

a	6		**d**	2
b	5		**e**	3
c	4		**f**	1

Then with a partner, students discuss if they think any of the paragraphs could be joined together.

Possible answers

2 and 3 could be combined to give the reason for writing and an introduction together, and also 4 and 5, putting the writer's opinion and conclusion together.

6 Alone, then pairs

For this activity, students need to 'notice' the language used by the writer which makes the style formal, for example the absence of contractions.

Possible answers

a great cause for concern, a young man, my personal view, let's not forget that, I am completely confident, people would agree with me, if I am not mistaken, we should all be concerned, yours sincerely

7 Alone, then pairs

There are many possible answers here. Encourage students to come up with as many variations as possible.

Possible answers

something which worries me a lot, in my opinion, from my point of view, as far as I'm concerned, I am completely sure, everyone will have the same opinion, everyone should worry about

> **TOP TIP**
> Students sometimes worry about whether or not they should include addresses and a date when they write a letter, so this **Top Tip** clarifies the issue for them.

8 Pairs

Tell students to read the task, then agree with their partner about what they have to do. They do not need to write anything yet. They should conclude that the question is asking them to write a formal letter to the school magazine editor, in which they need to give their views about spelling. They can use the ideas given, as well as their own.

9 Pairs

Working with a partner, students look at the letter written by an IGCSE student, then identify and correct any spelling and grammar mistakes. They do <u>not</u> need to rewrite anything.

Suggested answers (mistakes in **bold**)

The letter contains a lot of repetition (*I think*) and errors in subject/verb agreement, as well as misuse of the verb *make* (which should be followed by *–ing*). However, the student has given their views and has used the prompts in the question.

Hello ESS

January 29

I **had seen** your article today in my school magazine and I want to give you my reasons on the subject **spelling is so important**. I want to throw away my dictionary and I **do** not worry any more about making spelling mistakes. But I **think** spelling is difficult and I **think** we need help to avoid **to make** mistakes.

I **think** communication is more important than spelling words correctly. I **think** correct spelling shows that you care about how you **to** write and I **think** we need help to avoid **to make** mistakes but I **think** correct spelling shows that I care about how **you** write.

So I **think** spelling is important but if we don't care about spelling then we probably don't care about other mistakes that I make.

Best wishes

Bruno

10 Pairs

In pairs students look at the second letter and discuss in what ways it is a better response than the previous one. This letter has a better overall style, without repetition, and clearly responds to the question prompts, with few language errors.

> **TOP TIP**
> There are no set rules for the number of paragraphs required in a letter, but you may find that students benefit from some general guidance. Also point out the importance of using the correct opening and closing phrases for a formal letter.

11 Alone

This activity gives students the chance to write their own answer to the task, using the same format and style as discussed in the unit so far. Go through the question carefully again, making sure students understand exactly what they have to do, and the important information they should include to make their answer effective.

Here are two good sample answers written by **i** an **IGCSE Extended** student and **ii** an **IGCSE Core** student.

i Core

Dear Editor,

After reading your article in the school magazine, I have decided to express my belief that spelling is a very important part of the English language. The way we spell words tells us a great deal about the history of the language, its roots. Also, I think that if people spell words in the way they choose too, there will be a lot of confusion and difficulty understanding what has been written. The rules that exist for spelling are there to make English easier to learn and also to prevent a word from being spelt lots of different ways. For these reasons, I strongly believe that people's spelling mistakes should be corrected and not overlooked.

Yours faithfully,

Ronan Bolero [121 words]

ii Extended

Dear Editor,

Language is all around us and I believe that yes, spelling is important. Although I do not agree with one of my friends who said that correct spelling shows that we care about what we write, I do think that knowing how to spell correctly shows that you care about the language. I believe that while English spelling is sometimes very difficult and it is okay to make mistakes, no English person will know if you have bad spelling when you are talking about the weather and communicating. But if you send somebody an email which is full of English spelling mistakes, this does not look very nice.

If you find spelling in English difficult then I think it is a good idea to start reading an English book or get a friend to look at your writing and help you correct any mistakes before you hand in your work to your teacher. Reading newspapers and surfing the internet also helps! Spelling is important but it is not everything so don't give up if you are having trouble spelling things in English, you will get much better with a lot of practice and patience!

Yours faithfully,

Annabelle White [200 words]

F Reading and writing

1 Alone, then pairs

Explain that students are going to read a text and then write a further formal letter. First students work alone and read the text, and then join with their partner to discuss the questions (**a–f**).

Answers

a   business and social functions, casual conversation

b   in the book *Adventures in Speaking and Writing*

c   by what you say and how you say it

d   it has certain fundamental rules and principles

e   to acquaint readers with easy-to-follow rules for developing speaking and writing skills

f   email, visit the website

2 Pairs

Students work together to give meanings for the words and phrases (**a–d**). Then they use the words and phrases in sentences of their own.

Answers

a   be very beneficial,

b   have very high results,

c   display interest and eagerness,

d   people will respond well to you

3 Whole class, then alone

Students are going to read the *Dear Editor* letter and then write their own response to it. Go through the letter with the whole class, making sure they understand what the topic is (crowds of young hooligans outside the café), what the writer's views are about it (he thinks the young people's behaviour is unacceptable) and what he thinks the solution is (these louts should get a job and learn some manners).

Then ask students what they think about the behaviour of young people today, and how they will respond to the writer's views. During the whole class discussion, you can encourage students to make notes, which they can then use in their own writing.

Here are two sample answers written by **i** an **IGCSE Core** student and **ii** an **IGCSE Extended** student. Both these attempts would probably score in the top mark band for both content and language.

i Core

Dear Editor,

I am writing this letter in response to the letter sent by Mr. David Davies about the hooligans in Market Street. I do agree that it is not very nice to see them there and that young people should learn to behave in a more respectful way to society and to their elders in general, but I also think that Mr. Davies behaved very badly too. Why did he not ask the 'hooligans' as he called them to move out the way instead of getting so angry with them?

Anti-social behaviour is negative for all of us but treating people disrespectfully does not help the situation either. Instead of being angry, maybe Mr. Davies should try to understand how difficult life is for young people in the 21st century, how many challenges face young people and instead try to help as best as he can.

Yours faithfully,

Nikita Mavromatta. [*150 words*]

ii Extended

Dear Editor,

I am writing to express my anger at a letter I recently saw in the weekly newspaper, written by Mr Davies.

I believe his description of teenagers to be very disrespectful and unfair. He seems to be under the impression that because he came across a group of 'young hooligans', all teenagers are sure to be like them. Although I am aware that my generation's behaviour can be very often rude and disrespectful, I do not like the fact that he is of the opinion that all teenagers are lazy and should get a job!

Mr Davies should also understand, that a lot has changed since he was our age, and it is wrong of him to think that our behaviour, and the way we pass our time would be the same as himself when he was young. Not all teenagers spend their free time shouting in the streets. The majority are hard-working, normal young people who are focusing on their future. These sorts of generalisations are what give teenagers a bad reputation, and it is neither fair nor correct!

Thank you for your time.

Yours faithfully,

Marinos Papakyriacou [*192 words*]

Reflection

Use the **Reflection** to remind students of what they have achieved in the unit. Students should set themselves a **personal goal** based on their scores for Unit 8.

Exam focus

Writing, Exercise 6

1   Here are two sample answers written by **i** an **IGCSE Core** student and **ii** an **IGCSE Extended** student. Both these attempts would probably score in the top mark band for both content and language.

i   Core

Dear Sir/ Madam,

I am writing to express my delight at the new cinema complex that has recently opened in our town. There aren't many fun places for young people to visit in our town, so it's nice to be able to go to the cinema when we want to hang out with friends.

The old cinema complex didn't have much choice, but with this new one we have six screens to choose from, so there is always a film that we can enjoy. Also, even if we don't fancy watching a film, we enjoy going around the shops that are in the complex and sitting at one of the cafes. We're very lucky that we can spend our time in a friendly modern environment with lots to do!

Thank you again for opening the new cinema complex.

Sincerely,

Ling Zhang [*141 words*]

ii   Extended

Dear Mr. Panayides,

I am writing this letter to congratulate you on the opening of the new cinema complex in Larnaka. The old cinema that has now closed had been there for ten years and was in need of renovation! It was dirty, smelly and everything inside it looked grey. This new cinema complex on the other hand, is brand new, looks amazing and smells fantastic!

Many people have said that this new cinema was not necessary and that it was a waste of money but I personally disagree. This new cinema complex has given me and my friends opportunities to work and has brought life to a town that was beginning to look like a ghost city. We also now have somewhere to go at the weekends to have a coffee and relax instead of sitting on the pavements with nowhere to go and annoying many people with our presence.

The new cinema complex is a place that can be enjoyed not only by us young people but also by the older generation. I

really *do* think it is a success and wish to thank you once again for the great idea!

Yours faithfully,

Christiana Grey [*197 words*]

2   Here are two sample answers written by **i** an **IGCSE Core** student and **ii** an **IGCSE Extended** student. Both these attempts would probably score in the top mark band for both content and language.

i   Core

Dear Sir

I am sending this email to ask about the course in healthy eating and learning how to prepare healthy meals. I believe this course is useful for my schoolmates and I to attend and I would like to ask a few questions.

Firstly, could you please tell me when the course takes place and also how much will it cost? It is very important that we do not miss any lessons as we are still at school! Also can anybody join the course or do you need to have any knowledge about healthy eating? Is it possible for any age group to join the course?

We are very interested and we hope to learn how to be able to cook a few healthy meals and to be able to go to the supermarket and buy ingredients that are healthy and good for us!

Yours faithfully,

Alex George [*149 words*]

ii   Extended

Dear Sir/Madam,

I am writing to enquire after the healthy eating course which I saw advertised in my local supermarket. I believe the course could be useful for myself and my friends, but I would like to know more about it before we apply.

Firstly, could you please tell me where the course actually takes place and how much it will cost, as this will affect our final decision. There is also the question of whether or not there is an age restriction for the course. My friends and I are all under the age of 18, and my mother is also interested in joining, so does it matter what ages we are?

My friends and I are very keen on joining the course. We believe that it could be a very enlightening experience for us, and will open our eyes to a healthier lifestyle. We really want to come out of this experience, knowing more about eating healthy meals and also learning to prepare them on our own. I hope you can get back to me soon.

Sincerely,

Abel Dourand [*181 words*]

NOTE on Assessment Objectives (AOs) for Listening Exercise 4 (multiple-choice questions): Students listen to a discussion between two speakers and answer multiple-choice questions. The discussion is informal between two speakers, with a host to introduce the discussion.

Students need to show understanding of the connections between ideas, opinions and attitudes (L3) and understand what is implied but not directly stated, e.g. gist, speaker's purpose, intention and feelings (L4).

Learning objectives (LOs)

Suggested activity: Start the unit by focusing for a few minutes on the LOs box, making sure that students understand what they are going to be doing. Using the first LO as an example, ask students to identify where in the unit they can find the activities for the other four LOs. Get students to say which of the activities appeal to them the most, and ask them for their reasons.

A Watch, listen and talk

1 Whole class, then alone

Explain that your students are going to watch and listen to some IGCSE students talking about **interviews**. As your students watch and listen, they should make a note of **a** three different ways of preparing for a part-time job interview that the speakers think are effective, and **b** three part-time jobs that the speakers mention. Play the video a second time so that students can check or add to their notes.

Answers

a The best ways to prepare for a part-time job interview: any **three** from: research everything about the position, research the company, be enthusiastic, practise in front of a mirror.

b **Three** part-time jobs mentioned by the students: working in a charity shop, working in a coffee shop, freelance illustrator.

2 Pairs or small groups

Depending on the size of your class, put students into pairs or small groups. They can discuss their notes and then talk to each other about what they think are the best ways to prepare for an interview. Do not interfere too much, but make sure you get feedback from the class so that they know their efforts have been worthwhile. If time permits, you could write their ideas on the board and rank them according to your students' preferences.

B Speaking and vocabulary

1 Whole class, then pairs

You could introduce this unit by asking if any students have (or would like to have) a part-time job. Then, get students to work together and look at the five pictures. They need to speculate about what they think might have happened both before and after the pictures were taken. Obviously there are no right or wrong answers. Monitor the discussions, but do not interfere, and be ready to provide positive feedback.

2 Pairs

Your students in pairs discuss questions **a** and **b**.

3 Small groups

Check if students know what the abbreviation CV stands for (*curriculum vitae*). This is a Latin phrase meaning 'course' (*curriculum*) 'of life' (*vitae*) and it is used to give employers detailed information about a person's life to date. Students agree on what information a CV should include and make a list of headings. Obviously 'Education' is an important part – other headings are mentioned in the next activity.

4 Pairs

Students look at the list and compare it with the one they made in the previous activity. They should also think about the best order for the headings to appear in a CV.

C Listening

1 Alone, then whole class

Prepare students for the listening activity. Ask them who Janine Mesumo is (a careers adviser) and what they think her job involves (e.g. giving advice to students about future careers and about studying). Then students listen to the interview and check the order of the headings in Activity B4.

CD1, Track 17

Pablo Selles: We are very lucky to have in our studio today Janine Mesumo, who works as a careers adviser at an international school in Madrid. Her main role is to advise students who have recently completed their IGCSEs, AS and A Levels on what they should do next. Part of this is giving them advice on writing their first CV. Have I got that right, Janine?

Janine Mesumo: Absolutely, Pablo. Actually, a great deal of my time is spent in helping students draw up their CV, which can be quite problematic when you haven't yet had any work experience.

PS: What areas should first-time CV writers include?

JM: I think the key here is not to try to include too much. Prospective employers need to be able to get a quick overview, rather than a detailed biography of someone's life – that can come at the interview. However, there needs to be enough information, so that the employer can decide whether or not to call the applicant for an interview.

PS: Hmm, I see. So what information would you say is essential?

JM: Start with personal details: name, address, contact details. You'd be surprised how many people forget to put their telephone number and email address on their CV! Then, education and qualifications. Some people recommend combining these two areas; so, for example, you might say '1999–2001, International School, Madrid, six IGCSEs in Maths, English …', and so on, rather than listing the qualifications in a different section.

PS: That's an interesting idea – I like that! What comes next?

JM: Well, this is where some students become rather worried, because usually the next section is work experience.

PS: But often students don't have any work experience!

JM: Exactly, and so they worry about leaving a blank. But as a school- or college-leaver, nobody is going to expect you to have an employment history, so there really is no need to

worry. However, it is worth mentioning weekend or after-school jobs, or any work for charities, or voluntary work.

PS: OK, and after that? What about hobbies and interests?

JM: Yes, it is important to include leisure interests, but a common mistake is simply to list things, for example: 'reading, football, music'.

PS: So what should our listeners do?

JM: Instead of simply giving a list, explain in what way these things interest you or what skills you have developed through them. For example, if you put reading, give details about what you like to read …

PS: … and if you list music, what types of music you like listening to.

JM: Exactly, but also, music might mean playing an instrument, so give that information as well. Or if you're the captain of a sports team, include that information as it demonstrates leadership skills.

PS: Any other sections which need to be included?

JM: Well, two really. The first should include any skills which have not been mentioned before, such as IT skills, proficiency in other languages (don't just put 'French'!), and details of any organisations or clubs which you belong to. And finally, give the names, addresses and contact details for two referees.

PS: Which are what?

JM: A referee is a person who would be willing to write about you in a positive way! Always check with the person before you put their name on your CV.

PS: Janine, we're coming to the end of our time. Thank you very much for a very informative chat. If any listeners would like more information on writing their CV, just go onto our website and you'll find everything you need.

Answers

Personal details, Education and qualifications, Work experience, Hobbies, Languages, Referees

TOP TIP
Remind students to read all three options before they choose the best one.

2 Alone, then pairs

Students read through the multiple-choice questions (**a–h**), and predict the answers (**A**, **B** or **C**) for each one. Encourage them to look for key words in the questions,

61

but they do not need to finalise their answers yet. Allow some time for students to check with their partner.

3 Alone, then whole class

Play the audio again and get students to confirm their predictions from C2 as they listen. Then gather class feedback, checking that everyone understands the reasons for the answers.

Answers

a	A,	d	C,	g	C,
b	B,	e	A,	h	A
c	A,	f	C,		

4/5 Pairs

Students work in pairs to remember and write notes about some of the content of the interview. Students need to answer four of the interviewer's questions. Refer them to the audioscript in Appendix 3 of the Coursebook.

D Writing

1 Pairs

In this section, students will finally write their own CV. Before doing this, they look at the example in Activity D1 and identify the mistakes that the writer (Sophie Labane) has made in her own CV. She has omitted some important information (such as her phone number) and has put some information in the wrong place (e.g. referees should appear at the end).

Possible answers

Curriculum Vitae

Personal details

Name: Sophie Labane

Email: labane.sophie@swazimail.com.sz

Phone number: 54928519278

Address: PO Box 4321, Manzini, Swaziland

Education and qualifications

2011–today: Manzini High School, Swaziland

Studying for High School leaving certificate as well as IGCSEs in three different subjects: Maths, French and Music.

I received grade B for IGCSE English as a Second Language in 2014

Before 2011: Manzini Primary School, Swaziland

Work experience

None so far

Hobbies and interests

I love reading books and watching my favourite basketball team, the Bosco Steels.

Other skills

I speak Swazi and English, but Swazi is my first language, and I am competent in all skills in both languages.

I am a member of the Bosco Steels fan club.

Referees

Mr Al Faisal, Head Teacher, Manzini High School, PO Box 1234, Manzini, Swaziland w.thembu@mhs.ac.sz

Doctor Masia Lemba, PO Box 6789, Manzini, Swaziland lembamasia@swazimail.com.sz

2 Pairs

In pairs, students should discuss the information that could go into their own CV. They should also consider information that they would not include. Obviously 15–16-year-olds will probably feel that they do not have much to say about themselves, but they can definitely provide information for the Personal details, Education, Hobbies and interests, Other skills and Referees sections.

3 Whole class, then alone, then pairs

Go through the template with the class, checking again that they understand what needs to be written in each section. If students genuinely feel they do not have enough to write, tell them that they can make up some of the details (e.g. for the section on Work experience). Then students can share their CVs and check the content.

Sample answer
Personal details

Name:	Benilda Dantos
Address:	10, Jimmy Abbad Street, Manila, Philippines
Email:	benilda.dantos@hotmail.com
Telephone:	0063 78905634

Education and qualifications

Long Street Secondary School:
IGCSE Mathematics, IGCSE Chemistry, IGCSE English

Manila Primary School

Work experience

Cashier at 'Fashion Forward' department store

Hobbies and interests

I enjoy watching international movies with my friends at a small cinema in my neighbourhood. Also, I play tennis twice a week and I attend dance lessons.

Other skills

I am fluent in Filipino, French and have a good knowledge of English.
I am a member of the Red Cross.

Referees

Mary Johnson – English teacher, 0063 76379710
Ian Ocampo – Manager at 'Fashion Forward' department store, 0063 57140022

E Listening

> **LANGUAGE TIP**
> There are quite a few 'person' nouns in English with the suffix *-ee* or *-er*, with a change in word stress, but many are not relevant for your students. However, check if they can think of any besides the two given (*employee* and *interviewee*) – for example *evacuee*, *nominee*. Refer students to the exercise in the **Workbook**.

Job interview 1

1/2 Pairs, then whole class

Refer students to the job advertisement before Activity E3 of the Coursebook and explain that they are going to listen to a student being interviewed for the job with 'Winning Sports'. In pairs, they should write down possible questions the interviewer might ask the interviewee (two examples are given). Students should then move on to think about the possible answers the interviewee might give. Each pair of students will have similar questions and answers, but they will not be exactly the same, so you could spend some time asking the class which questions and answers they think are the best.

3 Alone, then pairs

Students listen to the interview and make notes about the interviewee's technique when answering the questions. She does not perform very well, using inappropriate language in many places (e.g. *Nope … I checked it out …* , *Er, yeah*) and she does not supply all the information the

interviewer asks for. Give students some time to compare their notes with a partner's.

CD1, Track 18

Interviewer:	Good morning, Miss Gupta. Please take a seat.
Abha Gupta:	Thanks.
Int'er:	Did you have any problems getting here?
AG:	Nope, I found the address very easily. I checked it out yesterday.
Int'er:	I see. Now, you've just left school with four IGCSEs. Is that correct?
AG:	Yeah.
Int'er:	And the subjects?
AG:	Oh, right, err, let me think now … Science, English, Art and Music.
Int'er:	Thank you. Which of those was your favourite subject at school?
AG:	I didn't really like any of them. The teachers were not very interesting. I must've been really lucky to pass them.
Int'er:	And which school did you attend?
AG:	The new one, behind the park at the start of the motorway.
Int'er:	I see. Now, tell me something about your interests, the things that you do in your free time.
AG:	Well, not much really. I like riding my bike. That's why I think this job would be good for me.
Int'er:	Because you like riding a bike?
AG:	Er, yeah. The job's to do with sport, isn't it?
Int'er:	Yes, Miss Gupta, it is. Have you had any work experience yet – for example a weekend job?
AG:	Well, yes, I had a job with my brother washing cars. We used to do it in our free time. We got loads of money to spend on clothes and DVDs, or for going to the cinema and other things.
Int'er:	What personal qualities do you think you could offer us here at 'Winning Sports'?
AG:	Well, like I told you, I like sports, especially riding my bike, and every weekend I go to the match, if they're playing at home, of course. What else do you want to know?
Int'er:	I think that's all for the time being, Miss Gupta.

AG:	Is that it?
Int'er:	Yes, thank you very much, Miss Gupta. That's all. Goodbye.
AG:	Did I get the job?
Int'er:	I'll be in touch. Goodbye.

4 Alone, then pairs

Students listen to four of the interviewer's questions, without any answers. This time students need to answer the questions themselves, using their notes from Activity E2, then compare their own answers with their partner's responses.

CD1, Track 19

Int'er:	Did you have any problems getting here?
Int'er:	Now, tell me something about your interests, the things that you do in your free time.
Int'er:	Have you had any work experience yet – for example, a weekend job?
Int'er:	What personal qualities do you think you could offer us here at 'Winning Sports'?

Job interview 2

1/2 Alone, then pairs

Prepare students to listen to the first part of another job interview. Refer them to the *Teen Weekly* advert to familiarise themselves with the job. As they listen, students need to write down three positive things about the interviewee's performance. Go through the example in the Coursebook to make students fully understand. After listening, students can compare their ideas with a partner.

CD1, Track 20
Part A

Lan Huang:	Hello, have a seat. My name's Lan Huang. And you are … Mr Hairilombus Papachristofer [*hesitantly*], is that correct?
Bambos:	Hello, pleased to meet you. Actually, the pronunciation is Haralambous Papachristoforou. Most people call me Bambos, for short. I'm Greek, on my father's side.
LH:	Really? How interesting! Did you have any trouble finding our office, ummm … Bambos?
B:	Not at all, Ms Huang. I came yesterday to make sure I knew exactly how to find you, and to check how much time I would need. And today I used Google

	Maps on my smartphone, just in case. I arrived two hours early!
LH:	That shows good initiative! Now, what is it about the job that interests you?
B:	Well, first of all, I visited your website when I saw the advertisement, and discovered more about the format of *Teen Weekly*, and that really interested me.
LH:	It did? Why?
B:	Basically, I just love writing. Ever since I was a child, I've been writing stories and trying to write poems too. I've also won three writing competitions.
LH:	Congratulations! Is there anything else that demonstrates your love for writing?
B:	Well, I've been editor of our online school webzine for two years, and I also publish my own monthly blog.
LH:	Excellent! Now, obviously our readership is teenagers, young people who are still at school. What do you think are the main interest areas for your age group?
B:	I guess for many teenagers, myself included, the most interesting topic is celebrity gossip and stories about film stars and musicians, sports people, important people – where they are, what they are doing, and so on. But not just gossip. I think many teens are interested in their society and culture, as well as global issues like the environment.
LH:	Good. Anything else?
B:	Well, for many teenagers, becoming an adult is a scary thought, and they often want to discuss their future education and careers.
LH:	Thank you, Bambos. Now, is there anything you would like to ask me?
B:	Well, yes, Ms Huang, I have some questions. I made a note on my phone – can I check them?
LH:	Please, go ahead . . . .

Possible answers

Bambos introduces himself politely; he gives some information about himself; he speaks clearly and accurately; he answers the questions fully; he uses a relaxed style, but is still quite formal and polite; he has questions prepared for the interviewer.

3 Pairs

Students work in pairs and predict the questions that Bambos might ask the interviewer, as well as Lan Huang's possible answers. Go through the example in the Coursebook before they start.

4/5 Alone, then pairs

Students listen to the audio and compare their predictions with what Bambos and Lan Huang actually say. They can work together and compare their answers, then refer to Appendix 3 of the Coursebook to make a final check.

CD1, Track 21
Part B

Bambos:	OK, firstly, what is the commitment in terms of time? I assume it's a part-time position, as I'm still at school?
Lan Huang:	Yes, of course. It's very part-time, so only 20 hours per month.
B:	Great. Secondly, would I be able to work from home?
LH:	Absolutely! In fact, we prefer you to do that. We would probably need you here for a meeting once every two to three months.
B:	Perfect. Umm … thirdly, the advertisement mentions 'competitions'. What type of things do you ask your readers to do for these?
LH:	Good question! To be honest, this is a new idea and something that we want the successful applicant for the job to consider.
B:	Really? That's awesome. OK, finally, is the salary paid weekly or monthly?
LH:	As it's a part-time job, based on monthly hours, the company pays at the end of each calendar month.
B:	Thank you. That answers all my questions.
LH:	Thank you, Bambos. It was a pleasure meeting you.

6 Whole class

Ask the class whether they think Bambos got the job. Make sure they give full reasons for their answers.

F Listening and speaking

1/2/3 Alone, then pairs

In this speaking section, students are going to interview each other for the Youth Club job (see Activity F1 of the Coursebook). Firstly, they need to read through the advertisement and check they understand everything (e.g. who should apply, what the job involves, how they can apply). Then, students prepare for the interview.

Student A should use the CV they wrote earlier in the unit and their ideas on interview techniques in order to prepare themselves. Student B should draw up some questions to ask Student A – again using ideas from the unit, and should refer to Student A's CV during the interview itself.

Differentiated activities

Support

Put all the As together and all the Bs together during the preparation stage, so that they can help and support each other.

Challenge

Have two interviewers per candidate instead of one. One interviewer is in favour of the candidate, while the other is not. They need to prepare their questions together and think carefully how they will perform the interview.

When everyone is ready, students pair up (A + B) and carry out the interview. If you have an odd number of students, make one group of one A (interviewee) + two Bs (interviewers). If you can video or audio record the interviews, this is an effective way for students to see and hear their spoken language. If time permits, students A and B can exchange roles.

4 Pairs

Allow some time for students to reflect on how they felt while they were being interviewed, to think about which questions were the most challenging, and which part of the interview was the most stressful. Encourage them to give reasons.

5 Pairs

B students give A students feedback on their performance, and inform them of whether or not they are getting the job!

6 Whole class, then alone

This is an exam-style practice question. Go through the instructions and the **Top Tip**, and check that students understand everything, as well as the seven statements **A**–**G**. Then play the audio. If you feel your students need more support, you could stop after each speaker (**1**–**6**) and discuss the answers that students have.

Answers

1D, **2C**, **3A**, **4G**, **5F**, **6B**

CD1, Track 22

Speaker 1 – female adult

I was terribly nervous before my first job interview, so it's not really surprising that I didn't get the job! It was all my fault*. I was very late, and when I did finally arrive I was hot and bothered and I looked a complete mess. Very unprofessional. Also, I had dropped my interview notes on the bus so I couldn't remember the questions that I wanted to ask. My advice of course is to be prepared, and don't copy my example, because that will only end in disaster!

Speaker 2 – male adult

If you go online you'll find pages and pages of advice about how to prepare for a job interview, and, to be honest, you can waste loads of time trying to find the perfect strategy. But in my experience the drawback* is that they all really give you the same advice, which is simply: relax and be yourself! Easier said than done, I think. However, no matter how well you have prepared yourself, if on the day you appear nervous and try to pretend to be someone else, you are definitely not going to do very well.

Speaker 3 – female adult (older)

I'm quite old now so I don't think I'll be attending any more job interviews! But during my life I've been to a few, and in the latter part of my career, up until about three years ago, I was the one doing the interviewing. I must've done over a hundred. It was interesting being the one asking all the questions, and watching the interviewee squirming in their seat when I asked a difficult question! Having said that, I think I was a good interviewer because I always remembered my own days in the hot seat!

Speaker 4 – male teenager

I've only had one job interview so far, for a part-time job in a supermarket. Even though the job was only stacking the shelves at weekends, I spent hours preparing for the interview, going online, trying to find the best strategies for doing well. I even got my parents and friends to do practice interviews with me. In the end, the interview only lasted about five minutes, and I was actually very disappointed, even though I got the job!

Speaker 5 – female teenager

I haven't had a face-to-face interview yet, but I did do an internet interview last year. It was for a part-time tele-sales job. Basically, the job was to phone people and try to sell them a different product each week, like make-up, or some other cosmetics. The interview wasn't difficult. It was an internet call and there was no video, so I've never actually seen the people who employ me, which is a bit strange. But I got the job and it's OK for now, but not something I want to do for the rest of my life.

Speaker 6 – male adult (older)

Since a very early age I worked with my dad in his carpenter's workshop, along with one of my dad's brothers. When my dad and his brother retired, I took over running the place, and stayed there until I myself retired, five years ago now. So, you may not actually believe this, but I have never had a job interview in my whole life! Does that make me very lucky or have I missed out on something special? I can't say it's something I've ever worried about, actually.

G Language focus: imperative verb forms

1 Pairs

The imperative (base form of the verb) is common in English, and can be used for various functions, as described in the Coursebook. Ask students for other functions (e.g. warning, request) and then they look at the three examples and discuss the function of each one.

Answers

a   advice, suggestion, recommendation,

b   offer,

c   advice, suggestion, recommendation

2 Alone, then pairs

Students work alone to decide on the function of each phrase, and then share with their partner.

Answers

a   warning,

b   request,

c   advice, suggestion, recommendation,

d   offer,

e   order, command,

f   request,

g   instruction,

h   advice, suggestion, recommendation,

i   offer

3 Alone, then pairs

Students read the audioscript interview in Appendix 3 of the Coursebook (between Pablo and Janine) and find more examples of the imperative form.

Answers

start with personal details, explain in what way, give details about, give that information, include that information, give the names, always check with, just go onto our website

4 Alone, then pairs

Students now practise producing the imperative form. They should work alone to think of their answers, and then discuss with a partner. There are many possible answers.

Possible answers

a   Please stop talking so loudly! / Can't you be quiet?!

b   Take some aspirin / Go and lie down

c   Have another slice / Try some more

d   Help yourself to anything you want / Have a seat / Make yourself comfortable

e   Listen carefully / Go online and find the map

f   Try asking yourself why it happened / Talk to someone at school

67

Reflection

Use the **Reflection** to remind students of what they have achieved in the unit. Students should set themselves a **personal goal** based on their scores for Unit 9.

Exam focus

Listening, Exercise 4, multiple-choice questions

CD1, Track 23

Joshua (teenage male): Good morning, Mrs Karima. Thank you for finding time to speak to me today.

Mrs Karima (adult female): Hello, Joshua, it's good to see you outside the classroom!

J: Mrs Karima, can you give us some advice about what we need to do in order to find our first job?

Mrs K: Well, with no or little real-world work experience, you may be concerned that you won't qualify for many jobs, or that there aren't many jobs available. However, your grades, school activities, club memberships and volunteer activities can demonstrate qualities that employers look for. A part-time job can be a first step into the working world.

J: The problem is that we don't have enough time to work during term time, especially when exams are getting close.

Mrs K: I appreciate that, Joshua, and of course you are right – studying must come first. But when the holidays arrive, you really should try to work. You can take on more hours and take on more responsibilities that will help you establish job experience.

J: Why is getting a part-time summer job so important?

Mrs K: Summer jobs often open doors for jobs during other parts of the year. Be sure to keep in touch with previous employers, as that may help you get hired again. Part-time jobs for teenagers can also lead to full-time employment and even future careers. Some jobs for teens may even include on-the-job training that will help you get started in your new position, or even start to develop a career.

J: How important is it to have a CV ready?

Mrs K: Even if you've never worked before, you should start to develop a résumé or CV. You can highlight your achievements at school or college, club memberships and social activities that demonstrate characteristics beneficial in a future job.
You'll definitely be one step ahead of most of your friends when you walk into an interview with a résumé which includes your current skill set.

J: So, Mrs K, let's say I'm interested in a job I've seen advertised. What should I do to be ready?

Mrs K: Most teen jobs will require you to go through at least a brief interview before you are hired. You should dress neatly, be well groomed, and be prepared to tell someone why you want the job. Most employers will understand that you're just trying to make some extra money. But if you can explain how getting this job will help you develop yourself, or even benefit others, then you'll be ahead of the game.

J: That also makes a lot of sense. What other things should I tell the interviewer?

Mrs K: Be ready to explain what skills you have that will allow you to perform this job successfully. For example, are you the one whose friends are always asking for computer help, or do you organise or run a club or committee at school, or are you just really good with people? Highlight your strengths and explain why you are their best choice for this job.

J: But doesn't that make me sound like a big-head?

Mrs K: Absolutely not! People in interviews who sell themselves are much more likely to be offered a job. Something else to remember is that jobs for teens are primarily part-time, and may only allow you to work as many hours as you are legally allowed to. In some cases, you can only work up to 16 hours per week, or a maximum of 70 hours in any one month. If you are slightly older, an A Level student, it's 18 and 80 hours. Make sure you understand the requirements of the job and that the employer knows how much time you are willing and available to work.

J: I hadn't thought of that. What's your final suggestion?

Mrs K: It's worth remembering that employers like to re-hire teens with a good work history. A part-time summer job or holiday job may be temporary work, but it could lead to bigger and better things! So, always try to leave on good terms with your employers, so that they can provide a good reference for you to use in your next job search.

J: Mrs K, thank you for talking to us.

Mrs K: You're welcome, Joshua.

Answers

a   B,

b   B,

c   A,

d   C,

e   C,

f   C,

g   B,

h   A

NOTE on Assessment Objectives (AOs): In the Cambridge IGCSE speaking examination, students need to communicate ideas/opinions clearly, accurately and effectively (S1), develop responses and link ideas using a range of appropriate linking devices (S2), use a range of grammatical structures and vocabulary accurately and effectively (S3), show control of pronunciation and intonation patterns (S4) and engage in a conversation and contribute effectively to help move the conversation forward (S5).

Learning objectives (LOs)

Suggested activity: Start the unit by focusing for a few minutes on the LOs box, making sure that students understand what they are going to be doing. Using the first LO as an example, ask students to identify where in the unit they can find the activities for the other four LOs. Get students to say which of the activities appeal to them the most, and ask them for their reasons.

A Watch, listen and talk

1 Whole class, then alone

Explain that students are going to watch and listen to some IGCSE students talking about **education**. As your students watch and listen, they should make a note of **a** the three best ways to study that the speakers mention, and **b** in what ways the speakers think exam studying is different from doing homework. Play the video a second time so that students can check or add to their notes.

Answers

a The best ways to study, any **three** from: using technology, using Google, printing past papers and mark schemes online, studying alone to concentrate, studying with a partner.

b In what ways do the students think that studying for an important exam is different from doing homework: homework is taking in knowledge and applying it, studying for an exam involves doing past papers.

2 Pairs or small groups

Depending on the size of your class, put students into pairs or small groups. They can discuss their notes and then talk to each other about what they think are the best ways to study. Do not interfere too much, but make sure you get feedback from the class so that they know their efforts have been worthwhile. If time permits, you could write their ideas on the board and rank them according to your students' preferences.

B Speaking and vocabulary

1 Pairs

Students look at the five pictures, which show students studying in different ways. Working in pairs, students name **at least two** things that they can see in each picture.

2 Pairs

Of course, everyone has their own preferences in terms of how they study, but picture **1**, which shows a teenager at their desk sleeping, is probably the least effective study method. Give students time to talk about each picture and to draw their own conclusions.

3 Pairs

Students look at the seven study methods (**a–g**) and discuss which might help them to study more effectively. Obviously there are no right or wrong answers here so allow students to discuss freely.

C Reading and speaking

The approach to reading in this section will generate multiple opportunities for students to speak to each other.

1 Whole class, then pairs

Tell students that the text they are going to read is called *Study Less, Study Smart*. Get students to tell you what they think this means and if they like the idea of *Study Less, Study Smart*. Then they look quickly at the text to do two things: **a** check which study methods in the previous section are mentioned (**a**, **b**, **d** and **f**), and **b** make a note of two further study methods mentioned in the internet article (any two of**:** Take good notes, Read textbooks effectively, Divide everything into two categories: facts and concepts).

2 Alone, then pairs

Students need to work alone to read the text in more detail and decide if the information (**a**–**e**) is true or false. Then they can compare with their partner, making sure they give reasons for their answers.

Answers

a true (*need a lot of time to truly understand it all*),

b true (*your ability to retain new information diminishes after about 25–30 minutes*),

c false (*Don't study where you do anything else*),

d false (*not often*),

e false (*is an acquired skill*)

3 Whole class, then pairs

Get students to re-read paragraph **7 Read textbooks effectively** and ask them to tell you what they think the SQ3R method involves and how it works. Then in pairs they talk specifically about the five steps: survey, question, read, recite, review, and what happens in each step. Do **not** let them read the paragraph in Activity C4 yet.

4 Alone

The paragraph introduces the SQ3R method in a little more detail, and gives an important piece of advice about reading. Give students a minute to read the paragraph and identify the specific advice.

Answer

Train your mind to learn while reading with SQ3R.

5 Whole class and then groups of four – A, B, C and D

Reciprocal teaching is an approach where students become the teachers, usually in groups of four. The teacher first of all demonstrates clearly what the students need to do, and then supports them in group discussions where they use four different strategies: clarifying, question generating, summarising, and predicting. Students take it in turns to apply each of the four strategies to different parts of a text or texts.

This is a **reciprocal reading activity**, in which different students do different things with the same piece of text. If you do not have enough students to make groups of four, students could work in pairs and each student completes two tasks instead of one. Ensure your students understand that each person in the group (or pair) will be doing something slightly different, even though everyone will be looking at the same text. This approach to reading is useful if you want to differentiate, because the four reading strategies offer different levels of challenge to students.

Firstly, **model the four strategies**: clarifying, question generating, summarising, and predicting, using the introductory paragraph, with the whole class. Get the **A** students to think of a clarifying question or statement, for example: *What does the word 'gain' mean?* or *I think 'recite' means to say something aloud*, and so on. Then the **B** students think of a comprehension question, for example: *What is the result of just 'doing it'?* Next, the **C** students summarise the information they have read, for example: *SQ3R has five steps which can help students to understand important information in a text*, and so on. Finally, the **D** students predict what they think they will read next, for example: *I believe we will read in more detail how the SQ3R method actually works*, and so on. When you are sure students understand what they have to do, tell them that they are going to read more about SQ3R, using the reciprocal reading approach.

6 Pairs

Ask students to look at the six words and phrases in the box, and then match them to the six underlined words and phrases in the text. They do not need to read the text in detail at this point.

Answers

concentrate = focus on,

get ready = prepare,

ignore = overlook,

support = aid,

understand = comprehend,

visuals = graphics

7 Groups of four – A, B, C and D

Either allocate different strategies to students (as per the instructions in the Coursebook) from Activity C5, or, if you feel students would be more confident using the same strategy they practised before, allow them to keep the same letter (**A**, **B**, **C** or **D**). Then, using the text from C6, students work in groups of four (or pairs) and apply their strategy. Various answers are possible. The important thing is to encourage students to interact in different ways with the text, and this interaction will lead to better understanding. Remember to give students time to share their questions and answers.

8 Groups of four – A, B, C and D

Working in the same groups of four, students are going to continue their reading, but now each student in the group is going to read a **different** short paragraph. Firstly, students should change letter one more time, and then find out where their text is at the back of the Coursebook in Appendix 2. Each student will not be able to see the other students' texts.

Explain to students that this time when they read, they need to make two or three written notes about the content of their paragraph. They do **not** need to apply the previous four strategies: clarifying, question generating, summarising and predicting. When students understand what they have to do, give them three to four minutes to find and read their text, and then write their notes. Tell students that they are going to use their notes to teach the others in their group.

9 Groups of four – A, B, C and D

When students are ready, each person in the group tells the others what they have read, referring only to their notes. They are not allowed to re-read nor refer to the text. When everyone in the group has had a chance to speak, students can read the other three texts that they have not yet seen, and compare the content with what their partners told them.

WORD TIP

These two words (*engage, concentrate*) appeared in paragraph **A** (Appendix 2) which students have just read. Refer students to the exercise in the **Workbook**.

D Language focus: 'alternative' conditional structures

1 Pairs

At this stage in their studying, students will no doubt have come across 'conditionals' on multiple occasions. This first activity gets students to recall what they already know by doing three things:

a writing example sentences which contain **different** conditional structures,

b analysing the form/structure of each one

c identifying the function of each one.

Give students time to work in pairs to answer the three questions.

Possible answers

a '0' conditional: *If you heat ice, it melts*, 1st conditional: *If you eat that, you could be sick*, 2nd conditional: *If he ran faster, he might get there more quickly*

b '0' present + present, 1st present + *will*, 2nd past + modal + infinitive, 3rd past perfect + modal + *have* + past participle

c '0' always true, scientific facts, 1st high probability present/future time, 2nd low probability present/future time, 3rd impossibility past time

2 Alone, then pairs

Students compare the sentences they wrote earlier in D1a with the four sentences (**a**–**d**) from the text they read, to identify if they used the same or similar structures, or completely different ones. The four sentences (**a**–**d**) show that conditionals do not always follow expected patterns. For example, in **b**: *If you're learning new material at school, it can be completely overwhelming*, the verb in the *if* clause is present continuous, and in the result clause the verb is modal infinitive. In **c**, the result verb is an imperative, and in **d** the *if* clause verb is present perfect followed by an imperative in the result clause.

LANGUAGE TIP

The **Language Tip** reinforces the point that conditionals do not always follow the rules, and that different combinations of structures are often possible. Refer students to the exercise in the **Workbook**.

3 Pairs

This activity further reinforces the point that conditionals do not always follow the traditional, fixed structure patterns that students have probably been exposed to and learnt over the years. Students work in pairs and match the structure combinations **a**–**d** to the four sentences in D2.

Answers

a	b,	**c**	c,
b	d,	**d**	a

4 Pairs

Give students a few minutes to study and discuss the pair of sentences and check their understanding of the difference between using *When* and *If*. Use *when* to imply that something will definitely happen, or is happening, and use *if* when there's uncertainty about something happening.

i   **When** you're learning new material at school or college, it can be completely overwhelming.

ii **If** you're learning new material at school or college, it can be completely overwhelming.

However, in some cases, there is very little difference in meaning:

i   **When** you heat ice, it melts.

ii **If** you heat ice, it melts.

5 Alone, then pairs

Students now go back to the texts in the unit and find more examples of conditionals. They should identify the structures that are used, and then see if their partner found the same examples.

Answers

When you <u>use</u> this technique, <u>reward</u> yourself during your breaks by checking your social media. (<u>present</u> + <u>imperative</u>)

If you <u>can teach</u> the information to someone else, it <u>means</u> that you have a solid grasp of the material. (<u>modal infinitive</u> + <u>present</u>)

… you <u>may need to</u> come up with a mnemonic device **if** you <u>want</u> to remember them easily. (<u>modal infinitive</u> + <u>present</u>)

If you <u>follow</u> the steps below, you <u>will learn</u> how to obtain as much information as possible from the text requirements for any class. (<u>present</u> + <u>modal infinitive</u>)

When your mind <u>is</u> actively <u>searching</u> for answers to questions, it <u>becomes</u> engaged in active learning. (<u>present continuous</u> + <u>present</u>)

But **if** you <u>can't answer</u> them, <u>look back</u> at the text again (as often as necessary) for help. (<u>modal</u> <u>infinitive</u> + <u>imperative</u>)

However, <u>don't move on</u> to the next section **if** you <u>can't provide</u> the answers from the previous one. (<u>imperative</u> + <u>modal infinitive</u>)

When <u>you've finished</u> reading the entire chapter using the preceding steps, <u>go back</u> over the questions you created for every heading. (<u>present perfect</u> + <u>imperative</u>)

If you <u>can't</u>, <u>look back</u> at the chapter and refresh your memory, <u>check</u> what you remember, and then <u>continue</u>

reading the subsequent chapters. (<u>modal infinitive</u> + <u>imperatives</u>)

6 Alone, then pairs

Students need to select **six** different conditional structure combinations that they have seen in the unit and use them to write their own sentences. If your students are already confident in using the more traditional conditional structures (0, 1st, 2nd, 3rd), encourage them to use the new ones they have learnt about. Give some time for students to share their sentences with each other.

E Speaking

1/2 Small groups

In Unit 5 students learnt about the introductory part of the Cambridge IGCSE speaking exam, and now they are going to focus on the rest of the exam. Put students into small groups to discuss and make notes about what they already know. Use the examples to get them started. After a couple of minutes, join the groups together to share their ideas and to find out what they can learn from each other.

> **TOP TIP**
> Students probably know that they will be given a topic card to talk about. This **Top Tip** informs them about how much time they have to study it, and reminds them they are not allowed to make any written notes.

3 Pairs

This activity helps students to differentiate between general advice for any speaking exam (e.g. *It's not a good idea to answer a question with just 'yes' or 'no'*) and exam-specific information. In pairs, students discuss further their ideas from E2 and add them to a copy of the table. There are many possible answers.

4 Whole class, then alone

Prepare students for listening to Fatima and Abdullah, who are discussing their speaking exam. Look at questions **a** and **b**, advising students that the first question tests their general understanding, while the second question is asking for a specific detail. Get students to predict the answers, then play the audio. Check their answers.

CD1, Track 24

Fatima: OK, Abdullah, let's do some practice for our speaking exam.

Abdullah: Good idea, Fatima. You go first – what's your presentation about?

F: Come on, Abdullah, you should know by now that we don't have to do a presentation or give a speech in the exam.

A: Really? I thought that's what we have to do. So what is it then?

F: We have a discussion with the examiner about a topic. It lasts about 10 to 15 minutes, I think.

A: Great! I'm going to talk about fast-food restaurants and I guess you would choose animals or becoming a vet.

F: Unfortunately, we don't get to choose our topic, Abdullah. The examiner has a set of topic cards and we have to talk about the one he or she chooses for us.

A: But what if I don't know anything about the topic? I won't be able to say anything! Fatima, that's mean!

F: But it's not a test of knowledge about the topic. The topic is just to give us something to talk around. We are being tested on how well we can communicate in English.

A: OK, fair enough. What happens when we see the topic card? Can we make written notes?

F: No, but there are some ideas on the topic card which we can use and we have a couple of minutes to prepare. We should use that time properly, to think and plan for the discussion.

A: And then what happens? We start talking about the topic, right?

F: Yes, that's right. The examiner will ask us some questions, too, about the topic.

A: Do I lose marks if I get the answers wrong?

F: No, Abdullah, there are no right or wrong answers – the examiner just wants to hear you speaking in English. Try to use expressions like: *In my opinion … , I believe … , On the other hand … , On the whole … ,* and so on.

A: Hmmmm, so answering with 'yes' or 'no' is probably not a good idea, right? We need to use 'because' as much as possible.

F: Right! We need to explain ourselves with more ideas and reasons.

A: What happens if I don't understand something? Maybe the examiner will think I'm not very good.

F: Come on, Abdullah! Just tell the examiner if you don't understand, or you could ask them to give you an example, or say something like: *Do you mean … ?,* or ask the examiner to repeat something.

A: Like: *Sorry, could you say that again, please?*

F: Exactly!

A: OK, so let's have a look at one of these topic cards, then, so we can practise.

F: There are plenty in the back of our Coursebook, Abdullah …

Answers

a Fatima,

b in the back of the Coursebook

5/6 Alone, then pairs

Students listen again and add information and advice to their table in Activity E3. Let them compare with a partner, and then read the audioscript in Appendix 3 of the Coursebook to check they have noted all the important advice and information.

Answers

Advice	Information
Use preparation time to think and plan for discussion.	Don't have to do presentation or make a speech.
Use expressions like *In my opinion … , On the other hand …,* and so on.	Discuss topic with examiner, about 10 to 15 minutes.
	Students can't choose topic.
Avoid yes/no answers.	Not a test of the topic, test of communication skills in English.
Use *because* as much as possible to explain and give reasons.	Students cannot make written notes.
Tell the examiner if something is not understood, or ask for clarification.	Use ideas on topic card to help prepare (about two minutes).
	No right or wrong answers.

7/8 Whole class, then small groups

Talk through the activity with the class, making sure they understand what they have to do. Also look at the topic card so students are familiar with it, and ask them to decide who in their group is going to prepare which of the five points.

Then, working alone, students prepare notes about their point/s on the topic card. Set a time limit for this and then each group member shares their ideas with the rest of the group. Group members should ask each other questions. Use the example in the Coursebook to guide students.

Differentiated activities

Support

Just allocate one point on which to make notes. You may also want to provide students with a few words or phrases to get them started or put them in pairs so they can support each other.

Challenge

Try to allocate at least two points from the topic card and ask students to write at least three notes for each.

F Watch, listen and talk

1 Alone, then pairs

Explain that students are going to watch an IGCSE student talking about Education, responding to the same topic card prompts that they have already seen in E7. As they watch, they need to check to what extent the student follows the advice from E3.

2 Alone, then pairs

They now watch a second interview, using the same topic card prompts. Students need to decide if the second student performs better or worse than the first one, giving reasons.

G Listening

1 Small groups

This section gives students listening practice, specifically in matching six short extracts. Before they listen, students discuss questions **a–d** in their groups. As always, you may decide to set a short time limit for each question so that time is not wasted.

2 Small groups

Continuing in their groups, students look at the words and phrases in the box and predict which ones they think they will hear. Encourage them to supply reasons, but there are no right or wrong answers.

3 Alone, then small groups

Prepare students to listen for the first time. They should check if their predictions from G2 are correct.

Answers

air conditioning, assignments, cosmopolitan, digital age, learn Arabic, weather is awful

CD1, Track 25

Speaker 1

My home country, Nigeria, can be very hot at times, but nothing like the temperatures here in Dubai. I'm not sure I will ever get used to it! Thank goodness that everywhere has **air conditioning**, but even that doesn't help in the really hot summer months, when it is almost impossible to be outside during the heat of the day. At least the heat forces me to stay indoors to study, and that's the real reason why I'm here – to study and get my degree. I just wish I'd chosen somewhere a little cooler!

Speaker 2

Dubai is so **cosmopolitan** – it doesn't matter what you like or what you want to do, you can find it here somewhere. It's impossible not to be active doing something every minute of every day because there is just so much to entertain you. My biggest problem is making a choice! When I've done enough studying, it's time to think about which shopping mall to meet my friends at, or which café to go to for some much-needed relaxation. Now that's a challenge!

Speaker 3

My family told me that, in this **digital age**, I would never be apart from them when I came on my own to study in Dubai. Yes, we chat online every day, and send each other instant messages constantly, and I'm forever downloading photos of my sister's new twin babies, but it's not true – I am alone, and I miss them so much. I've made some friends, it's true, but at the weekends I don't go out much. I just think about my family and how much I miss them all.

Speaker 4

I thought studying here in Dubai would be much easier than back home in Sweden, but you know something? I've never studied so much in all my life! We have so much to read and so many **assignments** to complete every month, and there always seems to be yet another quiz or test to prepare for. I know it will all be worthwhile in the end, don't get me wrong, and I'm not afraid of hard work, but I'm still young and I want to enjoy this experience as much as possible. There never seems to be enough time for anything apart from studying. And do you know something? I haven't even been to the top of the Burj Khalifa yet, and I've been in Dubai for nearly two years!

Speaker 5

My reason for choosing Dubai as a place to study is mainly because of its location. I thought about a college in Europe, probably the UK, because obviously I speak English, but I decided against it. Not only is it difficult and expensive to travel outside Europe from there, but also the **weather is awful!** I'm from Brazil, remember?! So, now that I'm here in Dubai, it's easy to travel either east or west. I've already been to Egypt, but next trip I want to go east, maybe to the Maldives, or perhaps further. I'm not sure yet, but the sky is the limit!

Speaker 6

I tried at high school to start learning Arabic because I find the language and culture so incredibly interesting, but I failed miserably. It was so difficult to find a good teacher and to meet up with other people trying to **learn Arabic** so that we could practise together. I almost gave up. But then my dad suggested that I could combine learning Arabic with studying abroad, and that's how I ended up here in Dubai. At first I didn't want to leave home and, unfortunately, being in an international university means that nobody here uses much Arabic. But at least there are plenty of good teachers readily available, and there are plenty of opportunities to practise. An excellent choice, I think! Now I love living and studying in Dubai, and my Arabic has really improved.

4 Whole class, then alone

Go through the statements **Speakers 1–6** with the class, asking them to predict what they think the speakers will say. Then play the audio again and students check whether the statements are true or false.

Answers

1	false,	4	true,
2	true,	5	false,
3	false,	6	true

5 Alone

Finally, students listen again and do the exam-style questions.

Answers

a	6,	e	5,
b	1,	f	3,
c	not used,	g	4
d	2,		

6 Small groups

To round off the section and the unit, give students a few minutes to discuss questions **a–c**.

Answers for b

Nigeria, Sweden, UK, Brazil, Egypt, the Maldives

Reflection

Use the **Reflection** to remind students of what they have achieved in the unit. Students should set themselves a **personal goal** based on their scores for Unit 10.

Exam focus

Speaking, Part 2, topic cards

NOTE: The exam focus is on speaking, and involves students in looking at a new topic card, and then taking on the roles of examiner and student, using the prompts on the card.

1/2 Pairs

Students work together and look at the prompts, discussing how they might respond to each one. When they are ready, students take on the roles of examiner and interviewee, using the topic of Studying Abroad and the prompts on the card. Your job is to monitor and encourage where necessary, and provide any language students are struggling with. However, this should be an opportunity for students to build their confidence and fluency.

NOTE on Assessment Objectives (AOs) for Reading and Writing Exercise 2 (multiple matching): Remember that in a *multiple matching* activity students need to read a continuous text divided into sections, or a number of shorter texts, and answer a series of questions testing more detailed comprehension. Candidates match the correct answer to the question.

This type of activity requires more intensive reading, and students will need to understand things which are implied, but not directly stated (for example, gist, speaker's purpose, intentions and feelings) (R4). Students also need to identify and select relevant information (R1), understand ideas, opinions and attitudes (R2) and show understanding of the connections between them (R3).

Learning objectives (LOs)

Suggested activity: Start the unit by focusing for a few minutes on the LOs box, making sure that students understand what they are going to be doing. Using the first LO as an example, ask students to identify where in the unit they can find the activities for the other four LOs. Get students to say which of the activities appeal to them the most, and ask them for their reasons.

A Watch, listen and talk

1 Whole class, then alone

Explain that students are going to watch and listen to some IGCSE students talking about **achievements**. As your students watch and listen, they should make a note of **a** what the speakers think are humankind's three greatest achievements, and **b** what three other achievements the speakers think will be made in their lifetime. Play the video a second time so that students can check or add to their notes.

Answers

a Humankind's greatest achievements, any **three** from: medicine, antibiotics, aeroplanes, cars.

b Other achievements that the students think will be accomplished in their lifetime: better care for the environment, curing cancer, helping other people.

2 Pairs or small groups

Depending on the size of your class, put students into pairs or small groups. They can discuss their notes and then talk to each other about what they think are humankind's

best achievements and what achievements will be made in their lifetime. Do not interfere too much, but make sure you get feedback from the class so that they know their efforts have been worthwhile. If time permits, you could write their ideas on the board and rank them according to your students' preferences.

B Speaking and vocabulary

1 Whole class, then pairs

Many students will be familiar with *Guinness World Records*, so there are plenty of ways to lead in to this topic. With books closed, check their understanding of what *record* means, then, in pairs, get them to discuss any records they know about. If necessary, prompt them with some well-known examples (e.g. Usain Bolt's 100-metre world record speed).

2 Whole class

Tell students to open their books and focus on the three pictures in Activity B2. Ask them what records they think are being broken. Allow any answers at this stage – they will find out what the records are later in the unit.

3 Pairs, then whole class

Students work with their partner to discuss questions **a–d**. Set a time limit for each question to keep students focused and so that time is not wasted. Then do class feedback so that students can hear each other's ideas.

4 Whole class, then pairs

You will need to check carefully that students understand what they need to do in this activity, so go through the instructions and do a couple of examples. Tell students that the missing word in the first gap is always a superlative, so elicit some examples as a way of checking understanding. The word in the second gap is always a number, and students will need to look carefully at the context in each question to predict what the number might be. Then students work together to do the remaining questions. Do not provide any answers at this point.

5 Pairs

Students look at the words in the box and discuss which one completes each record, and see if any are the same as the words they thought of in B4. There are **three** extra superlatives which are **not** needed.

Answers

a	youngest,	e	highest,
b	largest,	f	greatest,
c	longest,	g	heaviest,
d	most,	h	fastest

6/7 Pairs

For this activity students need to do two things. Firstly, they need to decide which set of numbers goes with each record, and, secondly, choose one number from each set to complete the second gap in each record. If you have internet access, students can go to http://www.guinnessworldrecords.com/ to check their answers. If not, you can supply the information.

Answers

a   4   **7**   10   13

b   **14 410**   17 410   20 410   23 410

c   37   47   57   **67**

d   43   **83**   123   163

e   36.7 °C   46.7 °C   **56.7 °C**   66.7 °C

f   40 000   50 000   60 000   **70 000**

g   **62.71 kg**   67.71 kg   72.71 kg   77.71 kg

h   3.78 seconds   4.78 seconds   **5.78 seconds**   6.78 seconds

8 Whole class

Ask the whole class how many questions they got right, and which world record surprised them the most, and why. You could write a ranked list on the board, in order of surprise, popularity or another criterion.

9 Whole class

Continue the discussion with the whole class. If you prefer, split the class into small groups and monitor as they discuss the prompts.

> **LANGUAGE TIP**
> Students should be familiar with both the form and use of superlative adjectives. However, this **Language Tip** reinforces how and when to use them. Refer students to the exercise in the **Workbook**.

C Reading

1/2 Pairs, then whole class

Students discuss the questions in Activities C1 and C2. Make sure they look carefully at the five pictures, particularly 2

and 4, as they are not what they first appear to be! Get their ideas, but do not tell them yet if they are right or wrong.

3 Alone, then pairs

Put students into pairs and tell them to choose who is **A** and who is **B**. Give them time to check the meaning of the words in their list. If you prefer, you could put all the **A** students into one group to work together and all the **B** students into one group. This will save time and will offer support to students. When everyone is ready, pair them so that they can share their findings.

4 Alone, then whole class

Students skim the text and use the words from Activity C3 to fill in the gaps. In preparation for this, tell the students to first think about the type of word needed in each case – noun, adjective, verb, and so on.

Answers

a	(noun) debut,	f	(verb) slain,
b	(adjective) misleading,	g	(noun) sabre,
c	(verb) resemble,	h	(adjective) braided,
d	(noun) precursor,	i	(adjective) Precise,
e	(adjective) ignoble,	j	(noun) premise

Differentiated activities

Support

i   Students complete just five gaps (the ones from their list in the previous activity). Tell them which five gaps they do **not** need to complete.

ii   Another way to support students is to tell them the part of speech for each word in their list, as well as the type of word needed in their five gaps.

Challenge

After students have completed the gaps, ask them to rewrite some or all of the sentences/phrases that contain a gap, using their own words. They can use their ideas from Activity C3 if they need to.

> **LANGUAGE TIP**
> This **Language Tip** reminds students that in English, adjectives have only one form: they do not change from feminine to masculine nor from singular to plural. Go through the information with the class and check their understanding. Refer them to the exercise in the **Workbook**.

5 Pairs

Students work in pairs to fill in a copy of the table. They will need to look again at the text, this time in more detail, in order to find all the necessary information. (Note that the text does not include the Olympic debut location for all of the sports.) You could put the answers on the board or on a chart/poster for students to check.

> **TOP TIP**
> The **Top Tip** next to Activity C7 of the Coursebook reminds students that looking for key words in questions will help them to identify where (in a text) an answer is likely to be.

Answers

Sport	Olympic debut (where + when)	Final Olympic appearance	Equipment	Other information
Solo synchronised swimming	Los Angeles + 1984	1992	none	swimmer performs 'water ballet'
Live pigeon shooting	Paris + 1900	1900	gun	300 birds killed, 21 shot by winner
Race walking	1904	On-going	none	two distances for men, one for women
Rope climbing	1896	1932	rope	rope shortened from 15 metres to 8
Club swinging	1904	1932	clubs	only in two Olympics
Roller hockey	Barcelona + 1992	1992	roller skates	only in one Olympic Games
Swimming obstacle course	Paris + 1900	1900	boats, pole	held only once, using River Seine
Trampolining	2000	On-going	trampoline	men and women compete
La canne	1924	1924	cane	similar to fencing
Tug-of-war	1900	1920	rope	country could win multiple medals

6 Alone, then pairs

Students work alone to further check their understanding of the text by answering questions **a–j**. There is one question for each sport, and the answer for each question is simply the name of the sport. When students have finished, they can check with their partner.

Answers

a tug-of-war,

b trampolining,

c *La canne*,

d solo synchronised swimming,

e roller hockey,

f club swinging,

g race walking,

h rope climbing,

i live pigeon shooting,

j swimming obstacle course

7 Alone, then pairs

Students work alone to write **six** more questions based on the text they have read. The questions should be similar to the ones they have just answered in C6, i.e. starting with the words *Which sport …?*. Then, with a partner, students exchange their questions and answer them by saying which sport each question refers to.

D Reading and vocabulary

1 Whole class, then alone

With books closed, ask students if they have heard of Robert Scott (often referred to as Scott of the Antarctic) and if they know anything about him and what he did. You could show them a picture of Scott. Also, elicit the meaning of the words and phrases in D1: *one month, explorer, perished, return journey, South Pole*. Then students open their books and complete D1.

Answers

a South Pole,

b explorer,

c one month,

d perished,

e return journey

2 Alone, then pairs

Students are going to read part of a biography about Robert Scott, which describes his and his team's deaths. To help with some of the vocabulary, ask students to match the words with the definitions, and then to check with their partner.

Answers

stumbled = walked unsteadily and almost fell

blizzard = severe snow storm

dissuade = try to stop someone from doing something

amputation = the action of cutting off a person's arm or leg

rations = a fixed amount of food or water

depot = a place where food and other things are stored

legible = written clearly enough to be read

Not needed: full of liquid or gas; a situation where something cannot continue

3 Alone

Tell students to quickly look through the text in order to find the words from Activity D2 and to make sure that they understand them in context.

4 Alone, then pairs

For this activity, students need to look at the text in more detail in order to complete a copy of the table. When students have finished, let them compare their table with a partner's.

Answers

Date	Event
January 1912	Only five team members remained
17 January	Reached the Pole, but Amundsen got there first
16 or 17 March	Oates wanted to stay in his sleeping bag, but struggled on when others insisted
day after	Oates left tent and disappeared
20 March	Raging blizzard, Scott's right foot a problem, blizzard stopped them continuing
29 March	Scott made last diary entry
12 November	Search party found tent

Differentiated activities

Support

i   Give students the key dates that they need to make notes about: January 1912, 17 January, 16 or 17 March, day after, 20 March, 29 March, 12 November.

ii   Give students the 'event' information and get them to match it with the correct dates.

Challenge

i   Encourage students to find and make notes about more information for the second column.

ii   Tell students to read the text in detail, without making any notes, then to complete the table with their books closed.

5 Alone in exercise

Students should scan the text and note down brief answers to questions **a–j**.

Answers

a   Wilson was too weak

b   they lost track of the days

c   there was a blizzard

d   frostbite

e   the blizzard

f   he wouldn't kill himself

g   sent to his wife

h   buried in snow

i   eight

j   he was starving and frozen

TOP TIP

The **Top Tip** reminds students that they do not need to understand everything they read in a text and offers some suggestions for things to do (strategies) for working out what a word means.

6 Alone

This activity gives students an opportunity to use a specific strategy to help them understand a phrase which they may not know.

Answer c

7 Small groups

To finish off this section, put students into small groups to discuss the two questions, and then do class feedback so that everyone can hear all the ideas.

E Language focus: past perfect simple

1 Whole class

Go through the information about the past perfect simple tense and then check students' understanding by getting them to answer (i) and (ii).

Answers

a   *In the 1900 Games in Paris, swimmers **(ii) climbed a pole**, before which they **(i) had crawled over and swum under boats** …*

b   *On 17 January, they **(ii) reached the pole**, only **(ii) to find that** a Norwegian party, led by Roald Amundsen, **(i) had beaten them** there.*

2 Whole class

Ask students to look at the two example sentences again and tell you how the past perfect simple is formed.

Answer

had + past participle

3 Alone, then whole class

Give students a few minutes to look back at the two texts in the unit to find more examples of the past perfect simple tense.

Answers

Olympics text – *swimmers climbed a pole, before which they had crawled over and swum under boats …*

The rope was 8 metres long, but previously had been nearly double the length.

Robert Scott text – *a Norwegian flag was a record of the five who had been the first to reach the pole*

It appeared that both had died peacefully in their sleep. But Scott was lying half out of his bag with one arm stretched out – he had been the last to die

Remarkably, Scott had been able to find the strength, despite being half-starved and three-quarters frozen, to write 12 complete, legible letters.

4 Alone

Students practise using the past perfect in a narrative style by combining pieces of information in three different newspaper articles. They need to write three sentences for each article, making a total of nine. Use the example for paragraph 1, asking students which actions happened first and second. You could use a timeline on the board to further highlight the sequence of events.

Possible answers

There are several possibilities and acceptable variations

TEXT 1

1   Jim is a member of his university basketball team which had won the local league three weeks previously.

2   The opposing team had managed to break through Roston's defences but Jim stopped them from scoring a goal.

3   Before saving a penalty in the second half of the match, Jim had made four amazing saves in the first half.

TEXT 2

1   Before arriving back in Brazil last night, Gabriela Rodrigues had worked for three years in India.

2   Gabriela had qualified as a doctor before signing up as a volunteer.

3   Gabriela's experience had been very positive and made her a better person.

TEXT 3

1   Maha Fahmy opened the new superstore yesterday in a location close to where she had grown up.

2   Before Maha was recruited by a Dubai-based company, she had completed various degrees.

3   Before returning to Egypt in 2005, Maha had been sent to four different continents for work.

F Speaking, listening and writing

1 Whole class, then small groups

Go through all the questions (**a–h**) with the class, checking that they understand each one, and the type of answers that are required (a person's name: Jim, Gabriela or Maha). Then put students into small groups, and give them a time limit for each question so that they stay focused. Allow time for class feedback so that they can share their ideas and encourage them to give reasons for their answers.

Answers

a Gabriela, **b** Jim, **c** Maha, **d** Maha, **e** Gabriela, **f** Jim, **g** Gabriela, **h** Maha

2 Small groups

Students work in their groups to discuss questions **a–d**. If you wish, you could ask students to make written notes about their discussions, and then refer to these during class feedback. There are no right or wrong answers; the questions are designed to encourage students to give their own and ask for others' opinions about achievements and heroes/heroines and heroic acts.

3 Alone, then pairs

Students listen to two different opinions about Maha, then share their opinion with their partner about what Maha did. Make sure students give reasons for their opinions, if possible.

CD1, Track 26

Male teenager: I really do believe that Maha is a special type of hero. Just think about what she has done so far in her life, and how much she has sacrificed in order to provide for other people. All that time living abroad after she had studied for so many years in Alexandria. I think that is real sacrifice and dedication, which is why she is now so successful and admired by so many people. Look at all the awards and prizes she has won, and I'm sure that she will continue to win many more. For me, Maha is definitely a hero.

Female teenager: I absolutely don't agree with you! All Maha has done is to be a successful businesswoman, but you make it sound as if she is the only such person on the planet! Yes, she has done some amazing things, but I expect she has made a considerable amount of money too, and for me that doesn't make her a hero, far from it. I'm happy that she is providing things that people need, homes to live in and places to go for shopping

and entertainment, but I don't believe she's done something heroic.

4 Alone, then pairs

Ask students to read the audioscript in Appendix 3 of the Coursebook and notice the way the two speakers give their general opinion about the question at the beginning (*I really do believe that Maha is a special type of hero.* and *I absolutely don't agree with you!*) and then proceed to give specific reasons. Students now need to find the different reasons that each speaker gives to support their opinion, and to tell their partner.

Answers

Male: made sacrifices in order to provide for other people / living abroad / studied for so many years / awards and prizes / will continue to win many more

Female: only a successful businesswoman / not only such person on the planet / made a considerable amount of money too / hasn't done anything heroic

5/6 Alone

Students work on their own to plan and write a paragraph about someone whom they consider to be a hero/heroine. Make sure students think of reasons before they start writing, and to use the audioscript in Appendix 3 as a model for their own writing.

Reflection

Use the **Reflection** to remind students of what they have achieved in the unit. Students should set themselves a **personal goal** based on their scores for Unit 11.

Exam focus

Reading, Exercise 2, multiple matching

Answers

a	B,		f	D,
b	B,		g	B,
c	A,		h	A,
d	C,		i	D,
e	A,		j	C

NOTE on Assessment Objectives (AOs) for Reading and Writing Exercise 6: Students need to demonstrate that they can write a report, a review or an article in response to a short stimulus, which may take the form of pictures and/or short prompts. The question includes information on the purpose, format and audience, as well as the word count and how the marks are allocated.

Specifically, students need to show that they can communicate information/ideas/opinions clearly, accurately and effectively (W1), organise ideas into coherent paragraphs using a range of appropriate linking devices (W2), use a range of grammatical structures and vocabulary accurately and effectively (W3), show control of punctuation and spelling (W4) and use appropriate register and style/format for the given purpose and audience (W5).

Learning objectives (LOs)

Suggested activity: Start the unit by focusing for a few minutes on the LOs box, making sure that students understand what they are going to be doing. Using the first LO as an example, ask students to identify where in the unit they can find the activities for the other four LOs. Get students to say which of the activities appeal to them the most, and ask them for their reasons.

A Watch, listen and talk

1 Whole class, then alone

Explain that students are going to watch and listen to some IGCSE students talking about **organisations**. As your students watch and listen, they should make a note of **a** what the speakers think are the benefits of joining a youth organisation, and **b** what three activities the speakers say youth organisations arrange for their members. Play the video a second time so that students can check or add to their notes.

Answers

a The benefits of joining a youth organisation, any **three** from: find new friends in different years, talk to other students you haven't before, closer school environment, helping other people.

b Activities that youth organisations arrange for their members: sports days, proms, charity days, visiting zoos, parks, water parks, teaching.

2 Pairs or small groups

Depending on the size of your class, put students into pairs or small groups. They can discuss their notes and then talk to each other about their experiences as members of a youth organisation. If they haven't been a member, they can discuss reasons why they aren't a member of one. Do not interfere too much, but make sure you get feedback from the class so that they know their efforts have been worthwhile. If time permits, you could write their ideas on the board and rank them according to your students' preferences.

B Speaking and vocabulary

1 Pairs

Get students to focus on the five pictures and discuss the questions. If necessary, provide them with any key vocabulary.

2 Pairs

The five icons are from an activity holiday web page. Students need to decide what the icons represent, then match them to the pictures in Activity B1.

Answers

Icons from left to right represent pictures 1, 2, 4, 3, 5

3 Pairs

There is sometimes confusion or disagreement over how many continents there are. Some people consider that there are seven: North America, South America, Antarctica, Europe, Asia, Africa and Australia. Some people consider the North and South American continents to be just one landmass, referred to as the Americas. Europe and Asia are also sometimes combined and referred to as Eurasia. Other classifications include the Middle East as a separate continent, while others combine Australia, New Zealand, the island of New Guinea, and neighbouring islands in the Pacific Ocean, referred to as Australasia. In Activity B3, there are six icons for six continents, including Australasia. Students look at the six icons then answer the questions.

Answers for a

Icons from left to right represent North America, South America, Africa, Australasia, Europe, Antarctica.

C Reading

1 Whole class, then pairs

Go through the instructions for this activity carefully, checking that students fully understand what they need to do. Clarify that this travel company arranges summer adventure holidays in four different locations around the world: Galapagos and Ecuador, Leeward Islands, British Virgin Islands, Australia. For each location, students need to make notes about: location, size, population, climate, geography, flora and wildlife, etc. Students will need access to different reference sources to find the information.

> **WORD TIP**
> It will be useful for students to know the difference in meaning between these two words, and to be able to use them correctly. Refer students to the exercise in the **Workbook**.

2 Whole class

If you have a classroom map or a projector, students can show you exactly where the four locations are. Alternatively, get them to point to the relevant place on the map in the Coursebook.

3 Alone, then pairs

Students read the four pieces of information and decide which of the four locations each piece of information matches. Even if they are not sure about which piece of information matches each location, this is an opportunity to find out more and to see new vocabulary in context. Students can then see if a partner came up with the same answers.

Answers

a   Galapagos and Ecuador,
b   British Virgin Islands,
c   Australia,
d   Leeward Islands

4 Groups of four

Each person in the groups of four reads about **one** of the four locations discussed so far in this section. The four texts are on different pages in the Coursebook, positioned so that students can only refer to one text. Students need to skim their text but not look at the other texts, then

check which of the pieces of information from Activity C3 it includes.

5 Alone

Students read through questions **a–h** and decide which two refer to their text. Make sure they understand that there are **two** questions for each of the **four** texts, so there are **eight** questions in total. When they have decided which two questions refer to their text, they find and then write the answers.

6 Groups of four

Students tell each other which destination they have read about, then ask each other the remaining six questions in Activity C5 to find the answers.

Answers

a   Great Barrier Reef (Australia)
b   Sir Francis Drake Channel (British Virgin Islands)
c   Galapagos Archipelago (Galapagos and Ecuador)
d   Australia (Great Barrier Reef)
e   Leeward Islands
f   Galapagos and Ecuador
g   Leeward Islands
h   Leeward Islands

7 Groups of four, then whole class

Students work together and discuss questions **a–c**. Monitor but do not interfere, and make sure there is sufficient time for each group to report back to the whole class. Give positive feedback.

D Listening

1 Pairs

In pairs, students discuss what they know (if anything) about WAGGGS – the World Association of Girl Guides and Girl Scouts. If you think students may struggle with this, prepare some picture prompts to give them some ideas.

2/3 Pairs

Students work together to match the words with their definitions. There are two extra definitions that are not needed. All the words appear in the listening text. Allow students to use reference sources to help them do the matching.

Answers

fundraising = collecting money, inspired = motivated, involvement = activity/contribution, issues = subjects, judge = evaluate (not needed = solutions and concerned)

4 Pairs

Phrases **a–e** all appear in the listening text. Students work together and use the words from D2 to complete the gaps.

Answers

a   judge,   d   issues,

b   involvement,   e   fundraising

c   inspired,

5 Alone, then pairs

Students listen and find out three things: **a** where the conversation takes place; **b** the number of people talking; **c** the topic of conversation, and then compare their answers with their partner's. They should also check the answers to D4, if possible.

Answers

a   local studio,

b   two (Kigongo Odok and Namono Alupo),

c   WAGGGS but specifically World Thinking Day (WTD)

CD1, Track 27

Kigongo Odok: Hello, my name is Kigongo Odok. Welcome to another edition of Youth Uganda. Today I am very happy to welcome to our local studio Namono Alupo, who works for WAGGGS, the World Association of Girl Guides and Girl Scouts.

Namono Alupo: Thank you so much for inviting me, Kigongo!

KO: Namono, I've heard about something called World Thinking Day, which takes place every year in February, am I right?

NA: Yes, on February 22nd, to be exact.

KO: To be honest, I know absolutely nothing about it! What's it all about? What actually happens on World Thinking Day?

NA: Well, the whole idea is to get our members thinking about important international issues, and to connect with the worldwide network of Girl Guides and Girl Scouts. In recent years, we have had record numbers of our members celebrating WTD in 90 countries. We also produce an activity pack, and last year more than 53 000 were downloaded in four different languages: English, French, Spanish and Arabic.

KO: Wow, that's an incredible achievement, but who exactly are your members?

NA: All age groups, from young children to adult, including adolescents …

KO: And an adolescent is …?

NA: Good question! Neither children nor adults are adolescents: they are young people in the years when everything about themselves is changing very quickly.

KO: Definitely a difficult transition period. And how else can you judge the success of WTD, apart from what you have already told me?

NA: Hmmm, let me think … Well, we also sold 100 000 badges, but, to be honest, nowadays it's all about social media, and we know that 14 319 of our members uploaded profile pics during their WTD involvement.

KO: So on a typical WTD, what do your members actually do, apart from upload selfies?!

NA: We want people to be inspired by the history and impact of our global movement, and to take action and speak out on the issues we most care about.

KO: For example?

NA: We want to make a global difference by fundraising for projects around the world. The activity pack gives our members ideas on how to do this, and invites them to explore and celebrate the meaningful connections that make our lives better. Sometimes neither a parent nor a school teacher is available to help young people do these things, and this is when WAGGGS can get involved.

KO: And who exactly do you want your members to connect with?

NA: That's a good question, and an important one. Connections could be with the people closest to us, to a place we care about, or to a Girl Guide or Girl Scout friend on the other side of the world.

KO: And how do they do this?

NA: Well, the activity pack, which I've already mentioned, contains various activities which our members are encouraged to participate in. Each activity has a different objective, for example, connecting with a community and helping to bring about change, or learning about the WAGGGS Cabana World Centre in Mexico or the Sangam World Centre in India.

KO: So is there any sort of challenge involved?

NA: Yes. The activity pack encourages members to make four special connections, and in doing so they collect four puzzle pieces. Then they put together their puzzle, and share their connections with the world.

KO: And I guess the connections are the ones you described earlier? With the people closest to us, ummm, and to a place we care about, and …?

NA: … to a Girl Guide or Girl Scout friend on the other side of the world.

KO: Now it all makes sense! How can our listeners find out more information?

NA: They can find out more by visiting our website, which is www.wagggs.org, and follow the link for World Thinking Day. From there you can download the activity pack to your PC or tablet, and there's a special printer-friendly version to save paper and ink. You can also check where your local WAGGGS group meets and easily connect with them.

KO: Excellent! Thank you very much for talking to us today, and good luck with the next WTD.

6 Whole class, then alone

During the second listening, students need to complete the notes about WTD. Before they listen, go through the notes and ask students to say what type of word is needed in each gap, and what the possible answers might be. Do not worry if they are unable to supply too much.

Answers

WTD happens annually on **February 22nd**

Main aims: encourage members to consider **important international issues** and connect with **worldwide network** of GGGS

WTD celebrated in **90** countries

Number of activity packs downloaded = **more than 53 000**, available in four languages: English, **French, Spanish, Arabic**

Best indication of success is use of **social media**

WAGGGS wants members to take **action** and **speak** out on issues

Also wants members to connect with family, places, or GGGS **members** internationally

Activity pack contains different activities with different **objectives**

Challenge is to complete a **puzzle** and share connections

More information from website **www.wagggs.org**

Special **printer-friendly** version of activity pack available.

7 Alone

Students look at the audioscript in Appendix 3 to check their answers.

E Reading

1 Pairs

Students are now going to read a text about a different youth organisation. Before they read, students look at pictures 1–5 and match them with the five interest areas (**a–e**).

Answers

1 **c**, 2 **d**, 3 **b**, 4 **e**, 5 **a**

2 Pairs, then whole class

There are two words or phrases in the box for each of the five interest areas. Students work together and decide in which area they would expect to read the words and phrases, and give reasons. Do not supply any answers at this stage as students will find out when they read the text. However, do class feedback to check that there are no misunderstandings about the words and phrases.

3 Alone, then pairs

Give students a few minutes to quickly read the text and check their answers. Do not allow too much time or they will try to read the text in detail, which is not necessary at this stage.

4 Alone, then pairs

Now students need to look at the first paragraph in more detail, and make some written notes about three areas (**a–c**). When they have finished, they can check with their partner.

Answers

a to be independent, democratic and modern, to offer knowledge and new ideas to young people in Cyprus, to reinforce ideals of good citizenship, to raise awareness of the environment;

b more than 150 members in five groups, divided into four age groups, each group has a leader and two or three assistants;

c experienced in working with young people, university or college graduates, high ideals and want to give something back to society.

5 Groups of five

If you are unable to work with groups of five, you can adjust the activity to suit your particular class. Each student in the group selects one of the five interest areas and re-reads their paragraph. After reading, they should write at least one clarification question for the other group members to answer. Use the example clarification questions in the Coursebook to check students understand what they need to do. When everyone is ready, the five questions should be shared between the group members, and then everyone in the group reads the four paragraphs they did not read, and tries to answer the questions.

F Language focus: non-defining relative clauses

Non-defining relative clauses provide extra information about the subject, but they can be removed from the sentence without having an impact on the overall meaning. Furthermore, their removal will not affect the grammatical accuracy of the sentence. Non-defining relative clauses are composed of a relative pronoun, a verb, and optional other elements such as the subject or object of the verb. Commas are always used to separate a non-defining relative clause from the rest of the sentence.

1 Pairs

Write your own example sentence on the board and ask students to identify the non-defining relative clause, as well as other important elements, such as the subject of the main sentence, the relative pronoun, etc. Then students work in pairs and decide if the information (**a–f**) is true or false. Do not supply any answers yet – they find the answers in the next activity.

2 Alone, then pairs

Students read the seven examples (**a–g**) from the text and use them to check the answers to Activity F1.

Answers

a   true,

b   true,

c   true,

d   false (a relative pronoun is always needed),

e   true,

f   false (it can appear in the middle or at the end of a sentence)

3 Alone

You will probably need to do at least one example to check that students understand what they need to do. In the example here, the non-defining relative clause is underlined:

Example: a Victor de Leon, <u>who is a professional videogamer</u>, set the record for youngest player in New York, USA.

Possible answers (non-defining clauses underlined), but variations acceptable

b   Superlative adjectives, <u>which often end in -est</u>, show the most or least of something.

c   Both men and women compete in trampolining, <u>which debuted as an Olympic sport in 2000</u>.

d   On 17 January, <u>when they reached the pole</u>, they found that a Norwegian party led by Roald Amundsen had beaten them there.

e   Robert Scott successfully reached the South Pole, <u>where he found that Roald Amundsen had got there before him</u>.

f   The village of Roston, <u>which has its own football team</u>, was saved from embarrassment by the team's goalkeeper.

g   Footballers give up their lives and devote themselves entirely to perfecting their bodies, <u>which means they can excel on the football field</u>.

G Writing

1 Pairs

Get students to think about the words: *explain*, *describe*, *suggest*, then ask them to decide which information (**a–c**) matches each key word.

Answers

a   suggest,

b   explain,

c   describe

2 Pairs

Students discuss and decide if they could use phrases **a–l** to explain, describe or suggest.

Suggested answers

	Explain		Describe		Suggest
b	If we did this …	c	My school is located …	a	I think we should …
c	My school is located …	e	She was born in the early 1940s …	b	If we did this …
d	Our school would benefit by …	f	The building is more than 30 storeys tall …	d	Our school would benefit by …
g	The country is planning to …	i	The organisation was established …		
h	The Head Teacher has told us that …				
i	The organisation was established …				
j	The project is attempting to …				
k	There are several reasons for this situation …				
l	There is no reason not to …				

3 Pairs

Students need to think carefully about what the question is asking them to do and write five notes about this.

TOP TIP

The **Top Tip** focuses on the importance of reading questions carefully, to make sure that all parts of the question are addressed in the answer.

4/5 Pairs, then whole class

Students work together and read the sample answer to the exam-style question. It is not a perfect answer and there are things that need to be addressed. Students should identify anything they think is wrong. Remind them not to just focus on grammar and spelling, but to look at the content too and decide whether or not the writer has answered the question. Go through the five points in G5

with your students, checking that they can identify at least one example for each point.

TOP TIP

Many questions of this type give the student prompts in the form of comments about the topic, or even pictures.

6/7 Alone, then pairs

Students now write their own answer to the exam-style question, using the notes to help them, but including their own ideas if they can. When they have finished, they can exchange their writing and, using the checklist in Activity G5, give each other some feedback.

Here are two sample answers written by **i** an **IGCSE Core** student and **ii** an **IGCSE Extended** student.

i   Core

Dear readers,

I have just spent the day with a girl Kayla Kalanga involved in the WTD project. Kayla comes from Botswana and is 17 years old. She was tall and she has three brothers and two sisters. Both of Kayla's parents both work as farmers.

During the day I spent with her I learnt that she is a member of WAGGGS and how this organisation deals with important international issues. It was created five years ago and connects with a network of girl guides and boy scouts. Its main aim is to raise money for worldwide projects.

If any of you are interested in learning about ways in which you could connect with WTD you can visit www.wagggs.com and download the activity pack to find out more, or check if there is a local WAGGG group in your area!

Hope you enjoyed reading,

Erika Hadid. [146 words]

ii   Extended

Only three days ago, I came back from a trip to Botswana where I was staying with Kayla Kalanga, who is a member of WAGGGS, an association where they learn about important international issues.

Kayla is a tall seventeen-year old, who lives in a small village in Botswana. Her parents are both farmers and she has three brothers and two sisters. During my time with her, she told me that she started taking part in the WTD project five years ago and has been taking part in three WTDs. She told me that being a part of this has helped her connect with different girl scouts and girl guides.

Her ambition is to raise money for projects around the world and she means to do this by using an activity pack which gives her lots of ideas for fundraising. She has set a challenge to make four special global connections and also told me that our school can download the same activity pack and find out more from their website, www.wagggs.com. This way we can find out where our local WAGGGS group meets, and we can take part.
[189 words]

Differentiated activities

Support

i   Allocate two or three points from the notes in Activity G6 to different students.

ii   Allocate different parts of the exam-style question to different students. Each of these approaches reduces the amount that students need to write. They can then join their pieces of writing together to make one complete answer.

Challenge

Students write the answer without using the notes given in Activity G6, and then use the notes to check that they have included all the necessary information.

Reflection

Use the **Reflection** to remind students of what they have achieved in the unit. Students should set themselves a **personal goal** based on their scores for Unit 12.

Exam focus

Writing, Exercise 6

1   Here are two sample answers written by **i** an **IGCSE Core** student and **ii** an **IGCSE Extended** student.

i   Core

Dear Madam

I am a member of our town's local youth group which focuses on finding ways for children and teenagers to become more involved in the community.

At the moment we are attempting to raise funds for the pet charity 'Pets and Tails', which tries to find permanent homes for stray dogs and cats. As a group we care a lot about animals and so we are doing whatever we can to raise money for this worthy charity.

We have organised dog walks, car washes, a small fair in the town hall and we have even taken it into our own hands to adopt some of the stray animals. We think it is a very worthy cause, and we hope you do too.

Yours faithfully.

Jorge Van [128 words]

ii   Extended

Dear readers,

I am currently volunteering for a youth group 'Survival' which helps young teenagers get back into sports after suffering from any sort of long-term illness or debilitating injury. It was created three years ago after my friend had a horrific accident while riding his bicycle. Unfortunately, after the accident, my friend was left paralysed from the waist down but he was so passionate about sport and exercise that he was determined to continue and help others at the same time.

Last year, a young boy called Tom suffered an accident after practising ice-hockey at his local sports centre. His accident has not stopped him playing, but in order to continue playing as a professional player he needs to buy a brand new wheelchair. We need your help!

I and a group of friends of mine are planning on running the London marathon in two months to raise as much money as we can in order to help buy the wheelchair. We are looking for sponsors, people who wish to run with us and anyone who is willing to donate any amount of money they can afford in order to help young Tom.

Yours faithfully,

Rosie Green. [198 words]

2   Here are two sample answers written by **i** an **IGCSE Core** student and **ii** an **IGCSE Extended** student.

i   Core

In this week's edition we are discussing taking holidays right here at home instead of going abroad. I have always loved going abroad for my holidays but this year I have chosen to have a holiday right here in England.

The countryside here is so beautiful; we have so many untouched beaches and amazing landscapes. Instead of giving my money away to foreign industries, I would rather it was spent here on the local economy, helping create more jobs and supporting the people who live in the areas I will be visiting.

I realised that I do not know my own country at all. I know Italy better than I do England and I feel that is a shame. So this summer holiday I am staying here and I shall hope for much sunshine! [134 words]

ii   Extended

Very recently, one of our own tourist organisations has been promoting the idea of remaining in our own country for our holidays. Although I believe it is a nice idea, I do not think it is very realistic, for various reasons.

Most people enjoy spending their holidays in new and exciting places, where you can see different cultures and try exotic cuisines in different locations. Furthermore, spending more time abroad means that you are broadening your horizons and becoming more open-minded about places and people that you are not used to. I also believe that when you travel, you learn to appreciate life and the beautiful world we live in, far more than if we stayed at home.

I don't deny that our own country has some beautiful places to visit and stay in. Moreover, by staying here for our holidays, we are helping people find jobs and helping the local economy through the money we spent. So, although it's great visiting other countries, we mustn't forget that our own has plenty to offer as well, and we should take advantage of this as much as possible. [188 words]

NOTE on Assessment Objectives (AOs) for Reading and Writing Exercise 5: Students write approximately 100–150 (Core) or 150–200 (Extended) words of continuous prose, in response to a short stimulus which may take the form of pictures and/or short prompts printed on the paper. The question includes information on the purpose, format and audience, as well as the word count and how the marks are allocated.

Specifically, students need to show that they can communicate information/ideas/opinions clearly, accurately and effectively (W1), organise ideas into coherent paragraphs using a range of appropriate linking devices (W2), use a range of grammatical structures and vocabulary accurately and effectively (W3), show control of punctuation and spelling (W4), and use appropriate register and style/format for the given purpose and audience (W5).

Learning objectives (LOs)

Suggested activity: Start the unit by focusing for a few minutes on the LOs box, making sure that students understand what they are going to be doing. Using the first LO as an example, ask students to identify where in the unit they can find the activities for the other four LOs. Get students to say which of the activities appeal to them the most, and ask them for their reasons.

A Watch, listen and talk

1 Whole class, then alone

Explain that students are going to watch and listen to some IGCSE students talking about **famous people**. As your students watch and listen, they should make a note of **a** what the speakers think people need in order to become successful or famous, and **b** how important the speakers think ambition is. Play the video a second time so that students can check or add to their notes.

Answers

a Things that the students think people need to become successful or famous, any **three** from: a good reputation, passion, talent, hard work.

b How important is ambition? Do they all agree? The students say that you can just do something shocking or weird to become famous, **or** you need to work hard. The students do not all agree.

2 Pairs or small groups

Depending on the size of your class, put students into pairs or small groups. They can discuss their notes and then talk to each other about what people need to do to become famous and which famous person they admire. Do not interfere too much, but make sure you get feedback from the class so that they know their efforts have been worthwhile. If time permits, you could write their ideas on the board and rank them according to your students' preferences.

B Speaking and vocabulary

1 Pairs

Get students to focus on the four pictures and discuss the questions. If students are unsure about who the people are, move straight on to B2, which gives the names and some facts about each person.

2 Pairs

If students are still unsure, the pictures provide some clues to which pieces of information match each person. Of course, it does not matter if students are not able to match correctly – the important thing is that they think about the task, and discuss things in English.

Answers

Sarah Attar, competed in 2012 Olympics, Saudi Arabian

Zaha Hadid, Iraqi-British architect, studied at American University Beirut

Mark Zuckerberg, co-founder of Facebook, born 1984

Bruce Lee, film actor, died 1973

3 Whole class, pairs

Firstly, check that students understand the meaning of each word in the box. For anything they are unsure of, either provide the meaning or give students time to find out for themselves. Then students discuss which words are connected with being successful and famous. There are no right or wrong answers, but you could probably argue that all of the words have some connection.

4 Pairs

Students should be better able now to think about the qualities of the four famous people. Once again, there are no right or wrong answers, but you might say that Sarah Attar needed skill, determination and strength to be successful as an athlete, whereas Mark Zuckerberg needed other qualities, such as confidence and fearlessness. Allow students time to discuss freely.

5 Alone, then pairs

Students think of a famous person and how to describe them, using the words from B3 as well as any others that are appropriate. Then they tell their partner about the famous person.

C Reading and writing: Making notes

1 Whole class, then pairs

Make sure students know who Eusébio was. Perhaps show them a video clip from YouTube or focus on the picture in the Coursebook (but do not let them read the text yet). Then get them to work in pairs to check the meaning of the words and phrases in the box.

2 Alone, then pairs

Students read phrases **a**–**i** on their own and decide if they think they will see them in the text. Then, with their partner, they give reasons for their decisions. Do not supply any answers at this stage as students will find out for themselves when they read the text in C3.

3 Alone

Students skim the text and check their answers to Activities C1 and C2. They do not need to write anything yet.

Answers to C2

a, **b**, **d**, **e**, **f**, **h**, **i**

4 Whole class, then alone, then pairs

Go through questions **a**–**g**, making sure students understand everything, including the vocabulary. Get students to tell you the key word/s in each question and remind them that this will help them to find the answers in the Eusébio text. They should also think about the type of answers required (e.g. 4c = a reason). When they are ready, students write the answers in their notebooks, then check with a partner.

Answers

a   Portuguese

b   Mozambique and Angola were both Portuguese territories

c   because of his physical and mental strengths

d   1966 World Cup

e   European Golden Boot

f   speed, technique, athleticism, accurate right-footed shot

g   his fair play and humility

5 Alone, then pairs

Writing effective notes or a good summary requires a clear understanding of the content of the text. In this activity, students need to decide (on their own) which three of the five headings given would help them to write their notes. They should be prepared to give reasons to a partner. The three best headings are *Nationality and family*, *Physical skills* and *Achievements in football*, because most of the content of the text is about these three areas of Eusébio's life. There is very little information about his home and education, nor about his hobbies and interests.

> **TOP TIP**
>
> Students' vocabulary and grammar is not usually assessed in note-writing exercises, but the **content** of the notes is. Only brief notes are required, but students must provide all the necessary information.

> **TOP TIP**
>
> Make sure students appreciate that a text may often contain more information than is required to answer the question. They should know that if there are three bullets for a particular heading, then there are three marks available – and only three pieces of information are needed (even if there are four or five pieces of information in the text).

6 Alone, then pairs

Students work alone first, to write three notes under each of the three headings: *Nationality and family*, *Physical skills* and *Achievements in football*. Before doing so, they should read the text in more detail, underlining the important information for each heading. Then they need to rewrite that information in note form. It is best if students paraphrase rather than copy the text, but as long as they identify the relevant information and write it under the correct heading, they would receive the marks available. When they have finished, allow students to check with a partner.

Answers

Nationality and family

- born in Mozambique,

- Angolan father,

- Portuguese nationality

Physical skills

- speed (100 metres in 11 seconds),
- athleticism,
- accurate right-foot shot,
- great free-kick taker,
- prolific goal scorer (733 goals in 745 matches)

Achievements in football

- top goal scorer 1966 World Cup,
- Bronze Ball award,
- winner of Ballon d'Or,
- played for Benfica for 15 years,
- 638 goals in 614 matches for club

Differentiated activities

Support

i   Reduce the number of headings under which students should make notes.

ii   Provide the answers jumbled up, so that students have to decide which note goes with which heading.

iii Direct students to the relevant paragraphs in the text.

Challenge

i   Ask students to find more information about each area, rather than the three pieces of information required.

ii   Students use their notes to write a short paragraph under each heading.

D Reading and vocabulary

1/2 Pairs

With a partner, students look at the words and phrases (**a–h**) in Activity D1 and predict what type of person they are going to read about. There are no right or wrong answers, so encourage students to speak freely and to give reasons for their choices. As soon as they are ready, they can look at the possible job types in Activity D2 and select which ones they think they will **not** read about. Try not to let students look at the text while they are doing these two activities.

3 Alone, then pairs

Tell students to skim the text to check their predictions and ideas from Activities D1 and D2. They should not worry about the gaps at the moment.

Answers

The text is about Helen Keller, an American author and campaigner for deaf and blind charities who became

deaf and blind as a young child and had to struggle to overcome her dual disability.

4 Whole class, then pairs

Check that there are no comprehension problems with phrases **a–i**, seven of which have been removed from the text (so there are **two** extra phrases that students will not need to use). Then let students work with a partner to look at the text again and decide where to put the missing phrases. If students need support, tell them which two phrases are not needed (a and h).

Answers

1 d	Helen Keller (1880–1968),
2 b	Born on 27 June 1880,
3 e	In 1886,
4 f	In the beginning,
5 i	Keller then,
6 g	Keller came,
7 c	From 1918

5 Pairs

For this activity, which is divided into four vocabulary-based questions (**a–d**), students work with a partner. They should be allowed to use different reference sources to help them find the answers.

Answers

a   i   campaigner [paragraph 1] = *someone who organises events in order to achieve something, for example, to collect funds or to raise awareness*

    ii   influential [1] = *having the power to affect how someone thinks, or how something develops*

    iii   de-stigmatise [1] = *to reduce the negative or unfair treatment of people or something*

    iv   rudimentary [2] = *very basic*

b   i   someone with a lot of knowledge and skills in a particular subject [3] = *specialist*

    ii   at the present time [3] = *currently*

    iii   unable to do [3] = *impaired*

    iv   started doing something [3] = *set about*

    v   continued [3] = *maintained*

    vi   annoyed at not being able to do something [4] = *frustrated*

    vii   learnt [4] = *picked up on*

c

Adjective	Noun	Adverb	Verb
rapid	rapids*	rapidly	X
quick	quickness	quickly	quicken
proficient	proficiency	proficiently	X
disabled	disability/ the disabled	X	disable
previous	X	previously	X
persuasive	persuasion	persuasively	persuade
difficult	difficulty	X	X
funded	funding	X	fund

rapids = part of a river where the water moves very fast

> **LANGUAGE TIP**
>
> The **Language Tip** focuses on adverbs ending in -*ly*, which are very common in English. However, students also need to know that some words ending in -*ly* are not adverbs. Refer students to the exercise in the **Workbook**.

d **i** [paragraph 2] completely, only, properly, badly, [3] currently, visually, [4] fully, [5] quickly, previously, [6] extremely, [7] badly, sadly

ii

Adverb	Adjective	Noun
completely	complete, completed	completion
only	only	X
properly	proper	X
badly	bad	X
currently	current	current
visually	visual	vision, visionary
fully	full	X
quickly	quick	X
previously	previous	X
extremely	extreme	extremity
badly	bad	X
sadly	sad	sadness

Differentiated activities

Support

i Allocate just one or two questions (from a, b, c or d) for students to work on.

ii Reduce the number of words students need to find.

Challenge

i Extend how much students have to do by getting them to produce their own sentences using some of the words from Activity D5.

ii Get students to complete as much as they can in 5c without looking back at the text.

6 Small groups

Students work in small groups and discuss questions (**a–c**). If a group has no answer for **a**, perhaps someone in another group can share their experience. Failing that, you could briefly tell students about someone that **you** might know. For **b**, do an example with a concrete noun *in a language that the students do not know*. It does not matter if you yourself are unfamiliar with the language – you just need to know what the word means and how to spell it. Choose something which you can easily find or bring into the classroom. Then follow the same procedure as Sullivan. Tell the volunteer student to close their eyes, or use a blindfold, and then rub the object you have chosen (e.g. a piece of paper, an orange, a pencil, a mobile phone) on the student's hand and at the same time write the word in the unknown language on the student's other hand. For **c**, if you have internet access at school, allow students 5–10 minutes to find the images. Alternatively, this could be set as a homework task.

> **WORD TIP**
>
> These two words are not often confused, but students are probably not as familiar with the word *obstacle*. It is a useful addition to their vocabulary. Refer students to the exercise in the **Workbook**.

E Language focus: discourse markers showing contrast

1 Pairs

There are many discourse markers in English, with different functions. They are extremely important in order to provide clues about what we want to say or write. This section focuses on discourse markers for showing contrast. Students work in pairs and study the nine phrases, and agree on which three show contrast.

Answers

Even though, In spite of, On the other hand

2 Alone, then pairs

Students think of more contrast discourse markers and then compare their ideas with their partner's.

Possible answers

however, in fact, in contrast, nevertheless, despite, on the contrary, though, although, yet, nonetheless

3 Alone, then pairs

Students now re-read the text and identify seven examples of discourse markers showing contrast, and check if any appeared in E1 or E2.

Answers

despite, however, nevertheless, in spite of, nonetheless, even though, although

4/5 Alone, then pairs

Students work alone and then check their answers with their partner's. Make sure students understand the structures used after the various discourse markers by completing the rules in E5.

Answers

Despite	her problems, having problems,	she became famous.
(a) *In spite of*		
(b) *Even though*	she had problems,	
(c) *Although (Though)*		
She had problems.	(d) *However,*	
	(e) *Nevertheless,*	
	(f) *Nonetheless,*	

a   *Despite/In spite of* + noun/noun phrase + verb phrase

b   *Although/Even though* + verb phrase + verb phrase

c   *However/Nonetheless/Nevertheless* + verb phrase

6 Alone, then whole class

In this activity students practise using discourse markers with phrases taken from the Keller text. Let them work alone and then do class feedback and allow everyone (if possible) to contribute some answers.

Possible answers

a   She had to struggle to overcome many obstacles. However / In spite of this, she obtained a university degree.

b   Although she could only communicate using signs, her young friend helped her to be more successful. / She could only communicate using signs. Nevertheless, her young friend helped her to be more successful.

c   Even though Sullivan was also visually impaired, she taught Keller how to communicate. / In spite of also being visually impaired, Sullivan taught Keller how to communicate.

Suggested answers (many are possible)

d   Keller was frustrated at her lack of progress. However, Sullivan helped her to start understanding.

e   Keller then progressed very quickly, even though she had to overcome a great many obstacles.

F Listening

1/2 Whole class, then pairs

Focus on the map and the picture. Explain who students are going to hear about (Nelson Suresh Kumar) and what he did (rode his motorbike on the world's highest motorable road). Ask students to predict what this involved and then in pairs they can work through questions **a–g** and Activity F2. Make sure you provide class feedback on all the questions, but remember that students have not yet listened to anything, so accept all their ideas and speculations.

Answers

There are no right or wrong answers to **a**, **b**, **c**, **e**, **f** and **g**.

d From left to right: glacier, gorge, gravel, mud, plain, sand dune, slush

3 Alone

Students listen and check their ideas from the previous activities F1e, F1f and F1g.

Answers

1f (Bactrian) camels, **1g** the world's highest battlefield

4 Whole class, then alone

During the second listening, students need to write answers to questions **a–h**. Go through the questions with the class, asking them to remember/predict answers, but do not say if anything is right or wrong at this stage. Then students listen, and after they can check with a partner, refer to the audioscript in Appendix 3, or you can supply feedback.

Answers

a   India

b   91 days

c   during the solo ride

d   a battle took place

e   three from: glaciers, valleys, mountain passes, snow, plains, mud, slush, snow, desert, lakes

f   three from: world's highest battlefield, villages, monasteries, water crossings, highways, narrow roads

g   covered in snow for other 8 months

h   double-humped

G Writing – Optional

1 Alone

This activity helps students to understand how a descriptive text is organised. Give them a couple of minutes to quickly review the two texts about Eusébio and Keller, and decide which one follows the plan.

Answer

Eusébio

2 Pairs

Students work together and analyse how the Keller text is organised.

Possible answer

- general and personal information
- early childhood and illness
- medical treatment
- learning to communicate
- education
- charity work and death

3 Alone

Students are now going to spend time planning for a piece of descriptive writing about a person they admire, or someone famous. The important thing is that they choose someone whom they know about, and whom they can write about. Then, using the ideas in the Coursebook, students make a list of things they could include in their writing.

> **TOP TIP**
> Use this **Top Tip** to remind students about style and level of formality for different audiences, as well as purposes for writing. You could review some of the sample exam-style questions in previous units and ask students to identify who the readers are and what the purpose of the writing is.

4 Pairs

To continue with the planning, get students to specify the information which should normally appear in an introduction and conclusion for this type of writing.

Suggested answers

Introduction – reason for choosing this person, birthplace, date, etc.; Conclusion – reiterate reasons for choosing this person, lifelong achievements/awards

5 Alone

Focus on the example notes and then get students to write their own notes, using their own headings. Remind students that they are going to expand their notes into a blog entry in the next activity, so they should make sure they have enough notes to work from.

Sample answer

Famous actress: Audrey Hepburn

Introduction: Audrey Hepburn, born Brussels, Belgium in 1929. Her father was of English descent and her mother was Dutch.

Background information: After the Second World War she moved to England to study ballet and took on small roles in theatres and films.

Work and achievements: Hepburn starred in many famous films, winning many awards including an Academy Award and a BAFTA. In later life, she became a Goodwill Ambassador for UNICEF and did lots of charity work.

Reasons for choosing this person: Not only was she a talented and beautiful actress, she cared about making the world a better place.

Conclusion: Has gone down in history as one of the most beloved and iconic Hollywood stars.

6 Alone

Students now write their blog, using their notes from Activity G5, but also trying to include relevant and appropriate discourse markers and vocabulary from the unit.

Sample answer

The Hollywood actress Audrey Hepburn was born in Brussels in 1929, to a father of English descent and a Dutch mother.

After the end of the Second World War in 1945, she moved to England where she studied ballet and also began to take on small roles in theatre plays and films. She soon began to star in musicals and romantic comedies in Hollywood. For her achievements in film, she won many awards, including a BAFTA and an Academy Award. As well as acting, she was also a Goodwill Ambassador for UNICEF and did plenty of charity work.

I chose Audrey Hepburn as my role model, because not only was she a talented and beautiful actress, she cared

more than anything about making the world a better place. She has gone down in history as one of the most iconic Hollywood stars.

Reflection

Use the **Reflection** to remind students of what they have achieved in the unit. Students should set themselves a **personal goal** based on their scores for Unit 13.

Exam focus

Reading and writing, Exercise 3, note-making

Answers

Where Garrett was educated

- age 5 went to Holland every weekend to study
- age 7 went to Lübeck Conservatoire   [1]
- home-schooled until 17   [1]

ALSO: after 17, studied at Royal College of Music, London; 1999 attended Juilliard School in New York.

Garrett's skills as a musician

- breathes life into classical music   [1]
- plays with confidence   [1]
- [Extended only] music takes on different shape and feel in his hands   [1]

Challenges in Garrett's life

- 340 days a year in hotels   [1]
- has to eat hotel room-service food   [1]
- lives out of a suitcase   [1]
- [Extended only] four hours' daily violin practice [1]

ALSO: no relaxation until after daily practice

[Total: 7 Core, 9 Extended]

Writing, Exercise 5

Here are two sample answers written by **i** an **IGCSE Core** student and **ii** an **IGCSE Extended** student.

i Core

Hi Celia

How are you? Last night I was lucky to go to a performance by the famous jazz band, *Jazz It Up!* Every year my home

town has a jazz festival and this year it was in the courtyard of the old castle right next to the river.

It was a beautiful, starry night and the jazz band was in the centre and the audience sat on chairs in a semi-circle around them. The performance lasted for an hour with a fifteen-minute break in the middle and it was the best thing I have seen in a long time!

It was a beautiful experience, the musicians were excellent and when you come into town next week then I really do advise you to buy a ticket and go watch the jazz band.

Bye!

Aviya [136 words]

ii Extended

Dear Grandma

I hope you're well. Last week my favourite singer Norah Jones came for a charity concert, in Hyde Park, London. She along with some other singers and musicians were all appearing at the performance in order to raise money for charity.

My friends and I arrived at Hyde Park two hours before the start of the concert! Already, there were lots of people standing in line. We arrived at the large stage and sat on the grass until the music started. The whole park was soon completely full. There was a great atmosphere; people were laughing and singing and calling out to the performers. The concert started and even though I was really enjoying myself, I was desperate for Norah Jones to come onto the stage.

Finally, Norah stepped on the stage, but just as she did it started to rain. Everyone was worried that the performance would be cancelled, but she started singing despite the pouring rain. Throughout most of the show I was cold and wet, but it was one of the best experiences in my life. I was awestruck by Norah Jones's singing and I can't wait to see her live again.

Love Katia [199 words]

NOTE on Assessment Objectives (AOs) for Listening Exercise 5 (Extended ONLY): Students listen to a talk and complete short notes either under bullet points or in a template. Then they listen to a short discussion based on this talk, and complete sentences using no more than three words. Students need to demonstrate that they can listen to a talk and complete gaps in notes based on what they hear.

Specifically, students need to identify and select relevant information (L1), understand ideas, opinions and attitudes (L2), show understanding of the connections between ideas, opinions and attitudes (L3) and understand what is implied but not directly stated, e.g. gist, speaker's purpose, intention and feelings (L4).

Learning objectives (LOs)

Suggested activity: Start the unit by focusing for a few minutes on the LOs box, making sure that students understand what they are going to be doing. Using the first LO as an example, ask students to identify where in the unit they can find the activities for the other four LOs. Get students to say which of the activities appeal to them the most, and ask them for their reasons.

A Watch, listen and talk

1 Whole class, then alone

Explain that students are going to watch and listen to some IGCSE students talking about **medical care**. As your students watch and listen, they should make a note of **a** what the speakers think the work of a nurse involves, and **b** if the speakers would consider nursing as a job for themselves. Play the video a second time so that students can check or add to their notes.

Answers

a The work of a nurse involves: caring for patients, healing patients, emotionally supporting the patient.

b Would the students consider doing a nursing job? Their **reasons**: Yes, but the student would prefer to be a doctor **or** no, because the students are not confident in their scientific ability.

2 Pairs or small groups

Depending on the size of your class, put students into pairs or small groups. They can discuss their notes and then talk to each other about other medical care jobs they know about. Do not interfere too much, but make sure you get feedback from the class so that they know their efforts have been worthwhile. If time permits, you could write their ideas on the board and rank them according to your students' preferences.

B Speaking and vocabulary

1 Pairs

Students look at the three pictures and, after checking that they understand what each picture shows, they make a list of as many words and phrases as possible connected with the topic (e.g. *healthcare*). There are two examples to get them started. You could set a short time limit for this activity and turn it into a competition to see which pair can write the longest (correct) list. Carry out class feedback to compare ideas.

2/3 Pairs

Students work together to check the meaning of the verbs in A. Allow them to use different reference sources for this before they match the verbs with the nouns in B.

Answers

alleviate suffering, diagnose and treat illnesses, perform surgery, prescribe and dispense medications, prevent illnesses/suffering, promote health, provide care/medications, restore health

4 Alone

Students read the short paragraph and find the phrases from Activity B2/3, checking that they have understood them correctly.

5 Whole class

Focus on the word *paramedic* and check that students understand its meaning. Make sure they know how a paramedic's work differs from that of a nurse.

6 Pairs

These nine words should not be too challenging for students, but ensure that they understand the meanings. They can use different reference sources for help.

7/8 Alone, then pairs

Prepare students for the listening activity. Before they listen, get them to predict which of the words from Activity B6 could complete the gaps (**a–g**) in the notes. Then play the audio so students can confirm their predictions. They can read the audioscript in Appendix 3 if necessary.

Answers

a	emergency,	**e**	injuries,
b	patient,	**f**	accidents,
c	treatment,	**g**	incidents
d	care,		

CD2, Track 2

Paramedics provide an immediate response to emergency medical calls. They are usually the first senior healthcare professional on the scene, and they are responsible for assessing the condition of a patient and providing treatment and care prior to hospital admission. A paramedic will attend emergencies, including minor injuries, sudden illness and casualties arising from road and rail accidents, criminal violence, fires and other incidents. They are usually in a two-person ambulance crew, with the other crew member being an ambulance technician or emergency care assistant who helps them. Some will work alone, however, using an emergency response car, motorbike or bicycle to get to a patient.

Adapted from www.prospects.ac.uk

9 Pairs

Put students into pairs to talk to each other about the differences between what a nurse and a paramedic do. Encourage them to use the words and phrases from previous activities.

C Listening

1 Whole class, then pairs

Check that students know who Florence Nightingale was. If they are unfamiliar with her work, use some pictures (including the one in this section) as prompts.

2 Pairs

In pairs, students look at the information in **a–f** and decide if it is true or false, giving reasons where possible. You do not

need to tell them if they are right or wrong at this stage, as they will find out the answers during the listening activity.

3 Pairs

Make sure students understand who they are going to hear (John is a nursing student and Dr Mary Winterson is a nursing specialist), and what the context is (i.e. an interview with questions about Florence Nightingale). Students listen for the first time and check their answers to C2, correcting any false information.

Answers

a Florence Nightingale was born in Florence, Italy. TRUE

b Her parents refused to allow her to become a nurse. TRUE

c She completed a three-month nurse training course in England. FALSE – the course was in Germany

d The British government asked her to work in British military hospitals in Turkey. TRUE

e Florence Nightingale received several medals for her nursing work. FALSE – she received one medal

f When she died, Florence had been blind for 15 years. TRUE

CD2, Track 3

John: Dr Mary, what can you tell us about Florence Nightingale's early years?

Dr Mary Winterson: Well, Florence Nightingale was born in Italy on 12th May 1820 and was named Florence after her birthplace. Her parents, Fanny and William, were wealthy and spent a considerable amount of time touring Europe.

J: How did she do at school? Did she get good grades?

MW: Yes, she did. As a schoolchild, Florence was academic and rarely had problems with her studies. She was attractive and the expectation was that she would marry and start a family.

J: But that didn't happen, did it?

MW: No, it didn't. Florence had different ideas. As a teenager she became involved in the social questions of the day, making visits to homes for sick people in local villages, and she began to investigate hospitals and nursing.

J: How did her parents react to this?

MW: Not very well, I'm afraid! Her parents refused to allow her to become a nurse as, in the mid-19th century, it was not considered a suitable profession for a well-educated woman. Because of the conflict which arose between Florence and her parents,

J: Not such a bad punishment! Where exactly did they go?

MW: The three of them travelled to Italy, Greece and Egypt, returning to England through Germany in July 1850. While in Germany, they visited a hospital near Dusseldorf, where Florence returned in the following year to undergo a three-month nurse training course. This enabled her to take a post at a clinic in London in 1853.

J: Wasn't Britain at war around this time? With Russia?

MW: Yes, you're absolutely right. In March 1854, Britain was at war with Russia. While the Russians were defeated in the autumn of that year, British newspapers criticised the medical facilities for the soldiers wounded during the fighting. In response to the criticism, the government appointed Florence Nightingale to oversee the introduction of female nurses into British military hospitals in Turkey and, on 4th November 1854, she arrived in Scutari with a group of 38 nurses.

J: What an amazing story! What happened when they got to Scutari?

MW: Well, initially, the doctors did not want the nurses there because they felt threatened but, within ten days, many more casualties arrived and all the nurses were needed to cope with this sudden influx of wounded soldiers.

J: So the doctors were forced to accept the female nurses? Were the nurses successful?

MW: Yes! The introduction of female nurses in military hospitals was an outstanding success, and the nation showed its gratitude to Florence Nightingale by honouring her with a medal in 1907. Throughout her life, she continued tirelessly to campaign for better conditions in hospitals and for improved health standards.

J: When did she die?

MW: She died on 13th August 1910, having been a complete invalid herself and totally blind for 15 years. She was a national heroine. Her far-sighted reforms have influenced the nature of modern health care, and her writings continue to be a resource for nurses, health managers and planners.

J: Yes, she was certainly an inspiring woman.

TOP TIP
Before working on Activity C4, go through the **Top Tip** with the class, as it contains useful information about multiple-choice questions.

4 Pairs, then alone
Prepare students for the second listening activity. Before they listen, students should read questions **a–h** and the possible answers (A, B, C) and consider which of the three options might be correct. Encourage them to give reasons if they can.

Answers

a	B,	d	B,	g	C,
b	A,	e	A,	h	C
c	C,	f	A,		

5/6 Whole class, then pairs
Go through the notes about Florence Nightingale, checking with students that they understand what type of information is required to fill each gap. Then in pairs they complete the notes, using a single word or a short phrase in each gap. Play the audio again for students to check their answers, or let them read the audioscript in Appendix 3.

99

Answers

a	academic, no problems,	f	Germany,
		g	1853,
b	hospitals and nursing,	h	38 nurses,
c	considered suitable for educated woman,	i	number of wounded soldiers,
d	Greece,	j	medal,
e	Egypt,	k	blind

WORD TIP
These two words are easily confused. Point out that *wound* is also a verb, whereas *injury* changes to *injure*. Refer students to the exercise in the **Workbook**.

D Language focus: future in the past

1 Whole class

In English, this is the use of *would* or *was/were going to* to refer to the future from the perspective of some point in the past. Use the example in the Coursebook for students to tell you which part of the phrase is about past events (*the expectation was*), and which part moves forward in time (*she would marry and start a family*). Use a time line on the board to help students to visualise this, if necessary.

2 Alone, then pairs

Students use the words in the box to complete the gaps in the information about *future in the past*.

Answers

a will,

b past,

c future,

d correct,

e past continuous

3 Whole class, then alone

Do this activity orally with the class, and then students write their answers. Point out that in order to use the past continuous tense, they will need to use an additional verb, for example: *plan, intend, expect*.

Answers

When doctors heard that Florence Nightingale was going to / would / was planning/intending/expecting to work with them, they felt threatened.

4 Whole class, then alone

This activity provides further written practice, but go through the questions (**a–h**) orally first, allowing different students to provide different possible answers.

Possible answers

a My parents were planning to move to Australia but they decided to stay in Bahrain;

b My sister was thinking of becoming a doctor but she changed her mind;

c I thought we would / were going to eat out tonight / I thought we were eating out tonight;

d He believed he would / was going to pass all his exams;

e I knew you wouldn't / weren't going to help him with his homework;

f Ali said Hamed would / was going to come / was coming with him but he came alone;

g She promised she would text her parents as soon as she arrived;

h I already told Sami when he arrived that we were going / would go to the cinema.

E Reading

1/2 Alone, then pairs

Working on their own, students recall the information about paramedics, matching the sentence halves. Then they check their answers in pairs and put the complete sentences into the same order as in Activity B8. Refer students to the audioscript in Appendix 3 to double-check their decisions.

Answers

3 + e, 5 + c, 1 + d, 2 + a, 4 + b

3 Whole class, then alone

Make sure students understand what they are going to read: an internet article about the qualifications needed to become a paramedic. On their own, students think about what they would like to find out (about the entry requirements) and write three questions. Focus on the example given first.

4 Alone

Students quickly read the text and check if any of their questions from the previous activity are answered. They do not need to read the text in any great detail at this stage.

5 Alone, then pairs

Remind students to identify the key word/s in each question and to think about the type of answer that each question requires. Then they write the answers to the questions. When everyone has finished, they can check with a partner.

Answers

a secure a student paramedic position with an ambulance service trust, or attend an approved full-time course in paramedic science at a university

b work their way up with experience and additional training

c English and Maths

d full manual driving licence

e successfully complete an HCPC-approved programme in paramedic science

f from two to five years

g students on full-time courses in paramedic science

F Speaking and listening: completing notes

1/2 Whole class, then pairs

Most students will be familiar with the ICRC (the International Committee of the Red Cross/Crescent), but if this is not the case, use some pictures – including the ones in the Coursebook – as prompts. Give them a few minutes to come up with ideas in response to Activity F2.

3 Pairs

Students work together to check the meaning of the words and phrases given. Some of this is quite demanding so be prepared to provide assistance if necessary.

4 Pairs

Students look at the three questions **a–c** and predict what the answers might be. If time is an issue, or if you think some students may struggle with the questions, allocate different questions to different students and then do class feedback.

5/6/7 Alone, then pairs

Students listen and check their predictions in Activity F4. Then they listen to the audio a second time and fill in the gaps, writing one or two words for each gap. Finally, students can check with a partner or refer to the audioscript in Appendix 3.

Answers

a	famine,	e	ethnic,
b	drought	f	political,
c	economic crisis,	g	economic,
d	political instability,	h	food,

i	water,	p	tools,
j	essential goods,	q	cholera,
k	hygiene,	r	typhoid,
l	medical care,	s	construction,
m	before,	t	engineering,
n	after,	u	humanitarian work,
o	seeds,	v	stress/pressure

CD2, Track 4

Marianna Milutinovic: Today we welcome Alvaro Solomou, one of the 1200 relief workers with the Red Cross, the ICRC, who is going to talk to us about the ICRC's approach to giving assistance. Welcome to the programme, Alvaro.

Alvaro Solomou: Hello, Marianna, and thank you for inviting me.

MM: Alvaro, can you tell us about how the ICRC assists victims of famine and drought and other natural disasters?

AS: Well, we should remember that, all too often, natural disasters happen in areas where there is already some other sort of problem, such as an economic crisis, or a period of political instability. Put the two together and the people involved become even more insecure and desperate.

MM: I imagine that different contexts also create extra problems, don't they?

AS: Yes, geographic context, as well as ethnic, political and economic, all translate into different needs and, therefore, the response the ICRC makes must be adapted to suit the context.

MM: How is that done?

AS: We use what is called the 'Assistance Pyramid'. This establishes that preference must be given in any relief situation to the foundations of the pyramid – in other words, to food, water and essential goods – before anything else is done.

MM: What about healthcare? Isn't that a priority?

AS: Hygiene and medical care take second and third places in the pyramid. Obviously, if a person is starving and thirsty, it does not matter how good the healthcare is.

MM: I see. Does the ICRC only assist when there is a crisis?

AS: No, not at all. In fact, in recent years, it has been the policy to provide help in developing countries once a crisis has passed, or even before one has occurred.

MM: How is that actually done?

AS: Well, for example, the ICRC assistance programmes have been extended, so that they now include seed and tools distribution, and the provision of veterinary care. The ICRC identifies priorities in a region, in order to provide the best possible assistance.

MM: Going back to the issue of water for a moment, isn't it true that millions of people across the world have difficulties gaining access to water? What can the ICRC do about this?

AS: Oh yes, that's absolutely true and, of course, in many places the water that is available is actually extremely unhealthy and may carry waterborne diseases, such as cholera and typhoid. The ICRC has a programme of assistance, which includes construction, engineering and providing access to water, along with hygiene and environmental protection, thus ensuring that water is clean and safe to use.

MM: Is it dangerous working for the ICRC?

AS: Well, in any crisis situation there are dangers, but all of us are strongly motivated by humanitarian work, and hopefully we can all cope with the stress and the pressures which are bound to exist.

MM: Alvaro, thank you for giving us such an interesting insight into the work of the ICRC.

G Speaking

1/2 Whole class, then pairs or small groups

If you prefer, students could work together in small groups to go through the discussion questions in this section. You should briefly go over the questions first, checking that students understand what they need to do.

Differentiated activities

Support

i   Give students some time to look back through the unit and at their notes in order to prepare for the discussion.

ii   Reduce the number of questions that students need to talk about.

Challenge

Tell students that they will need to make a written summary of their discussions after they have finished.

Reflection

Use the **Reflection** to remind students of what they have achieved in the unit. Students should set themselves a **personal goal** based on their scores for Unit 14.

Exam focus

Listening, Exercise 5, completing notes (Extended only)

Part A

CD2, Track 5

The world's transport crisis has reached such catastrophic proportions that road-traffic accidents now kill more people each year than malaria. I predict that by 2030, 2.5 million people will be killed on the roads in developing countries each year and 60 million will be injured. Even today, 3,000 are killed and 30 000 seriously injured on the world's roads every day.

These are really frightening statistics, but, of course, it isn't only road-traffic accidents which concern me. Air pollution from traffic claims 400 000 lives each year, mostly in developing countries, and some 1.5 billion people are exposed every day to levels of pollution well in excess of World Health Organization recommended levels.

We need to be aware of this because the damage being caused to people now, and especially youngsters, will follow them through until later life, and directly affect not only their health, but also their economic potential, and the health budgets of already strained national administrations.

Research shows us that the problems of the world's poor are multiplied by the car. It's a simple basic fact. Deaths and injuries take place mainly in developing countries and mainly to pedestrians, cyclists, bus users and children. The poor suffer disproportionately. They experience the worst air pollution and are deprived of education, health, water and sanitation programmes because the needs of the car now soak up so much national income. Advances in vehicle, engine and fuel technology are more or less irrelevant in Asian and African cities, where the growth of car and lorry numbers is dramatic and where highly polluting diesel is widespread.

Fortunately, I can report that in certain places, such as in parts of South America, something is being done. Transport budgets have been reallocated to improve the quality of life of poorer citizens and the results have been staggering. Bicycle- and pedestrian-only routes were planned, and cars were banned from certain areas. Parks were built on derelict land and car-free days implemented. This policy was radical and has improved the quality of life for the poor. This needs to be repeated all over the world.

Answers

The cause
Road-traffic accidents are just one problem; the other is *air pollution* from traffic.

The problem is greatest in *developing* countries.

1.5 billion people suffer from excess levels of pollution daily.

The damage
Young people's health and also *economic* potential affected.

Cars increase problems for poor people, as deaths and injuries occur mainly to pedestrians, cyclists, bus users and children.

Their levels of education, health, water and *sanitation* decline, as cars take economic priority over people.

The solution
Reallocation of *transport budgets* in South America has improved lives of poorer people.

Solution should be repeated all over the world.

Part B

Male teenager: Didn't that guest speaker give an interesting talk about traffic problems yesterday? It will really help us with that school project we have to do this term.

Female teenager: Yes, she was very interesting and she gave me some good ideas for our project too. I've already done some research.

MT: Since yesterday morning? Wow, that was quick!

FT: Well, I found out from my aunty, who's a police captain, that in the UK, the number of people killed in road accidents has fallen dramatically since 2000.

MT: Really? By how much? Maybe we can use the data?

FT: Well, in 2000, 3,409 people died, including pedestrians, cyclists, motorcyclists and all vehicle users, but last year that had dropped to less than 1800.

MT: That's incredible! That's nearly a 50% drop. I read somewhere that the annual death rate from road accidents in the UK is about five per 100 000.

FT: So for every 100 000 people, five die? That doesn't seem very high, even though, of course, it should be 0. I know that in some countries in Africa, it's more than 40 per 100 000.

MT: I think we could design a graph for our project – a line graph – showing how the death rate from road traffic accidents has changed over the past ten or 15 years.

FT: And we need to make it clear that nearly half of people killed are pedestrians, cyclists or motorcyclists – my aunty told me they are called 'vulnerable road users'.

MT: So they are more at risk because a car or a lorry gives you more protection. And we know that in South America even more 'vulnerable road users' are killed …

FT: … Yes, I spoke to the speaker yesterday and she told me the figure is nearer to 70%.

MT: I think we could put some focus on the effectiveness of bicycle- and pedestrian-only routes, and what happens when cars and other vehicles are banned from certain roads.

FT: Good idea. I know that locally more and more people are using their bikes to get to and from school and work, using the new cycle paths …

MT: … and that new pedestrians-only area downtown has really increased the number of shoppers. Banning cars has to be the way ahead.

FT: I agree. Well, I think we have enough to be going on with. Let's Skype later and discuss how to proceed. Bye!

MT: Great, talk later …

Answers

Information about problems with traffic

In the UK, death from road accidents has fallen by nearly *50%* since 2000.

For every 100 000 people in some *countries*, more than 40 people die on the roads.

Deaths involve *pedestrians*, cyclists and motorcyclists.

These are the *vulnerable* road users who are more at risk.

More emphasis needed on bicycle- and people-only paths and roads.

In many places, banning cars has resulted in more people going *shopping*.

NOTE on Assessment Objectives (AOs) for Speaking:
In the Cambridge IGCSE speaking examination, students need to communicate ideas/opinions clearly, accurately and effectively (S1), develop responses and link ideas using a range of appropriate linking devices (S2), use a range of grammatical structures and vocabulary accurately and effectively (S3), show control of pronunciation and intonation patterns (S4) and engage in a conversation and contribute effectively to help move the conversation forward (S5).

Learning objectives (LOs)

Suggested activity: Start the unit by focusing for a few minutes on the LOs box, making sure that students understand what they are going to be doing. Using the first LO as an example, ask students to identify where in the unit they can find the activities for the other four LOs. Get students to say which of the activities appeal to them the most, and ask them for their reasons.

A Watch, listen and talk

1 Whole class, then alone

Explain that students are going to watch and listen to some IGCSE students talking about **healthy living**. As your students watch and listen, they should make a note of **a** what the speakers say are the reasons for taking care of our health, and **b** what the speakers do to have a healthy lifestyle, and if they could improve it. Play the video a second time so that students can check or add to their notes.

Answers

a The reasons for taking care of our health: to stop us from getting sick, to live longer, show a good example to younger people.

b Things that the students do to have a healthy lifestyle: exercise, eat a balanced diet, get enough sleep.

How the students could improve their lifestyle: by eating healthier food, sports facilities being provided by their school.

2 Pairs or small groups

Depending on the size of your class, put students into pairs or small groups. They can discuss their notes and then talk to each other about how the lifestyles of other

people influence their own. Do not interfere too much, but make sure you get feedback from the class so that they know their efforts have been worthwhile. If time permits, you could write their ideas on the board and rank them according to your students' preferences.

B Speaking and vocabulary

1 Pairs

There are seven pictures of people doing things. Students work together and describe what they can see in each one.

2 Alone, then pairs

Each of the seven phrases can be matched with one of the pictures in B1. Students need to discuss the phrases and match them, and then add one further piece of information of their own to each picture.

Answers

1. reduces stress and high blood pressure
2. high in fat and calories
3. intense aromatic flavours
4/5 no pain no gain
6. couch potatoes
7. eat what you grow

3/4 Small groups, then whole class

Students work in small groups to discuss the questions. There are no right or wrong answers, so encourage students to speak freely. Do not interfere unless necessary, and save any language correction until students have finished. If time permits, do some class feedback, collecting students' ideas and perhaps writing the most popular ones on the board for further discussion.

C Reading and speaking

1 Pairs

Later in this section students are going to read about ginger and honey, two of nature's most amazing and healthiest foods. Firstly, students need to discuss the questions (**a**–**c**), which get them to focus on and to think about the two foods. There are no right or wrong answers. You may wish to set a short time limit for each question to keep students focused and to avoid time-wasting.

2 Pairs, then whole class

The information (**a–j**) is taken from the two texts students are going to read. They need to read each piece of information and decide to which food, ginger or honey, the information relates, giving reasons. Do not supply any answers at this stage as students will find out for themselves when they read the texts.

3 Alone, then A/B pairs

a Firstly, put students into A/B pairs. Then all the As find the text **Ginger – part of nature's pharmacy** and all the Bs **Honey – nature's oldest food** in Appendix 2.

b Students read their text and check their answers to Exercise C2. They should not speak to their partner nor look at the other text yet.

Answers to C2

GINGER **a**, **b**, **e**, **h**, **i**   HONEY **c**, **d**, **f**, **g**, **j**

c Students need to read their text again, this time in more detail, to answer questions (**i–v**).

Answers

	GINGER	HONEY
i	Widely used in Ancient China, dates back to 6th century BCE, introduced to Mediterranean before 1st century CE, 1585 Jamaican ginger first oriental spice grown in New World	Cave paintings show beekeeping in Spain 7000 BCE, honey bee fossils 150 million years old, earliest record of keeping bees 2400 BCE near Cairo, Egypt
ii	China, India, Jamaica, Mediterranean region, Middle East, New World, Europe	Spain, Cairo, Egypt, Greece, Sicily, Roman Empire, Europe
iii	Ginger plant, white and pink buds, yellow flowers, rhizome gathered and boiled and scraped to stop growth, perennial plant	Made using nectar of flowering plants, saved inside beehive
iv	Juice from roots used as spice, root pickled in vinegar, brewed in boiling water to make tea, dry ginger root used in cooking gingerbread, biscuits and cakes, also used in medicine and healthy living	Natural sweetener, mixed with cheese to make cheesecake, gift, ingredient in medicine, natural source of carbohydrates, boosts performance and endurance, reduces muscle fatigue
v	Various answers possible	Various answers possible

4 Pairs

Students now work with their partner and discuss the information they found out about in the previous activities.

5 Pairs, then whole class

The final activity in this section gives students an opportunity to further discuss ginger and honey, not only what they have read in the texts but also their own ideas. Limit the time for each question (**a–d**) so that students stay on task.

D Language focus: quantifying phrases

1 Whole class

Quantifying phrases are expressions that we use before a noun to give information about quantity, and they are very common in both spoken and written language. Look at the example in the Coursebook with your students, and ask for their ideas in response to questions **a** and **b**.

Answers

a it is plural (fossils)

b it agrees with the subject (fossils + date)

2 Alone, then pairs

Students work alone to find the nouns in the texts and identify the quantifying phrases which precede them. Then they check with their partner.

Answers

a a variety of (*other*) *luxuries*,

b a range of (*different*) *uses*,

c The majority of *studies*,

d a range of *sweetmeats and cakes*,

e a variety of *areas*,

f the amounts of *vitamins and minerals*

3 Pairs

Students work together to think of other nouns which are commonly quantified by *a pair of*.

Possible answers

a pair of sunglasses, trousers, socks, gloves, shorts, tights, stockings, pyjamas, slippers

4 Whole class

You could turn this into a competition, with students working in small groups or pairs to think of as many quantifying phrases + nouns as possible.

Possible answers

a bottle of vinegar, a slice of apple pie, a bar of chocolate/soap, a jar of marmalade, a scoop of ice-cream, a kilo of potatoes, a litre of milk, a carton of juice, etc.

5 Alone, then pairs

Students work alone to complete the gaps in the text using the quantifying phrases in the box. Then they check with their partner to see if there are any variations.

Answers

High-intensity exercise: Can less really be more?

Could just <u>a few minutes of</u> exercise a week be good for your health? Apparently it can. According to <u>a variety of/a large number of</u> studies (as well as <u>a large number of/a majority of</u> fitness fanatics who can't stop talking about it), short and intense 'High-Intensity Training' (HIT) workouts are the way to go. Of course, not every exercise is perfect, and <u>one of the</u> drawbacks of HIT is that if participants increase the level of intensity of each workout too quickly, they run the risk of incurring an injury.

E Listening and speaking

1 Pairs

In Unit 10 students discussed effective strategies for responding to questions in the speaking examination, and looked at role-play cards on the topics of Education and Studying Abroad. For this activity, students look at the role-play card about Healthy Living, and remind themselves of what they need to do.

Suggested answers

carefully read the topic, respond to all five prompts in the order given, no written notes allowed, try to develop the conversation, can introduce own related ideas, etc.

2 Alone, then pairs

Students work alone and carefully read the five prompts, deciding which ones they think are the least and most challenging. They should then discuss with their partner and give reasons for their choices. Generally speaking, the last couple of prompts tend to be more challenging than the earlier ones, but it may also be the case that these give students more to talk about.

3 Alone, then pairs

Students are going to listen to six different people responding to the five prompts in the topic card they have just been studying. As they listen, students decide which person matches each of the five prompts. There is one extra person speaking, who does not match any of the prompts. After listening, students work in pairs to compare their answers.

Answers

Adam 5th prompt: the suggestion that the people who profit from the health and fitness industry are not motivated by the right reasons

Hana 3rd prompt: the advantages and disadvantages of a healthy lifestyle

Mustafa X

Sara 2nd prompt: some people you know who try to have a healthy lifestyle and the reasons for this

Miska 4th prompt: the stresses and dangers of being obsessed with health and fitness

Layla 1st prompt: what you do to have a healthy lifestyle

CD2, Track 6

Adam:	I believe that health and fitness is a business like any other, and people have to profit from it.
Hana:	Obviously a healthy lifestyle makes you feel better. But in my opinion a healthy lifestyle can also be expensive.
Mustafa:	Healthy living is only for young people in my country, as far as I'm concerned.
Sara:	Some of my school friends have a healthy lifestyle. They are very keen on sports and play in different school teams.
Miska:	It seems to me that if you are really interested and involved in something, I think it can become stressful and dangerous.
Layla:	To be honest, I don't think I have a particularly healthy lifestyle nowadays. I guess that I'm too busy at school, doing homework, and helping out at home.

4 Pairs

Students now think about how the five speakers' introductory phrases could be expanded. There are

six phrases for students to look at and match to the **five** speakers (Mustafa has already been excluded) in E3. Students do the matching, decide which phrase does not fit, and then listen to check their answers.

Answers

a Layla,   c Hana,   e Adam

b Sara,   d Miska,   f does not fit

CD2, Track 6

Adam: I believe that health and fitness is a business like any other, and people have to profit from it.

Hana: Obviously a healthy lifestyle makes you feel better. But in my opinion a healthy lifestyle can also be expensive.

Sara: Some of my school friends have a healthy lifestyle. They are very keen on sports and play in different school teams.

Miska: It seems to me that if you are really interested and involved in something, I think it can become stressful and dangerous.

Layla: To be honest, I don't think I have a particularly healthy lifestyle nowadays. I guess that I'm too busy at school, doing homework, and helping out at home.

5 Alone

Students are going to listen to the five speakers again, this time responding to the prompts in the correct order, and adding some extra information to their responses. During listening, students need to match the speakers to the information (**a–e**).

Answers

a Hana,   d Layla,

b Miska,   e Sara

c Adam,

CD2, Track 7

a **Layla:** To be honest, I don't think I have a particularly healthy lifestyle nowadays. I guess that I'm too busy at school, doing homework, and helping out at home. But I know that I should do more. The longer you wait, the more difficult it gets to change. <u>In addition, and having said that, I think my diet is pretty healthy, and I play sports at school and walk everywhere. It could be worse!</u>

b **Sara:** Some of my school friends have a healthy lifestyle. They are very keen on sports and play

in different school teams. They all say how much they enjoy it, and they never seem to be bored with nothing to do. <u>Furthermore, they quite often ask me to join in, but I fear I won't be as good as them and make a fool of myself.</u>

c **Hana:** Obviously a healthy lifestyle makes you feel better. But in my opinion a healthy lifestyle can also be expensive. I think the key is moderation. If you do the right amount, it is obviously very beneficial, but too much could cause an injury. <u>So it's probably not a bad idea to programme your healthy lifestyle, by firstly including both physical and mental activity, and secondly introducing a balanced diet.</u>

d **Miska:** It seems to me that if you are really interested and involved in something, I think it can become stressful and dangerous. This type of lifestyle can take over everything you do, and I think that can be risky and cause you to worry. <u>Is it worth it? I don't think so. There's no need to be extreme about living in a healthy way. I'm young and I want to enjoy my life!</u>

e **Adam:** I believe that health and fitness is a business like any other, and people have to profit from it. I think that when you pay for something, it's up to you to make sure you are getting good value for money. <u>There are cheats and people who want to make more and more everywhere, and the health and fitness scene is no different. I'm afraid there's nothing you can do about it.</u>

6 Pairs

Students work together to check their answers and confirm by reading the audioscript in Appendix 3.

> **LANGUAGE TIP**
>
> Using fillers (or fixed phrases) makes spoken language sound far more fluent and natural, so it is a good idea to highlight this importance to students and encourage them to use fillers when appropriate. Get them to re-read the audioscript in Appendix 3 to find more examples.
>
> **Suggested answers**
>
> Sara: Furthermore,
>
> Hana: But in my opinion, So,
>
> Miska: It seems to me that, I think that, is it worth it?, I don't think so,
>
> Adam: I believe that, it's up to you, I'm afraid there's,

7 Whole class, then pairs

For the final activity in this section, students can role-play the examiner and candidate in a speaking exam, using the five follow-up questions (**a**–**e**). Go through the questions orally first, getting some possible answers from the class, then students perform the role-play. If time permits, they can exchange roles.

F Speaking

> **TOP TIP**
>
> Students often worry about their lack of knowledge about the topic. Reassure them that this is not a history exam in which they are assessed on facts. They need to demonstrate that they can communicate effectively in English, and the topic is just a starting point for the communication. Examiners are trained to deal with students who may not feel comfortable talking about a particular topic.

1 Pairs

Students discuss what criteria they think are used to assess spoken language, for example *vocabulary*. Students will probably also think of *grammar* and *pronunciation*.

2 Alone, then pairs

Do a couple of examples and then ask students to decide which area, *Structure, Vocabulary,* or *Development and Fluency,* the descriptions relate to.

Answers
Structure: **a**, **b**, **h**, Vocabulary: **e**, **g**, **i**, Development and Fluency: **c**, **d**, **f**

G Watch, listen and talk

1 Alone, then pairs

Prepare students to watch a video of a student practising a discussion with a teacher about **Healthy Living**. The student is responding to the same prompts that they have already seen in **Section E**. Students need to decide which, if any, of the criteria from Activity F2 could apply to the student, and give their reasons.

2 Alone, then pairs

Students now watch a second student responding to the same prompts and decide if they perform better or worse

than the first student, giving their reasons. They also need to decide again which, if any, of the criteria from Activity F2 could apply to the student, and give their reasons.

H Reading and writing

1 Whole class

With books closed, ask students question **a**. Do not supply an answer yet. Then move on to question **b**, which will give students the answer to the first question. Encourage students to think carefully about the question and to supply reasons why gardening is good exercise. Then move on to question **c** and again get specific ideas from students.

2 Pairs

Students open their books and do the matching activity.

Answers
a3 Besides the exertion involved, gardening has other pluses that makes it a good form of exercise and calorie burning.

b5 Gardening definitely has many health and therapeutic benefits.

c2 Gardening for 30 to 45 minutes a day can burn 150 to 300 calories.

d4 Gardening isn't usually enough exercise to replace your daily walk or swim.

e6 It takes at least 30 minutes of exercise several days a week, to really receive any health benefits from gardening.

f1 Lifting bags, pushing wheelbarrows and shovelling all provide resistance training similar to weight lifting.

3 Alone, then pairs

Remind students of the three paragraph headings **a** Is gardening good exercise?, **b** What makes gardening good exercise? and **c** How can I get the most exercise out of gardening?. Then they need to match each of the phrases from the previous activity to the correct paragraph heading.

Answers
a b5 and c2,

b a3 and f1,

c e6 and d4

4 Alone, then pairs

Students now read the text and complete the gaps (**a–f**) using the six sentences from Activity H2.

Answers

a   b5,   c   a3,   e   e6,
b   c2,   d   f1,   f   d4

> **WORD TIP**
>
> Sometimes students are familiar with using adjective form of a word, but are less confident about using the noun form. This **Word Tip** highlights two words which are probably more familiar to students as adjectives: *intense/intensive* and *strong*. Refer students to the exercise in the **Workbook**.

5 Alone, then pairs

Students now re-read the text and identify **one** piece of information in each paragraph that particularly surprises or interests them. They should tell their partner and decide if they agree or disagree with each other's choices, giving their reasons.

6 Whole class, then pairs

Go through the notes with the class and get them to give possible answers. Remind students that in these types of exercise there may be more answers than are actually required, i.e. while there may be three bullets, the text may contain four or five pieces of information. If this is the case, students must **not** try to include more than the required amount of information. After going through the notes, students on their own look at the text again and write their notes.

Sample answer from an IGCSE Core student:

Is gardening good exercise?

* Has many healthy and therapeutic benefits
* Just as effective as other moderate to strenuous forms of exercise, like walking and bicycling
* Gardening for 30 to 45 minutes a day can burn 150 to 300 calories

What makes gardening good exercise?

* Working the full range of major muscle groups: legs, buttocks, arms, shoulders, neck, back and abdomen
* Great deal of stretching involved with gardening
* Lifting bags, pushing wheelbarrows and shovelling all provide resistance training similar to weight lifting, which leads to healthier bones and joints

How can I get the most exercise out of gardening?

* It takes at least 30 minutes of exercise several days a week, to really receive any health benefits from gardening
* Break that 30 minutes up into shorter active periods throughout the day
* Incorporate a little stretching before and after gardening and take things slowly in extreme heat

7 Alone

Now students use their notes from the previous exercise to write a summary of the health benefits of gardening.

Sample answer

Gardening has many health and therapeutic benefits. It can be just as effective as other moderate types of exercise, because gardening for 30 to 45 minutes a day can burn from 150 to 300 calories. While gardening you are using a large number of major muscle groups and you are simultaneously stretching your body. Furthermore, all the lifting and pulling helps develop healthier bones and joints. In order to receive health benefits, you need to garden several times a week for at least 30 minutes. It is a good idea to break up 30 minutes of gardening throughout the day and to also make sure that you stretch before you garden and not to overdo it in high temperatures. [119 words]

Differentiated activities

Support

Students work in groups of three, with each student using their notes to write only one of the three paragraphs. Then they discuss each other's paragraphs and combine the three to make one summary.

Challenge

Students write their summary without using their notes, but only by referring back to the text. They can look at their notes after they have finished writing, to make sure they have included all the necessary information in their summary.

8 Small groups, then whole class

Finish off the final section by putting students into small groups to discuss the questions. Encourage students to give reasons for their comments, reminding them that this is one thing that examiners listen for in speaking examinations.

Reflection

Use the **Reflection** to remind students of what they have achieved in the unit. Students should set themselves a **personal goal** based on their scores for Unit 15.

Exam focus

Speaking, Part 2, topic cards

NOTE: The exam focus is on speaking, and involves students in looking at a new topic card, and then taking on the roles of examiner and student, using the prompts on the card.

1/2 Pairs

Students work together and look at the prompts, discussing how they might respond to each one. When they are ready, students take on the roles of examiner and interviewee, using the topic of Lifestyle Changes and the prompts on the card. Your job is to monitor and encourage where necessary, and provide any language students are struggling with. However, this should be an opportunity for students to build their confidence and fluency.

NOTE on Assessment Objectives (AOs) for Reading and Writing Exercise 2 (multiple matching):

Remember that in a *multiple matching* activity students need to read a continuous text divided into sections, or a number of shorter texts, and answer a series of questions testing more detailed comprehension. Candidates match the correct answer to the question. This type of activity requires more intensive reading, and students will need to understand things which are implied, but not directly stated (for example, gist, speaker's purpose, intentions and feelings) (R4). Students also need to identify and select relevant information (R1), understand ideas, opinions and attitudes (R2) and show understanding of the connections between them (R3).

Learning objectives (LOs)

Suggested activity: Start the unit by focusing for a few minutes on the LOs box, making sure that students understand what they are going to be doing. Using the first LO as an example, ask students to identify where in the unit they can find the activities for the other four LOs. Get students to say which of the activities appeal to them the most, and ask them for their reasons.

A Watch, listen and talk

1 Whole class, then alone

Explain that students are going to watch and listen to some IGCSE students talking about **social media**. As your students watch and listen, they should make a note of **a** what the speakers understand by the term 'social media' and the examples they give, and **b** what social media the speakers use most and with whom, and the reasons they give. Play the video a second time so that students can check or add to their notes.

Answers

a What the students understand by the term 'social media': sharing opinions/discussions with a lot of other people, interacting with people using the Internet.

Examples of social media they give, any **three** from: Instagram, Twitter, Snapchat, Facebook, Whatsapp.

b Social media they use the most: Instagram, Twitter, Snapchat.

What are their reasons: to communicate with friends and family, get opinions from other people

2 Pairs or small groups

Depending on the size of your class, put students into pairs or small groups. They can discuss their notes and then talk to each other about the social media they use and why they choose not to use others. Do not interfere too much, but make sure you get feedback from the class so that they know their efforts have been worthwhile. If time permits, you could write their ideas on the board and rank them according to your students' preferences.

B Speaking and vocabulary

1 Pairs

Students are going to look at some graphic information about the global digital age, but before doing so they need to understand some key phrases. Elicit meanings from your students, prompting them using different methods (for example, concept checking, asking for or providing opposites, etc.).

2 Pairs

The five icons appear in one of the graphics students will be looking at, but first they need to say what they think each icon represents by matching each one with an appropriate heading.

3 Pairs, whole class

Now students look at the two graphics and think about the general information that each one shows. There is no need for students to talk about specific details at this point, but they should match the two headings (i) Annual Growth and (ii) Global Digital Snapshot with graphics A and B.

Answers

A(ii), B(i)

4 Pairs

Allocate A/B to students in pairs. Student A looks at graphic A and Student B looks at graphic B. Give students a minute to tell each other in one sentence what their graphic shows, without including any specific details. There is a suggestion in the Coursebook to help students begin their sentence.

5/6 Alone, then pairs

Students now work alone to find the answers to three of the six questions (**a–f**), so firstly they need to decide which questions refer to their graphic. When they have answered the questions, they can share with their partner.

Differentiated activities

Support

i   Allow students to work in pairs to give each other some support.

ii Tell students which three of the six questions refer to their graphic.

iii Provide the answers to the three questions for students to match.

Challenge

i   Ask students to prepare two to three more questions for another student to answer.

ii Give students the answers to all six questions, and tell them not to look at the questions. They have to write the questions themselves and then check in the Coursebook.

Answers

a   332 million
b   7.395 billion
c   total number of active mobile social users,
d   growth in the number of active social media users,
e   number of active internet users, number of active social media users
f   31% (note that students will need to work this out themselves using the values in the graphic)

7 Alone, then whole class

The purpose of this activity is for students to re-present the information in their graphic using a different format, such as a chart, a table or a graph. If you think students will find this challenging, provide them with an example of your own first. Obviously there are many variations possible, but make sure students include all the necessary information and details in their presentation.

TOP TIP

Some examination questions may ask students to retrieve information from a graphic, rather than a text itself, and it is important to ensure students look at all the information given.

C Reading

1 Pairs or small groups

Questions (**a–d**) provide an introduction to the web article students are going to read in C3. Set a time limit for students to respond to each question. If time is an issue, you could divide up the questions between pairs or groups to discuss and then give whole class feedback. As students will be referring back to these discussions in C4, tell them to make some written notes.

2 Pairs

Students work together to check the meaning of the seven words and one phrase, which have been removed from the text.

Suggested answers

abstained = did not take part in something,

avid = very keen + multitaskers = people who can do more than one thing at a time,

compulsively = doing something a lot because you cannot control yourself,

mind-boggling = unimaginable,

self-esteem = confidence in yourself,

suppressed = controlled or stopped,

traits = characteristics,

tweens = young people aged around 10–14 years.

3 Alone, then pairs

Students read the text and fill the gaps using the words from C2. If you want to give some support, you could do this paragraph by paragraph, checking answers before students continue.

Answers

a   mind-boggling,
b   tweens,
c   avid multitaskers,
d   compulsively,
e   traits,
f   abstained,
g   self-esteem,
h   suppressed

4 Alone, then pairs

Students look at the text in more detail to check if their ideas and anything they discussed in C1 are confirmed or not. They should have made notes during these earlier discussions, so they can refer to these as they read.

> **WORD TIP**
> The word *while* is commonly seen and used to mean *during*, but it is seen less frequently when comparing two different facts. Point this out to students, and then refer them to the exercise in the **Workbook**.

5 Alone

For this activity students focus on the numbers in the first three paragraphs and identify what each one refers to. When they are ready, they can share their answers with a partner.

Answers

a   6.5 hours and 4.5 hours = daily time spent by teens and tweens on screen-based media for enjoyment purposes

b   60% = number of young people who say they text while doing homework, and 75% = number of young people say they listen to music while doing homework

c   50% = number of young people who believe that using social media made no difference to the quality of their homework

d   400 teens = number of teens in a study

e   62% = the amount of extra information written down by students who abstained from texting during a lecture

> **LANGUAGE TIP**
> This **Language Tip** highlights that *social media* is plural, not singular. There are some other words which have the plural ending *-ia*, but most of these are not commonly used in this way. For example: the plural of *curriculum* is *curricula*, but *curriculums* is also acceptable.

6 Alone, then pairs

Students look at the text one more time and write the answers to the questions (**a–i**).

Answers

a   nine hours

b   media used at school or for homework

c   half

d   they perform worse in tests

e   problems sleeping and a lower academic performance

f   because they are responding to messages and monitoring what is happening

g   the light from it

h   regulates your sleep cycle

i   it's the same type of light most common outdoors during daytime

D Listening

1 Alone, then pairs

Students are going to listen to part of a radio talk on the subject of social media. Before they listen, students look at the vocabulary from the listening in column A and match it with a suitable meaning in column B. Then check with a partner.

Answers

A	B
sedentary	inactive
detrimental	harmful
arteries	blood-carrying tubes
profound	extremely significant
gauge	assess
precursors	indications
disc	strong material between bones

2 Pairs

For this activity, students need to look at both columns of information to get a general idea of the content before they attempt to match the phrases. They will need to use common sense and logic as well as knowledge of grammar to make complete sentences, but it does not matter if they are unsure or get things wrong at this stage. Do not supply any answers as they will find out for themselves when they listen to the talk.

3 Alone

Students listen and check their answers.

Answers

a 6,   **b** 3,   **c** 4,   **d** 2,   **e** 5,   **f** 1

CD2, Track 8

The other unmentioned risk here has to do with the fact that media usage is often a **sedentary** activity. Children spend more than 60 percent of their waking day sitting down, and by some estimates children sit for an average of 8.5 hours a day. Furthermore, activity levels are thought to decline steeply after the age of eight, especially among girls. Researchers decided to study a small group of pre-teen girls (aged seven to 10 years) to determine if sitting is as **detrimental** to their health as it appears to be to adults. At the start of the study, all of the girls had healthy functioning **arteries**. However, after sitting for three hours, playing on tablets or watching movies, there was a 'profound' negative change in functioning arteries by up to 33 percent in the girls. This is alarming since a *1 percent* decline is known to increase heart disease risk by 13 percent in adults.

Fortunately, there were also some more encouraging findings. The girls' artery function had returned to normal a few days later when they returned to the laboratory for tests. And when the sitting time was interrupted by a gentle 10-minute cycling session, no decline was recorded. Still, no one knows what effect sitting for hours, day after day, has on kids' health, so it is best to encourage kids to stay active.

Not surprisingly, researchers have found that higher cell-phone use was linked to reduced physical activity and fitness. According to the authors, cellphone use may be able to **gauge** a person's risk for a multitude of health issues related to an inactive lifestyle.

Depending on the research you read, back problems are also a possibility. In a UK study involving ten year-olds, up to 10 percent may already have **precursors** to bad backs, and 9 percent of the kids showed worsening **back disc** problems with at least one disc. The researcher connected this to carrying heavy school books, watching TV, and playing video games, but texting may also play a significant role.

4 Alone, then pairs

Before students listen again, go through the multiple-choice questions (**a–d**) with them, offering a chance for them to answer from memory, or by guessing. Then play the recording again for students to answer.

Answers

a   A
b   B
c   B
d   C

LANGUAGE TIP

These two useful phrases *According to...* and *Depending on...* from the listening text can have different meanings, depending on how they are used. Go through the information with your students, and then refer them to the exercise in the **Workbook**.

E Language focus: *-ing* forms

1 Whole class

-ing forms are very common and can be used in many different ways. Go through examples **a–g** with your students, pointing out that it is not necessary for them to learn and remember all the different uses. However, it is important that they are confident in using them. For each example, ask students to replace the phrase containing the underlined *-ing* word with an alternative, for example:
a Before <u>entering</u> a cinema, switch off your mobile phone;
b <u>Speaking</u> during an examination is not allowed.

2 Alone, then pairs

If students are confident about the structures (i.e. the position of the *-ing* word in the phrase) in E1, they should be able to correctly match the examples below. Do the first one as an example and then students work alone before checking with their partner.

Answers

a   What is **shocking**, however, is just *how much* time they are actually **spending** doing this (g, e)
b   ... such as **lying** about the amount of time they spend **texting**, difficulty in **stopping** the behaviour, and **losing** sleep to text (c, f, a, c)
c   students who abstained from **texting** during a lecture (a)
d   students who texted or used Facebook while **doing** schoolwork (a)
e   teens are **staying** up late to respond to messages and monitor what is **happening** (e, e)

3 Alone, then pairs

Students read the audioscript in Appendix 3 and find examples of words ending in *-ing*, and say what their use is. Then they can compare with a partner's examples.

Answers

Children spend more than 60 percent of their <u>waking</u> day <u>sitting</u> down (g, c)

to determine if <u>sitting</u> is as detrimental to their health as it appears to be to adults (b)

At the start of the study, all of the girls had healthy <u>functioning</u> arteries. (g)

However, after <u>sitting</u> for three hours, <u>playing</u> on tablets or <u>watching</u> movies, there was a 'profound' negative change in <u>functioning</u> arteries by up to 33 percent in the girls. (a, c, c, g)

This is <u>alarming</u> since a *1 percent* decline is known to increase heart disease risk by 13 percent in adults. (g)

F Reading: multiple matching

1 Small groups

Students should be familiar with these (and other) social media. Working in groups, they tell each other which ones they use (if any) and what the advantages and disadvantages of each one are.

2 Small groups

Students look at the information about the four people who use different social media and predict what they think each one might say about how, why and when they use their chosen social medium. There are no right or wrong answers. You could alternatively put students into groups of four, with each student thinking about one person, and then sharing their ideas with the other group members.

3 Alone, then small groups

All the information (**a–h**) comes from the magazine article students are going to read in F4. Students work alone and speculate which person said each comment, then discuss in their groups and give reasons for their choices. There is no need to give any answers as students will find out when they read the article.

4 Pairs, then whole class

Students pair up as A/B, each one reading about two of the people, and checking their answers to F3. Then everyone shares their answers with the rest of the class.

Answers

a	B,	d	C,	g	A,
b	D,	e	B,	h	D
c	A,	f	C,		

5 Alone, then pairs

Students now do the multiple-matching task by reading all four paragraphs and choosing from the people **A–D** for questions (**a–j**).

Answers

a	C,	e	A,	i	B,
b	A,	f	D,	j	D
c	C,	g	D,		
d	C,	h	B,		

6 Alone

This is a writing activity to finish off the unit. Using the previous text as a model, students choose their own social medium and write about 150 words explaining why it is their favourite.

Reflection

Use the **Reflection** to remind students of what they have achieved in the unit. Students should set themselves a **personal goal** based on their scores for Unit 16.

Exam focus

Reading, Exercise 2, multiple matching

Answers

a A, **b** C, **c** D, **d** B, **e** C,

f C, **g** B, **h** C, **i** D, **j** B

NOTE on Assessment Objectives (AOs) for Reading and Writing Exercise 3 (note-making): Students need to demonstrate that they can make brief notes under supplied headings relating to an article/text (for example: from a newspaper or magazine) printed in the question paper. Specifically, students need to identify and select relevant information (R1), understand ideas, opinions and attitudes (R2) and show understanding of the connections between ideas, opinions and attitudes (R3).

NOTE on Assessment Objectives (AOs) for Reading and Writing Exercise 4 (summary writing): Students need to write an 80 (Core) or 100 (Extended) word summary about an aspect or aspects of a text printed in the question paper. To do this effectively, students need to identify and select relevant information (R1), understand ideas, opinions and attitudes (R2) and show understanding of the connections between ideas, opinions and attitudes (R3).

Furthermore, students need to communicate information/ideas/opinions clearly, accurately and effectively (W1), organise ideas into coherent paragraphs using a range of appropriate linking devices (W2), use a range of grammatical structures and vocabulary accurately and effectively (W3) and show control of punctuation and spelling (W4).

Learning objectives (LOs)

Suggested activity: Start the unit by focusing for a few minutes on the LOs box, making sure that students understand what they are going to be doing. Using the first LO as an example, ask students to identify where in the unit they can find the activities for the other four LOs. Get students to say which of the activities appeal to them the most, and ask them for their reasons.

A Watch, listen and talk

1 Whole class, then alone

Explain that students are going to watch and listen to some IGCSE students talking about **pollution** and the **environment**. As your students watch and listen, they should make a note of **a** what the speakers think are the main causes of pollution, and **b** what the speakers say about the measures being taken in their own country to reduce or control pollution and protect the environment, and how successful these are. Play the video a second time so that students can check or add to their notes.

Answers

a What students think are the main causes of pollution, any **three** from: fossil fuels, burning rubbish, lack of government funding, emissions from factories.

b The measures being taken in their own countries to reduce pollution and protect the environment: government asks factories to stop emissions for periods of time, none – it is not a priority for the government.

2 Pairs or small groups

Depending on the size of your class, put students into pairs or small groups. They can discuss their notes and then talk to each other about pollution in their country, what is being done to reduce or control it and how successful these measures are. Do not interfere too much, but make sure you get feedback from the class so that they know their efforts have been worthwhile. If time permits, you could write their ideas on the board and rank them according to your students' preferences.

B Speaking and vocabulary

1 Pairs, then whole class

In pairs, students look at the five pictures and work through questions **a–e**. There are no right or wrong answers so allow students to discuss freely without too much interference. You may decide to limit the time spent on each question so that students remain focused. During class feedback, students can compare their ideas.

LANGUAGE TIP

The **Language Tip** focuses on commonly confused phrases which we use when describing someone, something or somewhere. Students will need to use these phrases for Activity B1f and other activities in the unit. Go through the information with your students and refer them to the exercise in the **Workbook**.

Students now describe the five pictures in more detail, but this time making sure that they use the phrases from the Language Tip, as well as their words from Activity B1a. Make sure you allow time for students to share their ideas, and check for accuracy when using the introductory phrases.

2 Pairs

a Students work with a partner and decide if the names in the box refer to a continent, a country or region, or something else.

Answers

the Arctic = region, the Atlantic Ocean and the Pacific Ocean = areas of water, Europe = continent, Canada = country, Russia = country, Asia = continent, North America = continent

b Use a map for students to identify where the eight places are located. If you have a projector and a screen, you could use this and select students to come to the screen and point to or stick labels on the various places.

c–f Students discuss these questions in their pairs and then share their ideas with the whole class.

C Reading and writing

1 Whole class, then pairs

The newspaper article students are going to read is about a system used in Indonesia for recycling waste. Before anything else, check that students know where Indonesia is (you could ask them to show you on a map), and ask them what type of waste they think might be recycled there. Then in pairs students check the meaning of the words and phrases from the article. If time is short, you could supply possible definitions for students to match.

Suggested answers

shape the mindset = develop or change someone's opinion,
beverage = drink,
biodegradable = able to decay naturally,
consensus = agreement,
a cooperative = a company owned by the people who work in it,
discarded = thrown away,
brooches = pieces of jewellery usually pinned to clothing,
fertiliser and compost = substances used to help plants grow well,
gather = collect,
inorganic = without living material,
a glimpse of = a quick idea about something

2 Alone, then pairs

Based on the words and phrases, students consider what they are likely to read about in the text and make a list of two or three things. They then share their ideas and see if they agree.

3 Pairs

Students look at the five possible headlines for the newspaper article, checking that they understand what they mean. Then they quickly look through the text and select the most appropriate heading. Tell them not to worry about the gaps (**a–k**) and the words in boxes.

Answer

The original article was called *Earning from Waste*, so **b** *Earning Money from Waste* is the best answer. However, if students can make a good case for one of the other headlines, you should accept this.

4 Alone, then pairs

Students read the text again, completing the gaps (**a–k**) with the words and phrases from C1. Give them some time to check with a partner before you do feedback.

Answers

a	a glimpse of,	**g**	consensus,
b	a cooperative,	**h**	beverage,
c	inorganic,	**i**	Discarded,
d	gather,	**j**	brooches,
e	biodegradable,	**k**	shape the mindset
f	fertiliser and compost,		

5 Pairs

Working in pairs, students look at the exam-style question and discuss what they have to do. They do not need to write anything yet.

6 Pairs

This activity will give students a clearer understanding of the content of each of the five paragraphs in the newspaper article. There are six possible topics, which students need to match to the five paragraphs (there is one extra topic which they do not need).

Answers

a Changing attitudes [Paragraph 5],
b Handicraft products [3],
c How the BSM operates [1],
d Paying bills [not needed],
e Sorting, collection and delivery of waste [2],
f Selling products online [4]

7 Alone, then pairs

Students work alone to re-read the text in detail, and write two to three notes about each topic. Go through

117

the example in the Coursebook first. When students have finished their notes they can compare with their partner's. Do class feedback to check if everyone agrees.

Possible answers

1 How the BSM operates: *trash packed into bags and sacks, taken to be weighed, BSM cooperative is centre for trash collection and management*

2 Sorting, collection and delivery of waste: *organic and inorganic rubbish separated, organic recycled as fertiliser and compost, inorganic is non-biological, separated trash is weighed and then more sorting and packing, information sent to trash bank for payment*

3 Handicraft products: *umbrellas, handbags, hats, tissue holders, brooches*

4 Selling products online: *BSM provides advice on selling online*

5 Changing attitudes: *people's attitudes about waste changing, more people aware of careless dumping of waste*

8 Pairs

Students decide which of their notes from C7 they could use to answer the exam-style question in C5.

> **TOP TIP**
>
> While it may seem obvious, the number of bullet points tells students how many notes they need to write. There is one mark available for each note they write, so trying to write more information will not result in students' obtaining any extra marks!

9 Pairs

Students look at the sample answer in which a student has mixed up their notes under the wrong headings. Working together, students decide under which heading each note should appear, and give their reasons.

Answers

What happens after trash collection

• trash taken for sorting and packing

• trash weighed

• information sent to trash bank

Products made from recycled trash

• plastic sheets for making handicrafts

• everyday products such as umbrellas and hats

• jewellery: brooches

How BSM helps its members

• payments made

• assists with savings

• gives training

• advice on how to sell products

> **TOP TIP**
>
> Remind students that notes should always be brief and must relate to the text they have read. In other words, they cannot include their own ideas or information that does not appear in the text.

D Language focus: referring words

1 Whole class

Go through the information together with your students, pointing out that the phrases in red and green show how connections are made within a text using referring words and phrases.

2 Pairs

Students go back to the text and look at the boxed words in paragraphs 2–5. For each boxed word or words, students need to say which word or words it is referring back to. If you are short of time, you could allocate the four paragraphs to different pairs or groups of students to work on, and then allow some time for them to share their answers.

Answers

[2] The members of the BSM cooperative are from community units and school groups, as well as individuals[1], who (d) ___ and sort trash from their[1] homes and workplaces, separating organic[2] and inorganic[3] rubbish. The former[2] is (e) ___ and can be processed in the presence of oxygen, and can be recycled as (f) ___ later on, while the latter[3] is any waste of non-biological origin, of industrial origin or some another non-natural process, for example: plastics and synthetic fabrics. Group members[4] take their[4] separated trash for weighing to a local leader, while individual members[5] send their[5] trash directly to the central BSM location. Trash delivery time is based on a (g) ___ for groups, and once a month for individuals. The trash[6] is collected by dump trucks and taken for further sorting, packing and weighing by warehouse workers, and information is then sent to

the trash bank where calculations are made about its[6] value, and payments are made to individuals' or groups' bank accounts. Members[7] who strictly sort their[7] rubbish according to the 70 categories for inorganic trash can earn a lot more money, and information is readily available for them[7] on how to do this.

[3]   Used plastic[8] (h) ___ bottles[8] are directly processed into plastic chips after being separated from their[8] labels and caps and grouped by colour. (i) ___ plastic bags, paper, iron and bottle caps are packed and sent to factories in Malang and Subabaya, where some of what was once seen as trash will return to the central BSM in the form of plastic sheets for making handicrafts. Plastic packaging for food, soap, detergent, shampoo and coffee, among others, is also recycled into various everyday products, including umbrellas, handbags, hats, tissue holders and jewellery such as (j) ___.

[4]   As a BSM member, each person[9] receives training and learns skills in how to make handicrafts using recycled materials. They[9] are also advised about how to sell their[9] products online. Not all of the money earned through the trash bank can be distributed freely, especially for group members, as some of the earnings are spent on environmental development, such as a park construction or tree planting. Additionally, BSM assists members[10] with their[10] savings which can be exchanged for basic necessities, electricity bill payments and health insurance.

[5]   So far, only inorganic waste is handled by the BSM, leaving wet garbage to the Supit Urang landfill as the trash bank's land area is too small for a worm-breeding and compost-making site. However, BSM[11] feels it[11] has provided a solution for the problem of inorganic waste, and believes that its[11] efforts will gradually (k) ___ of locals[12] so that they[12] avoid carelessly and unnecessarily dumping waste.

E Speaking and vocabulary

1 Pairs

Students work together and, after reading the four phrases, they should decide what they think the text will be about. Give them freedom to speculate – they will find out when they read the text.

2 Pairs, then whole class

Based on their ideas from Activity E1, students make a list of words and phrases that they think might appear in the

text. Allow time for the whole class to share and compare their ideas.

3 Small groups

The words and phrases in the box all appear in the text. Students can use different reference sources to check the meanings if they cannot agree.

F Reading and writing

1 Alone

Students work alone and skim read the text, checking if their predictions in Activities E1 and E2 were correct. Tell them not to worry about the gaps in the text at this stage.

2 Alone, then pairs

For this activity students need to read the text in more detail, and complete gaps **a–e** with the correct word from the list. When they have finished they should check with their partner.

Answers

a	It,	**c**	Many,	**e**	its,
b	their,	**d**	they		

WORD TIP

These two words, *effect* and *affect*, are commonly misused, misspelled and even mispronounced. Go through the information and then refer students to the exercise in the **Workbook**.

3 Alone, then pairs

Students work alone and look at gaps **f–j** in the text. For each gap, they need to supply a suitable referring word. When they are ready, they should check their answers together.

Answers

f	their,	**h**	this,	**j**	we
g	its,	**i**	our,		

4 Alone, then pairs

Students write the answers to the questions. Before they begin, remind them to find the key word/s in each question and to think about the type of answer each question requires. After they have finished, students can give their answers to a partner for checking.

Answers

a   they are already suffering from the impact of climate change

b   because it affects our daily lives

c   [Students' own answers]

d   mild winters stop them migrating to warmer climates

e   because they are low-lying

f   significant snow loss, greater chance of avalanches

g   the areas most likely to be fully flooded by 2080 due to rising sea levels

h   due to combination of geographical and economic factors

i   EU will adopt ambitious targets for reducing carbon emissions

j   damage to societies, the environment, future prosperity

5 Pairs

Students read the exam-style question carefully and decide exactly what they have to do. Make sure they are aware that the summary is about *the impact of climate change in Europe*. Also, check the number of words required (100) and point out that students should use their own words as far as possible, as marks are awarded for language (up to 8) as well as content (up to 8).

6 Alone, then pairs

Students now re-read the text and locate the relevant information. There is some in paragraphs 1 and 6, but the main information students need to use can be found in paragraphs 2, 3, 4 and 5.

Answers

Their brief notes should include the following:

*   countries in Europe being affected by climate change, environments and economies at risk

*   Lithuania – birds dying because not migrating due to mild winters/warm weather

*   low-lying areas, Nordic Europe at risk of flooding

*   North Sea countries also at risk of flooding

*   50% of Danes worried about safety of their homes

*   ski tourism industry in French Alps and Pyrenees depressed, snow loss and more possibility of avalanches

*   some ski resorts may shut down

7 Alone, then pairs

Students should now be well prepared to write their summary. They should use the notes they have just written and can refer back to the text if necessary. Remind students that they need to check the accuracy of their language, as well as the content. When they have finished, students exchange their summaries and check each other's answers.

> **TOP TIP**
>
> The **Top Tip** reminds students that summary questions usually direct students to a specific part or parts of a text to summarise.

G Speaking

1 Small groups, then whole class

This activity asks students to discuss the topic of water in some detail, and questions **a**–**f** are designed to support them through the discussion. Briefly run through the questions, helping with any difficult vocabulary and making sure students know what they have to do at each stage. When they have finished their group discussions (allow plenty of time for this), open up the discussion to the whole class, making sure each group gets a chance to contribute. Your role is to monitor and not to interfere unless students specifically ask for your help. Be ready to provide positive feedback, as well as to comment on any language areas that you feel need attention.

Reflection

Use the **Reflection** to remind students of what they have achieved in the unit. Students should set themselves a **personal goal** based on their scores for Unit 17.

Exam focus

Reading and Writing, Exercise 3, note-making and Exercise 4, summary writing

1 Sample answer

i   Core

Results of hyponatraemia

- apathy and lethargy

- nausea

- dizziness and mental confusion

- lapse into coma and die

Advice about drinking water

- cut back how much water you drink

- prolonged drinking without ingesting salts

- drinking excessive water without eating

People at risk

- people who exercise for prolonged time

- very young or very old

- heat and humidity increase susceptibility

2 Here are two sample summary writing answers from **i** an **IGCSE Core** student, and **ii** an **IGCSE Extended** student. Both answers would probably score in the top band for both content and language.

i   Core

The report says how extreme weather is becoming normal across Europe. The report has a region-by-region analysis, showing how it affects each country. It explains how the developing world still remains the most vulnerable to climate changes. Europe must play a part in the discussion as the impact of it is already here. The EU released its targets for climate change for 2030 which recommends, a reduction by 45%. Lastly, the report says how important it is for Europe to meet targets as the damage to the planet is going to get worse if no measures are taken. [98 words]

ii   Extended

A study carried out by the Climate Action Network campaign group reveals the effects that climate change is already having on Europe. An analysis of each region in different countries of Europe showed the impact that the warmer weather is having across the continent. Also, not only are climates affected, but many geographical and economic factors as well. Wendel Trio, director of CAN Europe believes that the European Union can create targets in order to reduce the effects of emissions. Furthermore, he thinks we need to focus on helping the climate from within Europe. Europe can be the one to set an example and take on more targets for the reductions of greenhouse gas emissions by 2020. [117 words]

Focus on writing

NOTE on Assessment Objectives (AOs) for Reading and Writing Exercise 6: Students need to demonstrate that they can write a report, a review or an article in response to a short stimulus. This may take the form of pictures and/or short prompts. The question includes information on the purpose, format and audience, as well as the word count and how the marks are allocated.

Specifically, students need to show that they can communicate information/ideas/opinions clearly, accurately and effectively (W1), organise ideas into coherent paragraphs using a range of appropriate linking devices (W2), use a range of grammatical structures and vocabulary accurately and effectively (W3), show control of punctuation and spelling (W4) and use appropriate register and style/format for the given purpose and audience (W5).

Learning objectives (LOs)

Suggested activity: Start the unit by focusing for a few minutes on the LOs box, making sure that students understand what they are going to be doing. Using the first LO as an example, ask students to identify where in the unit they can find the activities for the other four LOs. Get students to say which of the activities appeal to them the most, and ask them for their reasons.

A Watch, listen and talk

1 Whole class, then alone

Explain that students are going to watch and listen to some IGCSE students talking about **hunger**. As your students watch and listen, they should make a note of **a** what the speakers think are the main causes of global hunger, and **b** what opinions the students have about global hunger. Play the video a second time so that students can check or add to their notes.

Answers

a The main causes of global hunger, any **three** from: funding from developed countries to poorer ones, the country doesn't have enough natural resources to feed the population, soil erosion, the government is not helping.

b What opinions do they have about global hunger: it's a serious problem, it's unfair, we should help people that we see in need, governments should get more involved.

2 Pairs or small groups

Depending on the size of your class, put students into pairs or small groups. They can discuss their notes and then talk to each other about whether they agree with what the students say. Do not interfere too much, but make sure you get feedback from the class so that they know their efforts have been worthwhile. If time permits, you could write their ideas on the board and rank them according to your students' preferences.

B Speaking and vocabulary

1 Small groups, then whole class

Quickly check that students know some chewing gum-related words and phrases, for example *chew, stick, piece/stick/packet of gum, make a mess*, then put them in small groups to discuss questions **a–g**. Set a time limit for each question to keep students focused and to avoid time-wasting. Students can compare their ideas during class feedback.

2 Small groups

There is some challenging vocabulary in these statements, so make sure students understand everything before doing the task.

Differentiated activities

Support

i Provide definitions for some of the more challenging vocabulary, such as *consumption, ingredients*.

ii Divide the information between students so the amount of information they need to work with is reduced.

Challenge

i Remove the dates and numbers from a, b, c, d and f. Then give students the dates and numbers and they decide which one completes the information.

ii When you allocate students to groups, challenge one student by asking them to teach and guide the others.

3 Small groups, then whole class

Students continue in their groups and discuss questions **a–d**. Give them the freedom to express themselves – monitor but do not interfere. Make sure you give positive class feedback when the group discussions are over.

4 Whole class

Ask students if they think chewing gum can be classified as a food, and get their reasons. They may, for example, say that it is not a food because it does not contain anything healthy, but accept all their reasons without criticism.

5 Whole class, then small groups – Optional

The graph shows the daily percentage confectionery intake of teenagers in Asia. Focus on the graph first and check students understand the information it is showing. Students refer to the graph and discuss the points in the task.

6/7 Alone, then pairs

Students use the information from this section to write a 'fact file' about chewing gum. They do not need to include all the information, only facts that they feel are important or particularly interesting. Make sure they do not exceed the 100-word limit (some students may want to write more). When they have finished, students exchange their writing and see if they included the same or different information as others in their class.

C Listening

1 Pairs

Prepare students for the listening activity by checking that they understand who (a dental expert: Dr Bealing, and Thomas) and what (an interview about chewing gum) they are going to listen to. Before students listen they work in pairs and decide on the meaning of six words and phrases.

Answers

bark = the hard outer covering of a tree;
mastic = another word for gum;
nicotine = poisonous chemical in tobacco;
hit = sensation;
saliva = liquid produced in the mouth to keep it wet;
stave off = stop something from happening;
hunger = the feeling when you need to eat;
weight gain = increase how much someone weighs;
cognitive = connected with thinking;
function = the purpose of something

2 Alone, then pairs

Students listen and answer questions **a** and **b**, then check with their partner.

CD2, Track 9

Thomas Sampson: Welcome to our weekly programme on health issues for young people. Today I have with me in the studio Dr Maria Bealing, a dental expert. Hello, Dr Bealing.

Dr Bealing: Hello, Thomas, and thank you for inviting me.

TS: Dr Bealing, people have been chewing gum since the ancient Greeks used the bark from mastic trees as a breath freshener. And today, gum is chewed for many more reasons, such as when we feel hungry, or to get a nicotine hit if you're trying to give up cigarettes. But is chewing a stick of gum actually harmful to the body?

DB: Well, the moment a person unwraps a piece of gum and tosses it into their mouth, the brain is alerted that the digestive process is about to begin, and bells start ringing up there! During what's called the cephalic stage …

TS: Sorry, the what?

DB: The cephalic stage … c-e-p-h-a-l-i-c … this is when the body anticipates the arrival of food and …

TS: Sorry to interrupt again but how does the brain know that food is on its way?

DB: Through the senses: we either see the food, in a cupboard or in the supermarket fridge, or smell it in a restaurant, or hear someone chopping it up in the kitchen, or hear a gum wrapper being opened, and so on.

TS: OK, I understand.

DB: And then the brain releases saliva to help us chew whatever is coming.

TS: That's why we use the expression 'mouth-watering'? It means that our saliva, the juices in our mouth, is ready to receive food?

DB: Exactly. And this gets our stomach juices excited too. But because no real substance is ever delivered, some people argue that gum chewing tricks the brain, which upsets the stomach.

TS: I've heard that people can lose weight through gum chewing. Is that correct?

DB: Scientific studies haven't successfully proven that gum can stave off hunger and lead to weight loss. Chewing gum jump-starts the digestive process and so it may, in fact, increase hunger, and this may, in turn, lead to weight gain.

TS: So are there any benefits in gum chewing?

DB: Well, researchers have found a benefit. Recent studies have shown that chewing gum during a task can increase cognitive function. In other words, chewing while doing can help some people concentrate.

TS: I must admit that I'm a bit of a gum-chewer, so should I stop, or can I carry on?

123

DB: My advice, if you really want to chew, is to try sugarless gum, but only after a meal. The saliva it helps to produce will clean your teeth and the minty or fruity flavour of the gum will sweeten your breath and possibly satisfy a sweet tooth.

TS: Thank you, doctor, that sounds very sensible to me!

Answer (b)

if you really want to chew, try sugarless gum, but only after a meal

3/4 Alone, then pairs

Go through the notes with your students, checking that they understand everything and reminding them that they can only write one or two words in each gap. Some students may be able to remember some information from the first listening. Students listen and complete the notes, then work with a partner to check their answers. They can refer to the audioscript in Appendix 3.

Answers

a Ancient Greeks chewed bark as **breath freshener**.

b Someone trying to give up smoking may need a **nicotine** hit.

c Chewing gum alerts the brain that digestive process is starting.

d In the cephalic stage the body gets ready for arrival of **food**.

e Brain uses senses to see, smell or **hear** food.

f **Saliva** released to prepare mouth for chewing and **stomach juices** also prepare to receive food.

g No proof that gum chewing helps to **lose weight**.

h One benefit: chewing can increase **cognitive function**, the ability to concentrate during a **task**.

5 Whole class

Ask students to refer back to question B1c: *Do you think chewing gum is good for you? Why/not?* Has their opinion changed in any way, and why?

WORD TIP

Breath and *breathe* are commonly confused terms. Give students some examples to compare, such as:
A breath of fresh air (noun)
The air that we breathe (verb)
Refer them to the **Workbook** for further practice.

D Reading

1 Pairs, then whole class

In the listening text students heard Dr Bealing say that *'scientific studies haven't successfully proven that gum can stave off hunger'*. Now students talk about what **they** do when they feel hungry. Give them a couple of minutes to discuss and then do whole class feedback to find out what everyone does.

2 Pairs

Students look at the introductory paragraph and match the underlined words with the correct definition (**a–g**).

Answers

a crop

b dynamic

c alleviating

d starvation

e biotechnology

f innovative

g invent

3 Alone, then pairs

Students work alone to complete the gaps in the table and then share their answers.

Answers

Noun	Verb	Adjective
alleviation	*alleviate*	alleviated/alleviating
innovation/innovator	innovate	*innovative*
invention/inventor	*invent*	inventive
starvation	starve	starving

4 Whole class, then pairs

Check that students understand the underlying idea in the question, i.e. that it might be possible to invent something (a machine?) which could produce enough food so that starvation would no longer be a problem. Then in pairs students discuss this and give their reasons in feedback.

5 Pairs

Students look at the eight ideas and discuss which six they think will appear in the text. When they are ready, give them the answers because in the next exercise they need to complete the gaps in the text using the six correct ideas.

Answers

d and **f** do not appear in the text

6 Alone, then pairs

Students quickly read the text and complete the gaps in each paragraph using the ideas from D5.

Answers
Paragraph **1** g, **2** b, **3** a, **4** h, **5** e, **6** c

7 Pairs or groups of three
Now students need to read the text in more detail to answer the questions about the content of each of the six paragraphs. Put students into pairs or groups of three and allocate three/two sets of questions to each student to answer. When they have found the answers, they can discuss and share these with each other.

Answers

a   i   get = obtain,

     ii   production = creation,

     iii   eat = consume,

     iv   world = global

b

Noun	Verb	Adjective
population	populate	populated
revolution	revolt	revolutionary
introduction	introduce	introductory
irrigation	irrigate	irrigated
billion	X	X

c   i   assumed = thought,

     ii   conquered = beaten,

     iii   aid = help,

     iv   spike = peak

d   Various possible answers

e   Various possible answers

f   i   it has helped to produce vast quantities of biotech seeds in 30 countries during the past 20 years

     ii   less fuel is needed, lower levels of soil pollution

E Writing

TOP TIP
The **Top Tip** refers to opinion-writing questions and shows students that they will usually be given some prompts – either as pictures or a list of ideas – as a way of helping them.

1 Pairs, then whole class
Students read the exam-style question carefully and decide exactly what they have to do. Make sure they are aware that they do not have to use the ideas given, and they should include some of their own ideas (as long as they stick to the topic). When students have discussed questions **a–c**, do class feedback to check that everyone understands how to approach this type of writing question.

2 Pairs
Students look at the choices given for introductory sentences, then decide which they think are the most and least effective, and why.

Suggested answer
b is probably the most effective introduction as it restates information from the question. **a** and **c** are not effective introductory sentences as they are both too general and off-topic.

3 Whole class, then alone
Students now think of **at least two** ideas to follow on from the introductory sentence: *The visit to the biotechnology laboratory provided us with an enormous amount of information about scientific food production.* Do this orally first with the whole class to help them generate some ideas, and encourage them to use their notes and ideas from previous activities. Then students do their writing – there are many possible answers.

Possible answer
The visit to the biotechnology laboratory provided us with an enormous amount of information about scientific food production. Before the visit I did not like the idea of science producing food for us to eat, but now I've learned so much and I understand that science is the only solution to produce more food. [54 words]

TOP TIP
The **Top Tip** reminds students that an introduction should be brief and to the point, but at the same time it should capture the reader's attention.

4 Pairs
Students look at the choices given for concluding sentences, then decide which they think are the most and least effective, and why.

Suggested answer

a is probably the most effective conclusion as it clearly states the writer's opinion. **b** and **c** are not effective concluding sentences. **b** introduces a contrary view (On the other hand …) while **c** continues an argument (Another point …).

5 Whole class, then alone

Students now think of **at least two** ideas to follow on from the concluding sentence: *In conclusion, and taking into consideration all the different arguments, my firm belief is that we should thank science.* Do this orally first with the whole class to help them generate some ideas, and encourage them to use their notes and ideas from previous activities. Then students do their writing – there are many possible answers.

Possible answer

In conclusion, and taking into consideration all the different arguments, my firm belief is that we should thank science. Without it, the problem of starvation would be much bigger than it currently is, and we would not be in a position to solve the problem. [45 words]

> **TOP TIP**
> Remind students that it is an effective technique to restate their opinion in the conclusion.

6 Pairs

Working in pairs, students read their partner's two paragraphs and give each other feedback.

7 Alone

Now students need to complete the main part of their article. This is often referred to as the 'body'. Check with students about how many paragraphs they need to write. While there is no set number, they will probably need to write two or three more paragraphs, making four or five in total (including the introduction and conclusion).

> **LANGUAGE TIP**
> Remind students to use sequence/discourse markers in their writing, as this will make it feel more natural and fluent.

8 Whole class

Let students read as many as possible of their friends' articles, as they can learn a lot from each other. Do not focus on the 'best' piece of writing, as this can demotivate students who need more support in writing.

F Reading and speaking

1 Pairs, then whole class

Students work together to discuss questions **a–d**. You could ask them to write notes and discuss their ideas with other students during class feedback.

2 Whole class, then pairs

Quickly go through the list of food types, checking that students understand what each one is. Then, with a partner, students answer questions **a** and **b**. You can check their answers during class feedback.

3 Whole class, then pairs

There are six phrases from the text, which students need to match with three of the food types in Activity F2 (two phrases for each food type). Read through each phrase, checking for understanding, and then students in pairs discuss which phrase goes with which food type, giving their reasons. The answers are shown below, but do not give students these yet, as they will find out in the next activity.

Answers

a and **c** = sugar,   **b** and **e** = rice   **d** and **f** = fast food

4 Alone, then whole class

Students work on their own and read the text in order to complete the gaps using the phrases from Activity F3. They will also be able to check their answers to the previous activity. When students are ready, let them work with a partner to check their answers.

Answers

(a) c,   **(b)** a,   **(c)** d,   **(d)** f,   **(e)** b,   **(f)** e

5 Groups of three

Each student in a group chooses one of the three food types they have just been reading about: sugar, fast food and rice. They should research their chosen food type, using different reference sources. In the final part of the activity, they report back to the group and when all three group members have reported back, the group decides who found out the most interesting facts. You could then extend this to the whole class, if time permits.

6 Whole class

Round off the section with a whole class discussion, prompting students with the questions in F6.

G Language focus: word building

1 Pairs

Get students to produce a table, similar to the ones they have already seen in this unit, giving the different parts of speech for the *-ion* words. Then they share with their partner and check each other's answers.

Answers

Noun	Verb	Adjective
exploitation (thing)	exploit	exploited
exploiter (person)		
realisation	realise	X
creation (thing)	create	creative
creator (person)		

2a Alone, then pairs

Students work alone on task 2a, and then check with their partner.

Possible answers

growth = noun, grow = verb
requirement = noun, require = verb, required = adjective
ill = adjective, illness = noun
negation = noun, negate = verb, negative = adjective, negatively = adverb
plentiful = adjective, plentifully = adverb
wasteful = adjective, wastefully = adverb, waste = verb
entirety = noun, entire = adjective, entirely = adverb

2b Alone

For task 2b, students complete the gaps in sentences **i–viii** using words from the previous activity. Point out that the required part of speech is given in brackets at the end of each line.

Answers

i	grow,	v	waste,
ii	plentiful,	vi	illness,
iii	excess,	vii	entire,
iv	negative,	viii	requires

Differentiated activities

Support

i   Instead of students doing 2a, supply them with the answers and they can use these in order to complete 2b;

ii   Inform students which word to use in each gap (**i–viii**), and then they change it to the correct part of speech.

Challenge

i   Remove the part of speech information at the end of each line

ii   When students have written their answers for 2b, ask them to choose four of their words from 2a and write sentences which include the words.

3 Alone, then pairs

Students work alone to write their own sentences, using the words given (**a–e**). For each word they should write two sentences, with the second sentence using a different form (part of speech) of the word. To support students, reduce the number of sentences they need to write.

H Writing

1/2 Alone, then pairs

Give students some time to read the exam-style question carefully and to think about the important instructions that they must follow, for example *word length*, *report style*, *try to include own ideas*. This question asks students to write a *report*, whereas the previous one asked for an *article*.

3 Whole class

Talk through the information with your students, making it clear that there is not one particular type of report style that students have to learn and use. However, as it says in the Coursebook, there are some general sections that should be included in all reports.

Ask students to think about the general sections with you, but they do not need to write anything yet.

Possible answers

a   A suitable title might be: *How food products affect the environment*.

b   *The purpose of this report is to show how food production impacts on the environment*.

c   Probably three, for each of the prompts in the question.

d   *Reasons for carrying out the research, The most interesting information, Further action*.

4/5/6 Alone

Now students work alone and follow the guidance for writing their answer to the question. They should use the ideas they discussed with you in the previous activity as much as possible.

127

7 Alone

Advise students to count how many words they have written so far, and to calculate how many more they need to write. Remind them that the word limits are Core 100–150 and Extended 150–200.

8 Whole class, then alone

Give students some useful words and phrases to use in a conclusion: *in fact, in conclusion, for these reasons, as a result of, to sum up, overall, ultimately, consequently.* Then they work alone to write their concluding paragraph, basing it on the content of what they have written in the earlier paragraphs.

TOP TIP

The **Top Tip** stresses the importance of good planning as the basis for an effective answer to a writing question.

Reflection

Use the **Reflection** to remind students of what they have achieved in the unit. Students should set themselves a **personal goal** based on their scores for Unit 18.

Exam focus

Writing, Exercise 6

i   Core

Scientific research now plays an important role in making sure that humanity has enough food to eat and that many of the crops that are now grown worldwide are resistant to many diseases, creating more produce at a cheaper price.

Lower costs and more food seem like a great idea but many scientists still debate about whether or not food that has been scientifically researched and genetically modified is safe to eat.

I personally understand the importance of scientific research and how science can help many people worldwide but I do not feel safe consuming such products. I believe science should not meddle with nature. I do not think that science has yet reached a level where it can compete with nature.

Scientific research does help humanity with its research into disease and sickness but I would rather it stayed away from food that humans consume. [146 words]

ii   Extended

We live in a world of excess, where everything has to be bigger, more attractive and exist in large quantities. In developed countries, food is one of the main things that we have in excess, and scientific research is one of the main causes for this. Due to this, I believe that scientific research needs to take a step back from the food industry.

It has come to the point, that we have so much food, a huge percentage of it goes to waste and is thrown away. Moreover, this excessiveness in food has led to people being able to buy food whenever and from wherever they want, something that in recent years has led to a rise in obesity. Furthermore, as the food industry tries to keep up with the high demand for products, they are finding new and unnatural ways to make fruits, vegetables, grains, etc. grow faster. Chemicals are injected into the produce to make it bigger and more attractive.

For the above reasons, I believe we must control scientific research in the food industry and reduce the amount of food that is produced, in order to avoid further problems. [193 words]

NOTE on Assessment Objectives (AOs) for Listening: Students need to demonstrate that they can identify and select relevant information (L1), understand ideas, opinions and attitudes (L2), show understanding of the connections between ideas, opinions and attitudes (L3) and understand what is implied but not directly stated, e.g. gist, speaker's purpose, intention and feelings (L4).

Learning objectives (LOs)

Suggested activity: Start the unit by focusing for a few minutes on the LOs box, making sure that students understand what they are going to be doing. Using the first LO as an example, ask students to identify where in the unit they can find the activities for the other four LOs. Get students to say which of the activities appeal to them the most, and ask them for their reasons.

A Watch, listen and talk

1 Whole class, then alone

Explain that students are going to watch and listen to some IGCSE students talking about **fashions**. As your students watch and listen, they should make a note of **a** what the speakers think fashion means, and **b** if the speakers believe that fashion affects them in a positive or negative way, and their examples and reasons. Play the video a second time so that students can check or add to their notes.

Answers

a What does 'fashion' mean: trends, following celebrities, it's individual to a person.

b How fashion affects the students in a positive or negative way: It doesn't, because fashion is just about shoes.

   What examples and reasons do they give: the students have their own style that they're comfortable with; as long as you like [what you wear], it doesn't matter what other people think or what it costs.

2 Pairs or small groups

Depending on the size of your class, put students into pairs or small groups. They can discuss their notes and then talk to each other about what fashion means to them and what they consider fashionable. Do not interfere too much, but make sure you get feedback from the class so that they know their efforts have been worthwhile. If time permits, you could write their ideas on the board and rank them according to your students' preferences.

B Speaking and vocabulary

1/2 Pairs, then small groups

Activities B1 and B2 provide prompts for students to discuss various aspects of fashion. As this is the penultimate unit in the Coursebook, students should be in a strong position for their speaking assessment, with the language skills and vocabulary to carry out this discussion with confidence.

In the first activity, students work in pairs, using the four pictures and four statements to give them some initial ideas. For the second activity, change the interaction and put students into small groups. Obviously there are no right or wrong answers, and students should have the freedom to express their ideas without interruption. Monitor but do not interfere. Give support if necessary and offer positive feedback at the end.

Differentiated activities

Support

Reduce the number of questions that students need to answer and/or remove the need for them to provide reasons for every answer that they give.

Challenge

Tell students to prepare an oral summary of their discussions, which they can present to the rest of the class.

C Reading

1 Whole class, then pairs

Firstly, check what students think the phrases *fast fashion* and *ethical fashion* in the headline mean. Then in pairs they predict **three** things that they think they might find in the text, giving their reasons.

2 Groups of three – A/B/C

Put students into groups of three for this activity, with Student A in each group looking at phrases **a–c**, Student B looking at phrases **d–f**, and Student C looking at phrases **g–i**. As an alternative, you could have all the As working together, all the Bs and all the Cs, so that they can support each other while checking the meanings of their three phrases. Students can use different reference sources for help, and you can provide some vocabulary support if necessary. Students may recognise certain words, but in these particular phrases the words may have a different meaning, or some words may just be unfamiliar. For example:

a *crop* = group of people or things with something in common, **b** *rich* = containing a lot of something good or useful, **f** *tapping into* = getting or making use of something, **h** *drawn* = caused a reaction, **i** *weave* = to make cloth, *looms* = equipment for making cloth.

If you decided to put all the As together in one group (and the Bs and Cs in their own groups), once they have checked the meaning of their phrases, they can go back to their original A/B/C groups to share their answers.

3 Alone, then groups of three – A/B/C

Students quickly read the first two paragraphs and do three things (**a–c**) on their own. Then they discuss their answers in their group of three.

Answers for c
1   Made in Vietnam,
2   Tradition, tradition

4 Groups of three – A/B/C

Still working in their groups, students look at the phrases in the box and speculate about which ones they think they will read in the rest of the article, giving their reasons. You could turn this into a 'word auction', asking groups of students to 'bid' for particular phrases, using a points system. Allocate 100 points, or IGCSE dollars, or paper clips, to each group, and then ask students to 'bid' for any words or phrases in the box that they want. The highest bidding group 'wins' that particular phrase, and points (or IGCSE dollars or paper clips) are deducted from their total. You will need to pre-teach relevant vocabulary, for example: *bid, bidder, auction, auctioneer*. You do not need to reveal which phrases appear in the text yet, as students will find out in C6.

5 Alone, then pairs

Students now work alone and look at the words and phrases in either column A or B, using reference sources to find out what they mean. Then they share their answers.

6 Alone

Students read the text and check their answers, and find out if they bid for the correct phrases in C4.

Answers
a   All the phrases appear in the text, apart from: *London and Paris*, and *shirts and dresses*

> **WORD TIP**
>
> These two words may seem interchangeable, but *global* is an adjective, whereas *world* is a noun. Refer students to the exercise in the **Workbook**.

7 Alone, then pairs

Refer students back to the list of possible paragraph headings in C3 to choose suitable headings for paragraphs 3–5.

Answers
3   It's all about colour,
4   Natural is best,
5   Changing skills

8 Alone, then pairs

For the final activity in this section, students read the text in detail to find and write answers to questions **a–j**, and then share with a partner.

Answers
a   save the country's rich ethnic heritage
b   maximise benefit to and minimise environmental harm
c   he learns techniques from them
d   hand looms
e   in fashion capitals (like Berlin and New York)
f   they were shocked
g   they are made with natural dyes and textiles
h   money
i   it is helping them to market their skills
j   Various answers possible: financial knowledge, managing people, marketing, etc.

> **TOP TIP**
>
> Questions which require students to identify people's feelings and attitudes, or to 'read between the lines' (to *infer*), can be quite challenging for some students. Question C8j is an example of where the answer is not actually in the text.

D Speaking and listening

1 Pairs

Students look at phrases **a–h** and speculate about which ones might appear in a discussion about fashion. Make sure they offer reasons for their decisions.

2 Pairs

Now students try to match the six pictures with the words and phrases from Activity D1. It does not matter if they are not sure, and there are no right or wrong answers, but encourage them to speculate and give reasons for their ideas.

3 Pairs

Once again, students need to speculate about which person from Activity D2 may have said each of the six comments. Giving logical, supporting reasons is far more important than anything else in this activity. Point out that there is one extra comment which students do not need to use (**g**).

4 A/B pairs

Students work in A/B pairs. Firstly, each student chooses three different people from the six in the previous activities, and then on their own writes down **two** words or phrases that they believe each person might think or say. This will give a total of six words or phrases. Then, in 4b, Students A/B take it in turns to read out their words and phrases for each person, with the other student guessing and giving reasons.

5 Pairs

Students need to read the exam-style question carefully and then answer the questions (**a–g**) with their partner.

Answers

a	six,	**d**	in the boxes,	**g**	six
b	fashion,	**e**	once,		
c	seven,	**f**	nothing,		

6 Alone, then pairs

Now students listen and answer the exam-style question. They can then check with a partner and refer to the audioscript in Appendix 3 for anything they are not sure about.

Answers

1a, 2f, 3e, 4c, 5b, 6d

CD2, Track 10

Speaker 1 male teenager

I've never been a really big fan of current fashion trends. Money of course is an obstacle for someone like me, so even if I want to be fashionable, I can't necessarily pay the prices that are demanded. So I think we should just wear what we feel happy in, and not worry so much about having all the latest gear. In any case, something fashionable today is out of fashion tomorrow, and clothes from the past often become popular again. Who can keep up with it?

Speaker 2 female young adult

For me the word fashion is a nightmare word! It makes me think of so many negative things. The way fashion controls people's lives is awful, and of course nowadays fashion is not just about clothes, but about the latest Ferrari or Lamborghini and watches and restaurants and even pets and the latest pair of trainers! People who only care about how much something costs, and how good they look, rather than anything else in life, are not in my circle of friends.

Speaker 3 male young adult

I don't understand all the negativity about trying to be fashionable. What's wrong with wanting to look and feel and smell great? Of course you need money, but tell me something that doesn't need money in today's world. I'm still studying right now and don't have a job yet and not much money, so I'm not in a position to buy the latest sunglasses and all the other things that I want. But as soon as I get my first wages after a couple of years, I'm going straight to the shopping mall!

Speaker 4 female adult

Something I learned at art college was that fashion is an incredibly complex subject, which is very difficult to define and really understand. Of course fashion has different meanings for different people, but fashion ultimately is a joining of not just art but also building design and engineering and even in many cases science and having an understanding of how the world works. Now in my job

I'm seeing that anything can be fashionable: it depends on how people view whatever it might be.

Speaker 5 male young adult

Fashion is not an option for me, it's an absolute must, and being 'in' is probably the most important thing that I think about every day. I don't care about the cost – I will find a way to buy whatever it is that I need in order to look my best. Cars and watches and trendy restaurants and furniture do nothing for me, but clothes and hair styles are the things that drive me every day. Work is great, but how I look and feel come first.

Speaker 6 female adult

Personally I have no interest whatsoever in fashion and alternative styles of clothes and so on. But my kids do and their demands can be very difficult to deal with, from the financial side. It's so difficult to say no when children ask for something that all their friends have or are wearing. Obviously there has to be a limit, but big businesses and advertisers are incredibly clever at making people and especially children feel inferior if we don't have something that others do.

E Listening

1 Pairs

Working with a partner, students discuss questions **a–c**. If necessary, for **a**, prompt them with some pictures of people wearing uniforms, or refer them back to the pictures of people in Unit 7 Jobs to give them some ideas. For **b** and **c**, encourage students to discuss freely as there are no right or wrong answers.

2 Pairs, then whole class

Either have all the pairs working on all the words and phrases, or distribute them randomly to different pairs. Students can use different reference sources for help. As students will need all the words and phrases for E3, make sure that you do whole class feedback so that everyone understands everything.

3 Alone, then pairs

Now students complete the phrases (**a–h**) from the talk they are going to hear using the vocabulary from E2. Then before they listen in E4, let them share and compare their answers. There is no need to confirm anything yet, as in the next activity they are going to listen to the talk about school uniforms.

4 Alone

Students listen to the talk and check their answers.

Answers

i   an atmosphere of pride, loyalty and equality,

ii   distractions,

iii   sweeping the nation,

iv   erase their individuality,

v   the latest peer-pleasing designs,

vi   merchandise,

vii avoid ridicule, embarrassment or abuse,

viii confrontation,

ix   mandatory

CD2, Track 11

The introduction of school uniforms in state schools is not a new subject. Schools have a long history of using school uniforms to create an atmosphere of pride, loyalty and equality among the student population. There has always been an image of professionalism associated with having students wear a uniform. It provides for a more businesslike approach to learning, removing some of the distractions normally encountered when children feel that they should possess the latest designer fashions, or follow the latest trend sweeping the nation at any given time.

School uniforms also tend to involve students more and make them part of a 'team' at the school. This is not so as to erase their individuality, but to include everyone on the same level, as far as image and dress are concerned.

Another important factor in the use of school uniforms has been cost. With fashions constantly changing from year to year, and even from season to season, parents have always felt the pressure from their children to provide them with the latest peer-pleasing designs. Uniforms reduce the cost of keeping up, since they remain the same – day after day, year after year. And their cost, in relation to fashion merchandise, is very appealing over the long term.

Wearing a uniform at school, as opposed to wearing the latest fashions, may also help the child avoid ridicule, embarrassment or abuse from others that can be caused when the 'have-nots' are compared with the 'haves'. Uniforms assist in avoiding such conflicts by removing the chance of confrontation over clothing, at least during the child's time at school.

The debate will continue. But more and more people in education – students, parents, teachers and administrators – are convinced that mandatory school uniforms lead to success. They point out that pupils in private schools, who achieve impressive academic results, have traditionally worn uniforms. As a result, most state schools have also adopted a school-uniform policy – and the trend seems set to continue.

5 Alone, then pairs

Students listen again and make a list of the reasons given to support wearing a school uniform. For example: *to create an atmosphere of pride, loyalty and equality among the student population.* After the second listening, give students some time to check their answers with a partner, and to refer to the audioscript in Appendix 3.

Answers

image of professionalism, more businesslike approach to learning, removing some of the distractions normally encountered when children feel that they should possess the latest designer fashions, tend to involve students more, make them part of a 'team' at the school, include everyone on the same level, uniforms reduce the cost of keeping up with fashions, wearing a uniform at school may also help the child avoid ridicule, embarrassment or abuse, uniforms assist by removing the chance of confrontation over clothing, private schools, who achieve impressive academic results, have traditionally worn uniforms.

6/7 Alone, then pairs

Before students listen, go through the task with them, highlighting that they can only write one or two words in each gap. Get students to give their ideas orally, and then play the audio. They can share with a partner and look at the audioscript in Appendix 3 to check their answers.

Answers

a   appearance
b   guidelines
c   acceptable
d   confrontation
e   badge

CD2, Track 12

Jan (teenage male): I don't have a problem wearing school uniform. At least when I can get home I can take it off and change into something more comfortable.

Cheryl (teenage female): Fair enough, but don't you think we look like penguins at school, everyone wearing the same clothes?

J: But that's the whole point, isn't it? 'Uniform' means the same, so at school there is no difference between us. Don't you know anyone whose parents can't afford to dress them in fashionable clothes at school? With school uniform, nobody has to worry if they look different.

C: But why should we be forced into wearing clothes that we don't like? Why don't they just give us some guidelines about what we can and can't wear? Wouldn't that be better? For example, no jeans, or everyone has to wear a white shirt or blouse?

J: Come on! You know as well as I do that everyone would soon find a way round the guidelines, and the teachers would find it impossible to know what is acceptable and what isn't.

C: Yes, I suppose you're right. On the other hand, if they treat us like penguins then they shouldn't be surprised if we behave like one! I think we're old enough to know what is acceptable and what isn't, in terms of school clothes.

J: Maybe, but that brings me back to my original point. What about those kids who are just going to show off in their new fashions, and the kids who can't really keep up? You know it will happen. Then we may get bullying and kids laughing at each other just because of their clothes.

C: Well, we certainly don't want any fights or confrontation over something like our clothes. Maybe the school should allow us to all vote and make a decision?

J: No way would we agree to wearing a uniform! But I would certainly vote for it. In any case, it makes me feel part of the school community, and I'm actually very proud of my school and my badge. Aren't you?

C: I guess so, but not wearing a uniform doesn't make me less proud than you, does it?

J: No, but we should feel proud to show off which school we go to, and one way to do that is by wearing a uniform. And another thing I've heard …

C: What's that?

J: Well, in schools where students have to wear a uniform, there's evidence that they achieve better academic standards!

C: Well, in that case …

F Language development: position of adjectives

1 Whole class

Look at the two example sentences and talk through questions **a–c** with the class.

Answers

a *different*, *hand-spun*

b the second (*hand-spun cotton*)

c the first (*they look different*)

Point out that adjectives usually appear before a noun, and in some cases after certain verbs: *be, seem, look, become, appear, sound, taste, feel, get.* Ask students what happens in their own language, and in any other languages they know.

2 Whole class, then alone

Go through the instructions with your students, checking that they understand what they need to do, and do the first part of the task (identifying the adjective in each phrase) together.

Answers

(adjectives underlined)

a <u>fermented indigo</u> leaves

b <u>contemporary</u> touch

c <u>traditional wooden</u> houses

d <u>complex</u> subject

e <u>alternative</u> styles of clothes

f <u>businesslike</u> approach

g <u>mandatory</u> school uniforms

h <u>fashionable</u> clothes

Possible answers for sentences

a The indigo-coloured leaves had been fermented.

b Her touch appeared contemporary.

c The houses were made in a traditional wooden style.

d The subject is getting complex.

e The styles of clothing appear more alternative.

f Their approach has become more businesslike.

g The wearing of school uniforms is mandatory.

h Those clothes look very fashionable.

G Speaking

1 Small groups

For this final activity, students discuss the question prompts (**a–g**) in small groups. To keep students on task, give a short time limit for each question. You might also think about allocating questions **a–e** to different groups of students. All the questions could also be used very effectively in a debate activity. As with all speaking activities, allow your students to speak freely and without interference from you, but always provide feedback at the end.

Reflection

Use the **Reflection** to remind students of what they have achieved in the unit. Students should set themselves a **personal goal** based on their scores for Unit 19.

Exam focus

Listening, Exercise 1, short extracts

CD2, Track 13

Question 1

V1 Good morning. May I help you?

V2 Yes, please. I need to buy this book for history at college.

V1 Do you want the book with or without the answer key?

V2 Well, the version without the answer key, please, as I think it'll be cheaper.

V1 Yes, it is cheaper. And we'll give you a free promotional history magazine with it as well.

V2 Ah, okay, thank you … and since we weren't told about the book with the answer key, I definitely won't take it, thank you.

Question 2

V1 Excuse me! I'm trying to find my way to the restaurant. Which floor is it on?

V2 Actually there are two in this store. It depends if you want to just have a coffee or sit and have a meal.

V1 Hmmm, I'm not sure. Maybe I should look for my friend in both.

V2 Well then, you need to go to the third floor if you arranged to eat a meal or on the ground floor for the café. The escalator is there on your left and you should find both of them without any problem.

Question 3

V1 Do you keep going to the same old places for coffee with your friends? Are you bored of the same old faces, the same old flavours of coffee? Yes? Then why not try 'Coffee Cup', a new place to go, with fresh new coffee flavours and a large outdoor seating area where you can relax with friends? Try our new promotional coffees with coffee beans from as far away as Jamaica and Cuba! The coffee beans are specially selected for you, because we know what you like best!

Question 4

OK children, listen to the schedule for today because we don't want any of you getting lost or being late like last time. The bus will be here in about 60 minutes to take us to the sports centre. When we get there you can choose your programme: either activities in the swimming pool or in the gym. But remember you're not allowed to play on the outdoor playing fields. We'll have about four hours at the gym with a break mid-way when we can go to the café for something to eat and drink. The bus to go back will be here at about two o'clock, just in time for your parents to meet you at school.

Answers

1a history
b **i** version without key,
   ii free history magazine
2a friend
b third and ground
3a fresh new flavours
b outdoor seating area
4a sports centre
b play outdoor fields

Listening, Exercise 2, note-making

Question 1

CD2, Track 14

Good morning, everyone. Today we're going to talk about one of my favourite topics: cats, or at least the domesticated cat, which is the one many of us have living in our homes and gardens. We now know that the domesticated cat has been part of human lives for about 12 000 years. Archaeologists found the skeleton of a cat on the eastern Mediterranean island of Cyprus in an area that is now named the Near East, but was formerly known as Mesopotamia. This particular cat had been deliberately buried alongside a human, most probably its owner, and would suggest that a special bond had existed between the human and the animal, many thousands of years ago.

Studies have shown that the domesticated cat descended from the African wildcat, and it shares its ancestry with lions and tigers from about 10–15 million years ago. These large cats in their turn have their ancestors from the region around west Asia.

Domesticated cats became an important addition to society when humans began to settle down, around 10 000 years ago, when more permanent living settlements were built. Because humans were not moving around so much, searching for food, crops like wheat and barley needed to be stored, and where there are crops, there are mice. So the cat became more of a friend when humans realised how the cat could control mice which were eating the crops.

The cat gradually became invaluable domestically due to its hunting skills, and since it was now living in close proximity with humans, it started adapting its characteristics to its new environment. It started to fit in: living with and appealing to humans, and so the process of domestication began.

One country where the cat has played a dominant role and where initially it was thought they originated from, is Egypt. But the domestic cat has actually only been part of Egyptian culture and tradition for the past 4,000 years or so. Egyptian culture was famous for its admiration of the cat through various humans during history commonly portrayed as a cat, or a woman with a cat's head. The word 'cat' itself comes originally from a North African word 'quattah'. This word was then adapted by most European countries in various different forms such as 'katze' in German, 'gato' in Spanish and of course 'cat' in English.

Today, not surprisingly, the cat is the most popular pet in the world for both men and women. Studies have shown that neither gender has a greater preference for cats. In the United States alone there are about 90 million domesticated cats and that accounts for 34 percent of Americans having a pet cat lying around somewhere in their home. The worldwide population of cats exceeds 500 million although unfortunately not all of them live the comfortable life of a pet. However, the cat has made a place for itself in our hearts.

Answers

a Talk about cats and how they became part of our lives. First domesticated cat found by archaeologists about **12 000** years ago. Lived on Mediterranean island of Cyprus. [1]

b Cat buried next to its **owner** in an area now known as the Near East although **formerly** named Mesopotamia. [½ + ½]

c Studies show domesticated cats **descended** from African wildcat. Ancestors were lions and tigers from about 10–15 million years ago. Originally from **west** Asia. [½ + ½]

d Domesticated cats settled down, around 10 000 years ago, when humans built **permanent** settlements, storing crops, for example: **wheat** and barley. [½ + ½]

e **Mice** attracted to these crops, so cats became important **friends** to humans. [½ + ½]

f Domestic cat only in Egyptian culture and **tradition** for around 4,000 years. The word 'cat' originally from North African word 'quattah'. **Adapted** by European countries, so 'katze' in German, 'gato' in Spanish and 'cat' in English. [½ + ½]

g Cat most **popular** pet in world with men and women. In the United States about 90 million domesticated cats and the **worldwide population** is more than 500 million. [½ + ½]

h Not all cats have **comfortable** lives as pets. [1]

Listening, Exercise 4, multiple-choice questions

Question 1

Answers

a	A		**e**	B
b	B		**f**	A
c	A		**g**	B
d	C		**h**	C

CD2, Track 15

Alfonso Fiore: Today I have the great honour of speaking to writer and fashion expert, Valentina Santini, winner of three World Fashion awards so far. Valentina has four homes, but we are meeting her in her home in Florence, the only one located in Europe, to find out what the word fashion means to her. Is it just the shoes and clothes that we see in magazines, or is it something else, something difficult to define? Judging by the look of your home, Valentina, you most definitely have an eye for everything that is tasteful and fashionable. It's a real pleasure to meet you!

Valentina Santini: The pleasure is all mine. I'm a great fan of your magazine, and of course your writing.

AF: Thank you! To begin with, can you explain to us what fashion actually means?

VS: Well, as someone once said: 'Fashion fades, only style remains the same.' I think the most important thing to remember when talking about fashion, whether you're referring to clothes, furniture, accessories or even food, is that it is constantly evolving and changing, just like the sea. This is how it differs to style, which is more personal, individual, more like a pond which doesn't move.

AF: So, when we use the word fashion, we don't just mean the clothes that start off on the runways of fashion houses and which eventually end up in clothes shops?

VS: Absolutely not. Of course, the fashion industry, as you yourself know, is massive, and the major sector is indeed the clothing industry. But we mustn't forget aspects of it such as makeup, hair trends and furniture, which are just as important.

AF: I see. Since we're talking about furniture, would you say that the pieces you currently have in your home are in fashion?

VS: As with clothes, there isn't just one or ten or even one hundred fashion styles for furniture, nor indeed for interior design in general. In fact, there are hundreds, going back thousands of years, and from all over the world. The list is endless! I would say this house is quite fashionable at the moment, and I feel very comfortable in my surroundings.

AF: I would expect that from a fashion expert such as yourself. Can you tell me a little about fashion and makeup?

VS: Social media is probably one of the main reasons that makeup today is so huge in our society. I mean, if you visit Pinterest, Instagram, YouTube, or any other social medium, you can find thousands of makeup tutorials, methods, makeup trends, and so on. It's come to the point where if you want to be fashionable, then you need to be able to keep up with this whole online bubble which is the fashion world.

AF: What would you say defines something as fashionable?

VS: As I said before, fashion is constantly changing. What makes it change are the great fashion houses whose job it is to design new and wonderful items. The reason that high-end fashion brands are the inspiration for the fashion world is not just because of the quality they offer and their celebrity status, but it's also because they are constantly raising the stakes. They are creating items that change every season, they *create* fashion, and everyone else just follows: celebrities, music and film stars. Everyone. For something to be considered 'fashionable' in today's society, it needs to follow the guidelines exhibited by these fashion houses.

AF: Do you agree with this? If that's the case, then we would be buying new furniture every few months just so we can consider ourselves to be in fashion.

VS: Perhaps that's a little extreme, but I have met people who do this. It's a vicious circle, I won't deny it, but it isn't all bad. In fact, I know for certain that the shirt you are currently wearing is from a very high-end and expensive fashion house!

AF: Guilty as charged!

VS: It's not a crime to love fashion, whether that love is for a pair of trainers or a designer sofa or a fast car. The best thing to remember is that if you love fashion, let it guide you, but not control you. A truly fashion-conscious person knows that you take fashion and you make it your own. In that way, it is *you* who defines fashion, and you don't let yourself be defined by it.

AF: I absolutely agree with you and really, it's been wonderful speaking to you, Valentina; a real eye-opener! Thank you so much for your time!

VS: It's my pleasure.

NOTE on Assessment Objectives (AOs) for Speaking:
In the Cambridge IGCSE speaking examination, students need to communicate ideas/opinions clearly, accurately and effectively (S1), develop responses and link ideas using a range of appropriate linking devices (S2), use a range of grammatical structures and vocabulary accurately and effectively (S3), show control of pronunciation and intonation patterns (S4) and engage in a conversation and contribute effectively to help move the conversation forward (S5).

Learning objectives (LOs)

Suggested activity: Start the unit by focusing for a few minutes on the LOs box, making sure that students understand what they are going to be doing. Using the first LO as an example, ask students to identify where in the unit they can find the activities for the other four LOs. Get students to say which of the activities appeal to them the most, and ask them for their reasons.

A Watch, listen and talk

1 Whole class, then alone

Explain that students are going to watch and listen to some IGCSE students talking about **technology**. As your students watch and listen, they should make a note of **a** what the speakers say about how technology has changed and developed, and **b** what technology the speakers could never give up, and their reasons. Play the video a second time so that students can check or add to their notes.

Answers

a How technology has changed and developed: it has changed quickly, technology has got a lot smaller but more powerful, technology has replaced some people's jobs.

b What technology could the students never give up: the Internet, mobile phones, medical machines.

Reasons they give: lack of communication, there would be no international companies, it would leave the student helpless in an emergency.

2 Pairs or small groups

Depending on the size of your class, put students into pairs or small groups. They can discuss their notes and then talk to each other about the technology they would like to see and use in the future. Do not interfere too much, but make sure you get feedback from the class so that they know their efforts have been worthwhile. If time permits, you could write their ideas on the board and rank them according to your students' preferences.

B Speaking and vocabulary

1 Whole class or small groups

If you are able to display the four images on a screen, this first task can be done as a whole class activity, with students calling out their ideas about each of the four technologies. Otherwise, students work in small groups and discuss each of the pictures. Whichever approach you use, remember that you want students to speculate and express their ideas, and there are no right or wrong answers.

2 Small groups

Deal with any vocabulary and then students discuss the information (**a**–**h**) and decide which piece of information could match each picture in B1, giving their reasons. There are two for each picture. There is no need to supply any answers yet as students will find out for themselves when they read the text.

3 Small groups

More speculation is needed for this activity. Students think about the four technologies in more detail and discuss and agree on at least three more words or phrases that they believe might appear in the texts. Encourage them, as always, to supply reasons for their choices.

4 Small groups

It may be the case that the questions in this activity have already been answered in previous discussion. If so, you can skip this and move on to B5; if not, students discuss and give reasons.

5 Groups of four – A/B/C

There are four texts, one for each of the four technologies, and each student in the group is going to read one text. Before reading, ask students to decide which of the six headings (**a–f**) could fit each technology. There are two extra headings which they do not need to use.

Answers

a   The problem solvers = 4

b   Hot new tech = not needed

c   Smart kitchen knows what's in the fridge = 3

d   A clean solution to energy needs = 2

e   The perfect thing for anyone going at a rate of knots = 1

f   Oceans on distant planets = not needed

C Reading and speaking

1 Groups of four – A/B/C/D

Students decide who is going to read each of the four texts, and then go to the correct page to find it. The texts are on different pages so that students only read their own text.

Students read their text and find the answers to B2 and B3. They then take it in turns to give feedback to each other about B2 and B3.

Answers

a   every single movement of its fleet D

b   sharpening their wearer's concentration A

c   from the supermarket aisle C

d   a 747 jumbo jet's 60 m wingspan B

e   the best possible repair solution D

f   the future is definitely beyond the horizon B

g   thousands of recipes C

h   automatically tightens the shoe A

2/3 Alone

Firstly, students look at the 12 questions (**a–l**) and select the **three** which they think they can answer from reading their text. Then they need to re-read their text and write the answers to their three questions. Finally, they should identify **at least two** things in their text that they find particularly interesting.

Answers

a   How can someone adjust the settings? **[A] Hold down one of the buttons**

b   How can the NCC teams predict a flight's arrival time? **[D] latest radar technology**

c   How is power provided to the trainers? **[A] by an internal battery**

d   How much power can six megawatts provide? **[B] enough energy for six thousand average households for a year**

e   What advantage do offshore turbines have over onshore turbines? **[B] bigger and produce more energy**

f   What help is available for people who do not want to go shopping? **[C] an app to help place a supermarket order**

g   What information does oven technology give? **[C] what is inside the oven and how to cook it**

h   What is the NCC compared to? **[D] NASA's Mission Control**

i   Where are the turbine components built? **[B] France**

j   Where can you find 'connected food' technology? **[C] fridges and ovens**

k   Which screen provides information about aircraft positions? **[D] the second one**

l   Who is most likely to buy the product? **[A] athletes**

> **WORD TIP**
>
> These two words, *internal* and *inside*, are probably not often confused, but *internal* may not be a word that students commonly use. Refer them to the exercise in the **Workbook**.

4 Groups of four

Students re-join their original group of four and discuss the answers to their questions, and tell each other what they found interesting in the text. They should do this without referring to the text, to avoid simply reading something for the others to listen to.

5 Groups of four

Students decide which of the other three texts they would most like to read, based on what they now know.

D Language focus: compound subjects

1 Whole class

Read through the information with the whole class and ask them to answer questions **a–d**. If you can put the four sentences on the screen, you will be able to more easily highlight the compound subject and main verb in each one.

Answers

a The sporting purpose of the neon blue light on the shoe's instep is unknown …

b … some aerial wind turbines are much smaller …

c … the new, brightly-coloured, hands-on appliances with embedded Wifi are too amazing to resist.

d In much the same way as NASA's Mission Control monitors all aspects of its space exploration …

2/3 Alone

Depending on how challenging students find this, you could skip D3, so that students only need to read one more text of the four in this unit. As they read, they need to find examples of compound subjects with a main verb. In order to assist students, specify that the compound subject must include **at least two words** (before the main verb).

Possible answers

STUDENT A: The perfect thing for anyone going at a rate of knots

1 Self-lacing trainers have arrived, not long after Marty McFly wore a pair in *Back to the Future Part II*. Nike has unveiled the HyperAdapt 1.0 trainer, featuring an 'adaptive lacing' system that automatically tightens the shoe the moment its wearer steps in. The trainers are powered by an internal battery that lasts for about two weeks between charges.

2 The sporting purpose of the neon blue light on the shoe's instep is unknown, but it looks a bit like the one from the Nike Mag trainers worn by Marty McFly in the 1989 film. McFly, who was played by Michael J Fox, put on a pair of self-tightening Nike Mag trainers after travelling forward in time.

3 Nike has pitched the trainers squarely at athletes, promising that they would reduce slippage caused by loose laces, thereby sharpening their wearer's concentration. Senior executives did not dare to suggest that their target market was actually people who could not be bothered to tie up their shoelaces.

4 The self-tightening system is activated when the wearer's heel hits a sensor inside the shoe, which instantly measures their weight and foot position. A series of motorised pulleys then pull together a mesh of filaments around the foot, tighter or looser where required. Plus and minus buttons on the side of the shoe allow the wearer to tighten and loosen their fit. Holding down the minus button for more than two seconds fully loosens the shoe so that it can be removed.

5 A study by scientists has found that we are hard-wired to be lazy, or at least, to conserve energy, as our caveman ancestors had to do. The research found that over time participants strapped into leg braces that caused them to strain would unconsciously adapt their walking gait to the most economic possible. Nike said that the HyperAdapt 1.0 trainers would learn the best fit for their owners' feet after being worn two or three times. After a while they would gather biometric data that would be relayed to other "smart" clothing and wearable technology.

[Adapted from: http://www.thetimes.co.uk/tto/technology/article4715973.ece?shareToken=3595c3268d6e9848eed6f90193938fe6 21/03/16]

STUDENT B: A clean solution to energy needs

1 The future is definitely beyond the horizon, with massive wind turbines out at sea and even airborne wind turbines above the clouds providing a clean solution to the world's energy needs. While Europe has always been at the forefront of wind energy technology, the United States has finally joined the party.

2 Deep-water turbines are extremely large, and each one alone can generate six megawatts of power – that's enough energy for six thousand average households for a year. Their height is twice as high as the Statue of Liberty, with a diameter that doubles the size of a 747 jumbo jet's 60m wingspan. On the other hand, some aerial wind turbines are much smaller, with a diameter of around 12 metres.

3 The clean energy company *Deepwater Wind* is building a wind farm of fifteen mega turbines to the south of Rhode Island in the state of New England, USA. Eventually, there could be as many as 200 such turbines, providing a significant proportion of southern New England's electricity needs. The turbine parts are manufactured in France and assembled on site, with great attention being given to ensure that clean energy is beneficial for everyone and everything, including the whales which inhabit the waters around Rhode Island.

4 Underwater noise is being controlled and all noise-producing activities will cease during the spring when the whales are present in the Rhode Island area. Furthermore, company boats will travel more slowly to create as little noise as possible. There has been worry among the fishing community, but the *Deepwater Wind* turbines will be up to 1.6 kilometres apart, providing plenty of room for fishing boats. Birds, too, are likely to be unaffected by the offshore turbines as studies show that migratory birds tend to fly near the coast and not out at sea where the turbines would be.

5 Offshore wind turbines have the advantage over onshore turbines in that they can be much bigger and therefore produce more energy. Transporting turbine parts over land to onshore sites is complex, involving high costs and time, whereas offshore turbine components can be transported on barges out to sea. This is a much cheaper and time-efficient solution.

[Adapted from: *Down to business: The future is beyond the horizon* in Royal Wings, Royal Jordanian inflight magazine, May/June 2016]

STUDENT C: Smart kitchen knows what's in the fridge

1 The experience is familiar to anyone who regularly cooks at home: you're at the supermarket buying everything you need for the next meal, but you can't remember if you have butter at home. So what do you do? To buy or not to buy? And now that you think about it, you did buy butter the last time you were at the supermarket, didn't you? And once you get home and look for the butter, you find out that you haven't got any.

2 But what if you could actually see the contents of your fridge from the supermarket aisle? Wouldn't that be something? In fact the technology is already here in the form of kitchen appliances with 'connected food' technology built in to fridges and ovens. There are even some options to 'upgrade' non-Wifi equipped fridges and ovens, but the new, brightly-coloured, hands-on appliances with embedded Wifi are too amazing to resist.

3 Once you have the appropriate app downloaded into your smartphone, you will receive a live feed from inside your fridge. Apart from showing what is already there, the technology will tell you what you can make with those ingredients by pulling data from an online store of thousands of recipes. The app will even help you to place an order for missing items, just in case you cannot be bothered to make the trip to the supermarket yourself.

4 The oven technology can 'sense' what is inside the oven and tell you how to cook it. It provides information on the correct cooking time and the right temperature, depending on the food's weight, the oven model and even the altitude of the place where the kitchen is located. There is even technology which

allows family members or friends to gather round a screen, choose a recipe and then make it together.

5 And for those who want some non-human company, you can install cameras in your kitchen ceiling, and the technology will enable you to watch yourself putting carrots on a cutting board. The app will tell you that yes, those are carrots, and will play back a video of you chopping the carrots while also giving you carrot recipes from the online store.

[Adapted from: *Smart kitchen knows what's in fridge*, in Gulf News, 31 May 2016]

STUDENT D: The problem solvers

1 When you have 200 000 passengers travelling an average of 530 daily flights through the Emirates hub in Dubai, keeping the network in perfect running order is not an easy task. That's where the NCC, Emirates' Network Control Centre, and the beating heart of the airline's entire operation, comes into play, playing a crucial role in the smooth running of the airline.

2 In much the same way as NASA's Mission Control monitors all aspects of its space exploration, the NCC manages every flight, every departure, every arrival, and every single movement of its fleet. Inside the airline's nerve centre is a 60+ strong team of highly specialised individuals, all monitoring, coordinating and problem-solving on a daily basis. Made up of 15 different departments, each has its own distinct area of specialism. For example, there are crew scheduling teams who focus timetabling crew for different flights, while the team of flight despatchers arrange flight plans and choose the best routes on any given day. A team of engineers, each trained on specific aircraft types, is able to recommend the best possible repair solution.

3 But despite the need for different departments, nothing is achieved in isolation, with all the teams working together, using their different skillsets to develop the best approach to each situation. It is the responsibility of everyone to ensure that flights stick to schedules as closely as possible, no matter what happens.

4 The NCC relies on a number of key pieces of technology to help ensure that flights operate on time. For example, using the latest radar technology, the teams can predict the exact time an aircraft will land, taking into consideration wind speed, the flight path and even the aircraft's optimal speed.

5 The focal point for the entire department is the giant floor-to-ceiling radar screen, which shows vital information such as aircraft holding patterns and

which runways are in use. A second screen shows all current aircraft positions, delivering a complete picture of the entire Emirates network at any given moment in time, and ensuring the highest level of connectivity for its passengers.

[Adapted from: *The problem solvers*, in Open Skies, Emirates in-flight magazine, May 2016]

4/5 Whole class, then alone

Talk through the information with the class, highlighting the use of *and* and joining phrases. Then students work alone to choose the correct form of the verb in sentences (**a–i**). There is also an exercise in the **Workbook**.

Answers

a   Eating, sleeping and reading **are** enjoyable activities.

b   Chocolate and strawberry **are** my favourite flavours of ice cream.

c   Neither the president nor her assistant **has** replied to my question.

d   Mum as well as Sharon **enjoys** chocolate ice cream.

e   Either the boots by the door or the flip-flops in the living room **are** John's.

f   Neither Marcos nor Carole **lives** in that house.

g   Wind and rain as well as snow **cause** problems at airports.

h   Either you or your brother **is** going to go first.

i   Either the chicken or the fish in the freezer **needs** to be thawed for dinner tonight.

E Listening and speaking

1 Alone, then pairs

Students work alone and carefully read the five prompts, deciding which ones they think are the least and most challenging. They should then discuss with their partner and give reasons for their choices. Generally speaking, the last couple of prompts tend to be more challenging than the earlier ones, but it may also be the case that these give students more to talk about.

2 Alone, then pairs

Students are going to listen to six different people responding to the five prompts in the topic card they have just been studying. As they listen, students decide which person matches each of the five prompts. There is one extra person

speaking, who does not match any of the prompts. After listening, students work in pairs to compare their answers.

Answers

Olaf	positive and negative effects of technological advances on our lives
Aisha	the suggestion that technology destroys privacy
Tom	skills you need to use technology effectively
Mari	
Pedro	technology you could not live without
Maryam	what you think the greatest technological development is, and why

CD2, Track 16

Olaf:	I can't think of any negatives! Technology is only positive.
Aisha:	I don't have a problem if people know about me. I've nothing to hide anyway
Tom:	My age group was born with technology and we've grown up with it, so we don't need special skills.
Mari:	My grandparents used different types of technology, but they still had it.
Pedro:	My phone. No need to even think about it.
Maryam:	There are so many amazing technologies, but for me all the smart apps take my breath away.

3 Alone

Students now think about how the five speakers' introductory phrases could be expanded. There are **six** phrases (**a–f**) for students to look at and match to the **five** speakers (Mari has already been excluded) in E2. Students do the matching, decide which phrase does not fit, and then listen to check their answers.

Answers

a	Aisha,	d	Tom,
b	Maryam,	e	does not fit,
c	Olaf,	f	Pedro

4/5 Alone

Students listen again and answer questions **a–e**. Then they can share with their partner and check the audioscript in Appendix 3.

Answers

a   Aisha

b   Olaf

c Tom

d Maryam

e Pedro

CD2, Track 17

Pedro: My phone. No need to even think about it. We all have one, in fact we've all had one for so long that we probably can't remember life without one. It's just normal to have one. <u>If you took my phone away from me, I just wouldn't be able to operate normally. Life would be meaningless!</u>

Tom: My age group was born with technology and we've grown up with it, so we don't need special skills. Of course, if a new technology comes along then perhaps we need to learn how to use it. <u>But I believe that we can easily transfer our skills from one technology to another – we're not stupid, are we?</u>

Maryam: There are so many amazing technologies, but for me all the smart apps take my breath away. It seems like there's an app for everything and anything you might want to do. <u>And the great thing is that every day a new app comes along, or friends make you aware of an app that they've tried and enjoy using.</u>

Olaf: I can't think of any negatives! Technology is only positive. Just think of how we use it every day. What's not to like about technology? <u>The point nowadays is that everything involves technology to some extent, so it's impossible for life to continue without it.</u>

Aisha: I don't have a problem if people know about me. I've nothing to hide anyway. I think the only people who worry about privacy are criminals. <u>I don't even think we have any idea of who knows what about us because nothing is secret in the 21st century.</u>

> **LANGUAGE TIP**
> There have been several examples in the Coursebook of introductory phrases and fillers for students to use in their spoken language. In this final unit, the focus is on introductory phrases for giving opinion.

6 Pairs

Students work together to discuss possible responses to the follow-up questions. Then they can role-play, and try to use expressions from this Language Tip and those in other units.

F Speaking

1/2 Pairs

Students think back to Section F in Unit 15 to remember how spoken language is assessed in the Cambridge IGCSE examination. Then they complete the gaps in the criteria (**a**–**f**) using the words in the box.

Answers

a The candidate uses a range of <u>structures</u> accurately and consistently.

b The candidate uses <u>simple</u> structures securely.

c Shades of <u>meaning</u> are achieved and some sophisticated <u>ideas</u> are communicated.

d The candidate uses a restricted range of <u>vocabulary</u>.

e Pronunciation and <u>intonation</u> are generally clear.

f The candidate makes an attempt to respond to <u>questions</u> and prompts.

G Watch, listen and talk

1 Alone, then pairs

Prepare students to watch a video of a student practising a discussion with a teacher about **Technology**. The student is responding to the same prompts that they have already seen in Section E. Students need to decide which, if any, of the criteria from Activity F2 could apply to the student, and give their reasons.

2 Alone, then pairs

Students now watch a second student responding to the same prompts and decide if they perform better or worse than the first student, giving their reasons. They also need to decide again which, if any, of the criteria from Activity F2 could apply to the student, and give their reasons.

> **TOP TIP**
> This **Top Tip** reminds students that they should respond to the prompts in the same order as they appear on the topic card.

143

H Reading and writing

1 Pairs, then whole class

The five pictures show technologies which were ground-breaking when they were first invented. Students work together to answer questions (a–d), and then do whole class feedback so they can share their ideas together. There are no right or wrong answers here.

2 Pairs

Before students match the words, ask them to say what they consider to be today's greatest technological inventions. Then they work together to find the ones in the table. When they have done the matching, ask them to answer questions a–f.

Answers

1 f,   2 a,   3 d,   4 h,   5 j,
6 e,   7 b,   8 g,   9 c,   10 i

Communication activity

For questions c and d tell students that they are working on a committee which has to select what they think are the top three most useful technological inventions from the list of ten. So, they need to discuss how to reduce the list. For question e, get them to discuss if they think there is anything missing from list and why they consider this item a 'great technological invention'.

In question f students are asked to read an article about technological inventions, and then write a summary of the ways in which technology has made our lives easier and more convenient. As a variation, divide the paragraphs between different pairs and get each pair to read their paragraph (or paragraphs) and note down two to three important points in it. Then in whole class feedback students find out about all the other paragraphs, and then write their

summary. Remind students that a summary is not usually about the whole text, but about a specific part or parts of it.

Here are some sample summary writing answers from **i** an **IGCSE Core** and **ii** an **IGCSE Extended** student. Both answers would probably score in the top bands for both content and language.

i   Core

Technology developed a lot over the centuries. Today our communication is made easier by mobile telephones, not only for phone calls but also for internet access. Food has been made easier and faster to cook with the invention of the microwave. GPS makes it almost impossible for a person to get lost and nowadays they are installed in most smartphones. The PC with the internet changed the face of the whole world and the mouse makes it easier to use. Digital music has reduced waste and remote controls make it easier to control appliances. We can immediately share photos from phones and have face-to-face conversations. [107 words]

ii   Extended

The article discusses technology's greatest inventions and begins explaining how technology continues to evolve throughout the ages, changing the way we live and work. It then mentions examples that have altered our lives such as the mobile phone, the microwave, the GPS and possibly the greatest of them all, the PC. The article also refers to the internet which is described as still being in its 'infancy'. It then goes on to mention inventions such as the remote-control which make our lives much easier. It ends with a reference to the idea of video-conferencing that would have been considered science-fiction-like 100 years ago. So many inventions and yet more and more technological inventions appear every day. [116 words]

Reflection

Use the **Reflection** to remind students of what they have achieved in the unit. Students should set themselves a **personal goal** based on their scores for Unit 20.

Exam focus

Speaking, Part 2, topic card

NOTE: The exam focus is on speaking, and involves students in looking at a new topic card, and then taking on the roles of examiner and student, using the prompts on the card.

1 Pairs

Students work together and look at the prompts, discussing how they might respond to each one. When they are ready, students take on the roles of examiner and interviewee, using the topic of *Life in 100 years' time* and the prompts on the card. Your job is to monitor and encourage where necessary, and provide any language students are struggling with. However, this should be an opportunity for students to build their confidence and fluency.

Unit 1: Free time

Exercise A1

free time

shopping centre

discount price

online puzzles

amazing app

resistance training

creative story

board game

loyalty scheme

Exercise A2

a   creative story

b   resistance training

c   board game

d   Online puzzles

e   amazing app

f   shopping centre

g   loyalty scheme

h   discount price

Exercise A3

a   *General*. All others are directly related to sports and fitness.

b   *App*. An app is a piece of software and a relatively new invention; the other terms are all traditional methods of providing information.

c   *Amaze* is a verb. The others are adjectives.

d   *Announced* is not a compound noun (a noun made up of two parts).

e   *Swimming* is the only sport that does not use a ball.

f   *Children* – the plural is not formed by adding an 's'.

g   *Stalls* because it is an individual place (plural here) but the others are group words.

Exercise A4

a   shopping mall

b   football

c   funny

d   adults

e   stalls

f   announced

g   delightful

h   app

Exercise A5

a   You should drink about 3 l (litres) of water each day.

b   This USB stick has 19 GB (gigabytes) of space left. Is that enough?

c   The speed limit on motorways in many countries is 100 kph (kilometres per hour).

d   A bag of sugar normally weighs 1 kg (kilogram).

e   Temperatures rise to about 45° C (Celsius) in our country in the summer – it's very hot.

f   A key on a laptop normally measures about 1 cm (centimetre).

g   My daughter is going to run a marathon, so she runs about 5 km (kilometres) every day to prepare.

h   The shop is only about 100 m (metres) away, I'm sure you can walk that far!

i   On a map 1 mm (millimetre) doesn't look very far, but in reality it can be a very long distance.

Exercise A6

a   original

b   original

c   unique

d   original

e   unique

f   unique

Exercise B1

No set answers

Exercise B2

Blog a. Three from:

Adjective	Noun
sizeable	family
delicious	meat
nutritious	milk
amazing	speed
exciting	sport
numerous	date trees
sandy	tracks

Blog b. Three from:

Adjective	Noun
free	time
Olympic-sized	pool
young	boy
empty	pool
large	dinner

Exercise B3

No set answers

Exercise B4

a   warmth

b   efficiency

c   stranger

d   delight

e   fascination

f   enthusiasm

g   firmness

h   impression

Exercise C1

a   true

b   true

c   false – the main ideas and key words

d   false – sometimes only one word is required

e   true

f   true

g   true

Exercise C2

a   <u>What</u> are the <u>six ways</u> that can help a person become <u>successful?</u>

b   <u>What</u> is the <u>minimum recommended</u> daily exercise?

c   <u>What kind</u> of books will <u>improve</u> your skill of reading?

d   Other than at school and college, <u>where</u> are <u>good places to learn</u>?

e   What are <u>two examples</u> of how you can <u>help</u> other people?

f   <u>Why</u> is it not healthy to <u>only focus</u> on your studies?

g   <u>What people</u> should you always give <u>priority</u> to in your life?

h   Is it important to include <u>all of the points</u> listed in order to be successful? Why/not?

Exercise C3

a   six words or phrases

b   a number

c   types of book

d   names of types of places

e   two types of activities

f   a reason

g   nouns

h   yes / no answer

Exercise C4

a   exercise, read, take classes, volunteer, hobbies, friends and family

b   half an hour a day

c   fiction and non-fiction

d   the internet

e   two from: clean up the highway, work in a soup kitchen, provide support to young people

f   stresses you out and prevents you from developing other skills

g   friends and family

h   no, only some of them

Exercise C5

a   physical

b   confidence

c   institution

d   underestimate

e   neglect

f   incorporate

Exercise D1

Example answer

I agree with the comments because I think young people waste a lot of time doing nothing in their free time except playing on their PCs or smartphones.

I personally have some hobbies like collecting football shirts from my favourite club, Manchester United. I spend time researching them and there are online sites for collectors like me. We discuss our favourite players, swap shirts and it helps me to forget about school and studying and exams.

I believe that getting the right amount of sleep helps you to be successful, and I always try to get around 8 hours per night.

Unit 2: Television

Exercise A1

a	v	d	ii	g	ix
b	viii	e	iv	h	i
c	vii	f	iii	i	vi

Exercise A2

No set answers

Exercise A3

mobile phones

voluntary work

social media

television programme

living standards

information leaflet

sound system

smartphones

pocket money

a	pocket money
b	smartphones / mobile phones
c	voluntary work
d	Mobile phones / Smartphones
e	sound system
f	living standards
g	social media
h	Information leaflets

Exercise A4

a	obviously	c	obviously
b	apparently	d	Apparently

Exercise B1

a	beautifully	e	fashionably
b	completely	f	generously
c	doubtfully	g	hungrily
d	eventually	h	incorrectly

Exercise B2

a	incorrectly	e	doubtfully
b	eventually	f	fashionably
c	hungrily	g	generously
d	completely	h	beautifully

Exercise B3

No set answers

Exercise C1

a	v	d	ii	g	iv
b	vii	e	i	h	vi
c	iii	f	viii		

Exercise C2

a True – in fact 79% [4].

b True – that milestone involved the adoption of digital TV [2].

c False – more people worldwide now pay for their TV than get it over-the-air [3].

d False – in Africa in particular, fewer than a third of the households own a TV set [4].

e True – nonetheless, many retailers worldwide have low expectations as shipments of TV sets continue to decline [5].

f True – we have to remember that the actual definition of television is rapidly changing [6].

g True – one thing is certain though: for the foreseeable future, television will continue to dominate how the world's population gets its information and entertainment [7].

Exercise D1

Core

Dear Sir/ Madam,

After thinking for quite a while, I have chosen two television programmes and I hope you agree with and like the ones I have picked.

My first choice is the *Great British Bake- Off*, a reality television show, which I think should be aired at seven o'clock in the evening. It's a very entertaining baking competition, which I believe can be watched and enjoyed by all the family, both adults and children. My second choice is the crime series *Silent Witness*. This choice is an adult programme which I believe should be aired at either ten or eleven o'clock at night, as there are some scenes which are disturbing for children. It is a good programme though for adults and teenagers.

Sincerely,

Jamie Brown

Extended

Dear Sir/ Madam,

I was greatly honoured to be chosen to select two programmes of my choice to be aired on national television. I very much hope that you will appreciate my choices.

The first programme I selected is a current affairs programme called *Panorama*, which investigates a wide range of current subjects which take place around the world. I think it would be wise to air this programme at around eight or nine o'clock in the evening. Although it is not inappropriate in any way, some of the subjects discussed are quite complicated and would not be understood by children and neither perhaps by young teenagers.

The second programme I chose is *Horrible Histories*. It is a series of children's documentaries which focuses on the more gruesome facts of history that are not taught in school. It is of course very light-hearted, comical and enjoyable for children and young teenagers, and I believe it would be good if it were aired around five in the afternoon, after school.

I hope that you have enjoyed my suggestions, and thank you again for this opportunity.

Sincerely,

Anastas Petrov

Unit 3: Food

Exercise A1

Possible answers

Apple	Noodles
Baked beans	Ostrich meat
Cake	Pasta
Dates	Quinoa
Eggs	Rice
Fish	Salami
Gnocchi	Tuna
Honey	Upside down cake
Ice cream	Veal
Juniper berries	Waldorf salad
Ketchup	Xigua
Lasagne	Yoghurt
Milkshake	Zucchini

Exercise A2

Possible answers

Fast food	Traditional food	Neither
Ice cream	Baked beans	Apple
Ketchup	Cake	Juniper berries
Milkshake	Dates	Ostrich meat
Noodles	Eggs	Quinoa
	Fish	Tuna
	Gnocchi	Upside down cake
	Honey	Veal
	Lasagne	Waldorf salad
	Pasta	Xigua
	Rice	Zucchini
	Salami	
	Yoghurt	

Exercise A3

						B	A	T	C	H				
						S	U	P	P	O	S	I	N	G
					C	A	B	I	N	E	T			
		D	O	N	A	T	E							
R	E	G	I	S	T	E	R	S						
				T	A	R	G	E	T					
				I	N	S	I	S	T					
						I	N	C	R	E	A	S	E	
						N	E	G	L	E	C	T	E	D

Exercise A4

a donate
b targets
c insist
d increase
e neglected
f cabinet
g registers
h Supposing

Exercise A5

a insist
b insist
c persists
d insist
e insist
f persist

Exercise B1

a Supposing they don't come,
b We'll leave the house
c We should get there on time,
d As soon as they told me,
e I think we've taken the right clothes,
f We'll definitely go and celebrate

iv then we'll have to go without them.
ii as soon as they come so we're not late.
vi providing that there's not too much traffic.
i I knew they didn't want to come with us.
v but that's supposing the weather is good.
vii providing you pass your driving test.

Exercise B2

a Does it take longer to cook brown rice than white rice?
b How long does it take you to write an essay?
c What time do you get up to eat breakfast?
d Where do you like to study each day?
e When do you sit down to watch television with your family?
f Why do we have to study grammar?

Exercise B3

No set answers

Exercise C1

a Health dangers of obesity
b Worldwide trends
c Shoppers' habits
d Statistics on the sales of fattening foods
e Sales of healthier products
f Not just what you eat

Exercise C2

a peer pressure
b being overweight and obese
c men (74% were overweight or obese)
d advertising to young people; it has no effect (children are just as overweight there)
e shoppers' behaviour
f fatty foods and fizzy drinks
g sales of fruits and vegetables have risen, cafés and restaurants have an increase in healthy eating, sales of salads increasing, more people joining gyms

Exercise D1

Core

Dear fellow students,

I recently contacted four major companies in the food industry, to find out about the contents of their products. I contacted two major fast food companies, a diet cereal brand and a health food company.

I'm hoping to compare the content of the fast food products with the healthy food products. This way, I believe we can start understanding more about what we eat and become more careful about the food we choose to put into our bodies. I would love to hear more ideas from you because we can really work as a school to promote healthy lifestyle and I would like everybody to be involved with the process. In order to make our school a healthier place, we need to work together, so, I'm expecting plenty of ideas from all of you.

Thanks,

Zoe Menelaou [140 words]

Extended

Dear friends and fellow students,

I've recently contacted four companies in the food industry, to find out what they put in the food that we eat.

I sent letters to a major fast food company in our area, a company which focuses on food for diets, an organic farm and a company which produces and sells cold cuts. I want to find out if the things they claim about their companies are true, and what ingredients actually go into the things that we so easily put into our mouths.

Once we get this information, I'm planning to carry out a survey to see how many of us actually know what we are eating, whether it's healthy or not, and if the information we receive from the companies adds up to our own views. This way, I hope that we can all be enlightened and understand better about eating healthily.

If any of you have got any ideas about how we can promote healthy eating, please contact me! I think it would be great if we could all get involved in this campaign and show that we care about living healthy and nutritious lives.

Yours,

Delmy Rodriguez [196 words]

Exercise D2

Extended

The local product I have chosen is the lemon, which grows everywhere here in Cyprus. Lemons are so abundant that people pick them up off the streets. Lemons are famous for their nutritional value as they contain high levels of vitamin C, far more than oranges and grapefruits. They contain fewer calories per 100g and no saturated fats or cholesterol. Because of the citric acid in lemons (up to 8%) they are excellent as a natural food preservative, but also as an aid to human digestion. So lemons benefit us both as a food and a natural medicine.

A popular imported product in Cyprus is breakfast cereal, which, because we eat it with milk, is supposed to be healthy. However, there is a lot of sugar and flavourings in packet cereals from the shops. Also, because there is very little protein in them, cereals do not make you feel full for a long period of time. Many people add sugar or honey to their morning bowl of cereals, and this risks making you put on weight.

Stick with natural products and stay healthy! [183 words]

Unit 4: Transport

Exercise A1

U	C	F	B	K	F	**B**	D	Q	W	P	Z	K	Y	M
Y	J	L	F	Q	**I**	E	L	O	**H**	A	X	P	Y	I
X	**R**	G	L	**C**	Y	F	D	**E**	C	N	I	A	**R**	**T**
K	**E**	**R**	Y	E	M	E	**K**	V	A	W	X	P	Q	F
V	**I**	**C**	E	**S**	L	**I**	Z	Z	O	U	K	E	J	Y
B	**L**	H	U	**F**	**B**	T	E	X	**C**	H	M	H	A	X
E	**O**	**B**	A	**R**	**B**	R	C	G	K	I	Z	M	Q	I
F	J	**D**	**O**	**O**	A	E	E	J	A	H	G	X	I	A
L	P	**T**	**A**	T	L	**A**	**E**	**R**	**O**	**P**	**L**	**A**	**N**	**E**
M	**O**	A	D	**B**	L	N	C	P	**C**	**A**	**R**	G	Y	C
M	K	T	S	F	**O**	W	D	S	B	E	F	U	C	L
D	W	O	B	M	**O**	**D**	M	B	A	U	G	Q	S	I
W	I	D	W	G	**N**	N	**A**	X	A	W	V	W	Q	K
F	A	P	R	H	G	P	T	Y	V	O	J	C	S	W
M	V	Q	G	H	Q	S	R	G	D	A	M	Q	U	B

Exercise A2

a   ferry

b   car

c   bicycle

d   coach

e   balloon

f   bus

g   motorbike

h   train

i   aeroplane

j   *boda-boda*

Exercise A3

a   disaster

b   disasters

c   catastrophic

d   disaster

e   any of: disaster/disasters/catastrophe/catastrophes

f   catastrophe

Exercise A4

a   The <u>roads</u> are so badly <u>potholed</u> that they are damaging my car.

b   The <u>river</u> <u>swelled</u> to dangerous levels that night after the rain.

c   It's not always possible to compare <u>people's livelihoods</u> as so many factors are involved.

d   A lot of <u>strain</u> was put on the family after the <u>divorce</u>.

e   There were many <u>fatalities</u> after the <u>accident</u> on the motorway.

f   <u>Women</u> have <u>campaigned</u> for equal rights in many countries.

g   If you use your <u>initiative,</u> imagination and <u>common sense</u>, then you should be fine.

h   There was a surprisingly high number of <u>participants</u> for the <u>marathon</u>.

Exercise B1

Example answers

a   I've always avoided talking to strangers

b   Last month I travelled to Uganda

c   you're staying

d   I'll write my many stories

Exercise B2

Noun	Verb	Noun	Verb
decision	decide	protection	protect
expression	express	examination	examine
admission	admit	suggestion	suggest
cancellation	cancel	subtraction	subtract
education	educate	graduation	graduate

Exercise B3

No set answer

Exercise C1 / C2

a   i   information
        have accidents

   ii   two pieces of information

       a trained driver and wear a crash helmet

b **i**   a piece of information

       because he was frightened

   ii   a place

       home from the hospital

c **i**   a reason

       he was recommended

   ii   a place

       the countryside

d **i**   information

       surprise because people trust so much

   ii   three nouns

       potholes, animals and children, and puddles

Exercise D1

a Segway

b balancing

c police

d battery

e American

Exercise D2

No set answers

Exercise D3

a the gondola

b because Venetians stand

c by travelling in a tangah

d it's uncomfortable and not fast

e electric generator engine

f poor railway tracks make it bumpy and only grass mat to sit on

g fast way of getting down the hill

h two drivers dressed in traditional white outfits

Unit 5: Holidays

Exercise A1

a snow-capped

b paramount

c husky

d popular

e thrilling

f volcano

g freshwater

h professional

i complex

j endemic

k actually

Exercise A2

Across:

2 complex

5 paramount

6 freshwater

9 snow-capped

10 thrilling

Down:

1 volcano

3 popular

4 professional

7 actually

8 endemic

11 husky

Exercise A3

a stationery

b stationery

c stationery

d stationary

e stationary

Exercise A4

a needy – the others describe having money

b satisfied – the others describe wanting/needing food

c calm – the others describe noise

d idle – the others describe doing something

e lacking – the others describe wholeness

f insignificant – the others describe importance/size

Exercise A5

a calm

b insignificant

c needy

d lacking

e idle

f satisfied

Exercise B1

All the husky dogs had <u>chocolate-coloured</u> fur which showed up against the <u>pure white</u> beauty of the freshly fallen snow. The dogs had to climb from the green fields of the lower hills to the peaks of the <u>snow-capped</u> mountains. On their paws they wore <u>shock-absorbing</u>, specially made leather boots, due to the pounding their legs would receive from the constant trekking. The dogs were used to a <u>leisure-filled</u> life living at ground level on the plains and rolling in the white sands of the freshwater lakes near their homes.

Exercise B2

a I live in an English-speaking country.

b Shakespeare is an author who is very well known.

c She never cooks and only buys ready-made food.

d He lives in a 20-storey building.

e It's a two-year-old cat and already it's fat.

f It's a very brightly lit room – I don't like it.

g She is a part-time worker because of the children.

Exercise C1

Actually / well / to be honest / hmm / let me think

Exercise C2

1 Let me think (2)

2 To be honest (3)

3 Well (3)

4 Hmm (2)

5 Actually (2)

Exercise C3

a Worrying doesn't help
  - You can prepare because the questions you will be asked are personal.
  - The questions are not there to challenge you.

b The questions in Part One
  - The examiner is there to help and guide you.
  - It's not assessed.

c Using your own language
  - Don't use your own language.
  - Tell the examiner you don't understand.

d Phrases to show you don't understand
  - 'I'm sorry but I don't understand what you mean.'
  - 'Could you repeat that please?'
  - 'Could you say that more slowly please?'

e Not having enough to say
  - Keep speaking.
  - The examiner will help you out.

f The topic
  - You are not being tested on your knowledge.
  - Tell the examiner but then talk about a related topic that you're more comfortable with.

g Pronunciation
  - They are not expecting you to speak like a native speaker.
  - Speak clearly so you're understood.

h Mistakes
  - You would be penalised particularly if you are difficult to understand.

Exercise D1

- search likely sections of the text
- read the question
- underline the key word/s
- ask yourself what information is the question asking for

Exercise D2

a <u>How many</u> methods of <u>transport</u> are available to reach the Isles of Scilly?

b <u>What</u> is *Scillonian III*?

c Name <u>four</u> '<u>treasures</u>' of the islands.

d <u>Which</u> other part of the world are the islands <u>compared with</u>?

e <u>How many people</u> live on the Isles of Scilly?

f What do you <u>need</u> to do <u>before</u> <u>travelling</u> between any of the islands?

g On <u>which island</u> is the Old Wesleyan Chapel?

h <u>Where</u> can you find the second-oldest lighthouse in Britain?

Exercise D3

a	isles	**d**	treasures
b	chapel	**e**	Isles of Scilly
c	lighthouse	**f**	transport

Exercise D4

a	two	**d**	the Tropics
b	a cruiser	**e**	2000
c	four from: exotic plants, wild flowers, ancient cairns, crumbling castles, sparkling white sands and azure seas	**f**	check times and tides
		g	St Mary's
		h	St Agnes

153

Unit 6: Learning

Exercise A1

a graph
b grammar
c guide
d college
e counselling
f career
g primary
h programme
i pronunciation
j facilities
k findings
l fees

Exercise A2

a fees
b pronunciation
c career
d grammar
e guide
f facilities

Exercise A3

a The students often go to the cafeteria to relax and have a break.
b You should go to the accommodation and welfare office if there's a problem with your flat.
c There are good banking facilities at the college, with ATMs everywhere.
d I felt very depressed about exams, so I went to the counselling service and they really helped me.
e I go every day to the sports centre to play table tennis.
f You're not allowed to talk in the LMRC because people study there.
g We are always busy at the weekends as the social and leisure programme is excellent and full of great activities.

Exercise A4

a practise
b practise
c practice
d practise
e practice
f Practice! Practice! Practice!

Exercise B1

a The dog tried to <u>befriend</u> the boy in the park.
b Because she <u>misunderstood</u> the instructions, she did the activity incorrectly.
c The exercise was <u>uncomplicated</u> and so she finished quickly.
d They wanted to <u>revisit</u> the area, as it was so beautiful.
e He missed the bus because he <u>overslept</u> again after a late night.
f She looked at him in <u>disbelief</u> because of the lies he was telling.
g If you <u>cooperate</u> better then you will finish the project quickly.
h Because the country's currency was <u>devalued</u>, prices rose drastically.
i She was <u>transformed</u> when she had her hair restyled.
j They did not <u>foresee</u> that the house would be destroyed during the hurricane.

Exercise B2

Across

2 transform
4 disbelief
7 uncomplicated
9 befriend

Down

1 revisit
3 oversleep
5 misunderstand
6 cooperate
8 devalue

Exercise B3

a availabi<u>lity</u>
b cheap<u>er</u>
c excite<u>ment</u>
d guid<u>ance</u>
e happ<u>iness</u>
f imagin<u>ation</u>
g luxur<u>iously</u>*
h lov<u>ing</u>

*Both -ious and -ly can also operate independently as suffixes.

Exercise B4

a carelessly
b grateful
c homeless
d beautiful
e harmless
f colourful
g worthless
h useless

Exercise C1

a   infested with hostile creatures

b   on the verge of

c   do physical damage

d   gaming addiction

e   can be so extreme

f   more likely to suffer

g   for hours on end

h   to eat properly

i   in poor physical condition

Exercise C2

a   hostile creatures

b   to another place

c   that your back aches, you are getting a migraine and you haven't had anything to eat or drink

d   the main nerve between the forearm and the hand is squeezed or pressed

e   migraines

f   when seated in the same position for hours

g   because they don't want to take the time to prepare anything

h   those already in poor physical condition

Exercise D2

Core

Dear Antonis,

Our parents are threatening to control how and for what we use our computers at school. We are going to suggest dedicating time for both physical and computer activities, because they are always complaining that we use our computers instead of being active.

We don't only play games on the computers, we also use them for research and for a lot of school work, like projects. I think the best solution would be for us students to promise to use the school computers only for homework purposes, and we can use our computers at home for fun. Do you have the same problems as us at your school?

Love to everyone,
Maria [114 words]

Extended

Dear Leila,

I'm sure you have to deal with this too, but our parents are constantly complaining that we sit at our computers all day and now they are threatening to restrict our computers at school. We've decided that we should campaign for physical and computer activities. That way, we can be more active and get exercise like adults want us to, but we also get to spend the time we want on the computers.

They think that we only use computers for fun, but on the most part, we need them for research and for school projects. So much of the information we learn is from the internet, so restricting our access will only make it complicated for us. I believe that we should be allowed a certain amount of leisure time on the school computers after we have finished our work, rather than completely controlling what we do and how we do it! Adults should respect our needs. What are your thoughts on this matter?

Lots of love,
George [171 words]

Unit 7: Jobs

Exercise A1

a   Surgeon – Many years at university are necessary to do this job, which can be very challenging and demanding. They play a very important role in our society in looking after people and making them well.

b   Teacher – Again, a university education is very important for this job. They play a very important role in our development as adults and we learn many interesting things from them.

c   Police officer – They maintain peace and security in our cities and wear a uniform so that they can be easily identified. Men and women are both necessary in this job.

d   Engineer – They do many different jobs in the building and construction of a city. Again, a university degree is extremely important as there are so many areas to learn about.

Exercise A2

a   also

b   in addition

c   besides

d   sometimes

e   furthermore

f   consequently

Exercise A3

Make clear	Contrast/difference	Detail	Result/consequence	Example	Summary
namely	however	specifically	consequently	for example	in other words
accordingly	in spite of	in this case	as a result	such as	for this reason

Exercise A4

a in other words
b specifically
c in spite of
d namely
e as a result
f in this case
g consequently
h such as

Exercise A5

a accept
b accept
c except
d accept
e except
f accept / except
g except
h accepted

Exercise B1 / B2

a If I were you, I'd visit the doctor soon to check that cough.

b I think it would be better if you came later, as I won't be ready.

c It might be a good idea to read the book before seeing the film.

d Why don't we take the dog for a walk now, before it rains?

e I don't think she should buy that car, as it's too expensive.

Exercise B3

1 b
2 f
3 a
4 i
5 e
6 h
7 d
8 g
9 c

Exercise B4

No set answers

Exercise C1a

ii They are normally jobs that other people do not want to do.

iii People get their clothes and bodies dirty.

Exercise C1b

No set answer

Exercise C2

a host
b duties
c alongside
d pilot
e juxtaposition
f wit
g hazards
h spin-off
i graphic
j inundated with
k commissioned
l concept
m honour

Exercise C3

a Dirty Jobs
b Discovery
c November 2003
d three
e September 2012
f the situations
g colourful personalities of the men and women who do the jobs
h the cameraman
i the crew
j hazardous/dangerous
k disgusting
l admiration
m respect
n father
o 'Somebody's Gotta Do It'

Exercise C4

No set answers

Exercise D1

Baggage handler tasks	What makes it a dirty job?
Loading baggage onto aircraft	Can be hot and sweaty
Offloading baggage from aircraft	Luggage travelled many places
Moving baggage to airport carousels	The vehicles they use

Exercise D2

Core

Three baggage handlers needed at Airport Terminal 1. Salary ranges from $10 to $17 per hour. The job offer is part-time or temporary, starting on the 31st of May. It is suitable for students as the work hours are 10 to 15 a week including weekends. Although we do not need academic achievements, we will show preference to applicants with IGCSEs in English and Mathematics. A uniform will be provided due to working conditions being in all types of weather. [80 words]

Extended

At Airport Terminal 1, three baggage handlers are needed for part-time or temporary employment. The payment ranges from $10 to $17 an hour, depending on shift hours, experience and age. It is a job suitable for students due to the working hours being only 10 to 15 hours a week including weekends and nights. All applicants must be fit and healthy due to the lifting and carrying that is involved. No academic qualifications are required, but it is possible preference may be shown to applicants with IGCSEs in English and Mathematics. A uniform will be provided for all weather conditions. [100 words]

Unit 8: Communication

Exercise A1

a   hundreds – 100s
b   one-fifth – 1/5
c   six hundred and eighty – 680
d   three hundred and fourteen thousand per cent – 314 000%
e   thirteenth – 13th
f   thirteen to nineteen – 13–19
g   one million – 1 000 000
h   four hundred and ninety-two – 492
i   sixty-three thousand and sixty-four – 63 064
j   ten – 10

Exercise A2

a   63 064
b   13th
c   680
d   492
e   1 000 000
f   314 000%
g   1/5
h   10
i   100s
j   13–19

Exercise A3

faucet – tap
check – bill
janitor – caretaker
diaper – nappy
license plate – number plate
résumé – CV
zucchini – courgette
zip code – postcode
trashcan – dustbin
sidewalk – pavement
truck – lorry
restroom – bathroom
fall – autumn
cookie – biscuit
gas – petrol

Exercise A4

a   license plate/number plate
b   résumé/CV
c   zip code/postcode
d   fall/autumn
e   faucet/tap
f   zucchini/courgette

Exercise B1

a   true
b   true
c   true
d   false
e   true
f   true
g   false

Exercise B2

a   The world's first known printed book is developed.
b   The first demonstration of an electric telegraph is given by the US inventor Morse.
c   The first personal computer known as 'Apple' is designed.
d   Homing pigeons are used as postmen in Baghdad.
e   A kind of paper made from bamboo is developed by the Chinese.

157

f The first postage stamp <u>is introduced</u> in Britain, called the Penny Black.

g The telephone <u>is invented</u> by an Italian called Marconi.

h The use of the first television <u>is demonstrated</u> in London.

i Writing <u>is developed</u> on clay tablets by the Sumerians.

Exercise B3

a It has been reported that the fire is out of control.

b It is thought that saving money is better than spending it.

c That ugly modern building was built for hundreds of thousands of euros (by the municipality).

d Different public holidays are celebrated (by countries) around the world.

e Another satellite for the weather has been sent up (by NASA).

f The film *The Lord of the Rings* was also enjoyed by people who loved the book.

Exercise B4

a 3100 BC … Writing was developed on clay tablets by the Sumerians.

b 1500 BC … A kind of paper made from bamboo was developed by the Chinese.

c 865 … The world's first known printed book was developed.

d 1050 … Homing pigeons were used as postmen in Baghdad.

e 1838 … The first demonstration of an electric telegraph was given by the US inventor Morse.

f 1840 … The first postage stamp was introduced in Britain, called the Penny Black.

g 1871 … The telephone was invented by an Italian called Marconi.

h 1926 … The use of the first television was demonstrated in London.

i 1976 … The first personal computer known as 'Apple' was designed.

Exercise C1

a abandoned – left alone

b engrossed – very interested in

c manipulated – controlled or influenced

d relentlessly – never ending

e dozen – twelve

f potential – leading to success

g solitude – being alone

h exemplary – excellent

Exercise C2

a true – *I realised it had been months*

b false – *what surprised me was the anger*

c true – *in the hands that we adults should be holding*

Exercise C3

a	dozen	**e**	manipulated
b	engrossed	**f**	exemplary
c	abandoned	**g**	potential
d	relentlessly	**h**	solitude

Exercise C4

a They were engrossed with their own private screen.

b The eyes of the parents are also fixed on their own devices.

c The nursery colours and baby names.

d They are hit by commercialisation.

e Advertising

f Children now interact with their smartphones instead of with their parents.

Exercise D1

Core

Dear Editor,

A great deal has changed since our parents' generation were children, but I believe one of the main advances has been in communication.

The telephone has developed into smartphones which have internet access, GPS; they have become mini computers. Furthermore, because of our unlimited access to the internet, social media has become a hub for us to communicate with friends and family, share our experiences and connect with people all around the globe. Our parents had none of this. They had to wait days for a letter or a postcard from a loved one, phone calls were ridiculously expensive and the only way they could communicate away from home, was through payphones.

There aren't that many differences between the two generations, but communication is definitely something that has developed gigantically over the years, and it will continue to do so.

Yours respectfully,

Marie Moreau [146 words]

Extended

Dear Editor,

Although there is not such a large generation gap between us and our parents, on the topic of communication, I believe that things have changed a great deal over recent years.

My generation has had the luxury of growing up in a time when the development of communications technology has radically evolved within a number of years. Take for example the mobile phone; we are able to communicate today with somebody within seconds through the use of a phone call, a text message, and now with smartphones, even through the internet. Our parents on the other hand, although they had telephones, they could not communicate with someone as they walked down the street or sat on the bus.

Nowadays, we have emails, and social media. We can catch up with anything and anyone within seconds. We no longer have the need for telegrams or letters like our parents did. Our friends and family don't have to wait days in order to receive a postcard from us telling them about our holidays, they can learn about it within an instant because of photos we posted only seconds ago. Everything has become easier, quicker and more widespread.

Yours respectfully,

Marco Verdi [201 words]

Unit 9: Interviews

Exercise A1

a	date	h	stress
b	watch	i	notice
c	referee	j	check
d	order	k	refuse
e	point	l	minute
f	fan	m	strike
g	leave		

Exercise A2

a	fault	d	drawbacks
b	drawback	e	drawback
c	faults	f	fault

Exercise A3

Doer	Recipient
employer	employee
interviewer	interviewee
trainer	trainee
payer	payee
nominator	nominee
adviser	advisee

Exercise A4

a	trainer, trainees	d	employer
b	interviewee(s)/ interviewer	e	nominee
c	payee	f	adviser

Exercise A5

a	CV	d	referees	g	name
b	qualifications	e	skill	h	hobbies
c	interview	f	education		

Exercise B1

Function	Example
A direct order	Come here!
To give instructions	Turn the pages slowly
To make an invitation	Come for dinner
On a sign or notice	Keep out!
To give friendly formal advice	Have a quiet word with her about it
Make an offer	Hello. Have a seat
Give a warning	Careful

Exercise B2

a	Don't wear	f	Be careful
b	Be smart	g	Make sure / tidy up
c	Don't shake	h	Take
d	Try	i	Be polite
e	Look interested	j	Accept

Exercise B3 (Other variations possible)

a   Don't say that you've got no experience.

b   Thank them at the end of the application.

c   Do type it rather than write it.

d   Read the instructions carefully.

e   Write clearly and not in pencil.

f   Complete all sections of the form.

Exercise C1

Speaker 1 – G

Speaker 2 – E

Speaker 3 – C

Speaker 4 – A

Speaker 5 – F

Speaker 6 – D

Exercise D1

I am 16 years old and live at home with my parents and twin sisters in a small village near Firenze in Italy. I am currently studying for my IGCSEs at an international school in Firenze. Because my mum is German, and I grew up learning German at home, I took my German IGCSE a few years ago.

For the past two years I've been helping my dad every Saturday in his workshop in the village. He's a craftsman who designs and builds special furniture. I enjoy working with him, it's like a hobby for me, but I do not want to do the same thing. I'm much more interested in sport.

But my passion is painting, and whenever I have free time, which is not very often, I like to paint buildings. We are lucky because Italy has so many beautiful old buildings and I love to record them in my paintings.

Unit 10: Education

Exercise A1

concentrate	diminishes
prepare	recognition
ignore	recollection
support	retention
understand	interact
examination	concept
homework	formulate
technique	topic
dedicated	cosmopolitan
overwhelming	

Exercise A2

a	dedicated	f	concentrate
b	diminishes	g	overwhelming
c	technique	h	interact
d	recollection	i	cosmopolitan
e	support		

Exercise A3

a	engaged	d	concentrate
b	Concentrate	e	concentrate
c	engaged	f	engage

Exercise A4

Across:

3	study	8	lecture
7	examination	10	homework

Down:

1	college	5	school
2	education	6	teacher
4	uniform	9	notes

Exercise B1 / B2

a present simple/imperative (iv)

b modal + infinitive/present simple (ii)

c present simple/future (vi)

d present simple/present continuous (v)

e present continuous/modal + infinitive (iii)

f imperative/present simple (i)

Exercise B3

a If they <u>don't have</u> time during the week, they'll go to the cinema on Saturday.

b If we leave quietly now, nobody <u>will notice</u>.

c If we <u>had known</u> about your money issues, we would've helped you.

d If I <u>were</u> you, I would not buy those green trousers.

e We <u>would have arrived</u> earlier if we had not missed the train.

f If I didn't have a mobile phone, my life <u>wouldn't be</u> the same.

g That's no problem; <u>I'll get</u> the food if you buy the drinks.

h If I <u>told</u> you something, you would be sure not to tell anybody.

i She <u>would have gone</u> out with you if you had invited her along.

j I wouldn't have read your notes, if you <u>hadn't hidden</u> them in such an obvious place.

Exercise B4

No set answers

Exercise C1

a connected to education – academic

b money you earn – salary

c not enough – short

d costs – expenses

e to begin with – initially

f add – contribute

g good name – reputation

h person who has a university degree – graduate

i rely – depend

Exercise C2 / C3

c not included

Exercise C4

academic [appears in paragraph 5]

salary [4]

short [4]

expenses [3]

initially [3]

contribute [3]

reputation [5]

graduate [3]

depend [3]

Exercise C5

a false

b false

c true

d true

e true

f false

g true

h false

Exercise D1

No set answers

Unit 11: Achievements

Exercise A1

a achievement

b ballet

c equipment

d event

e record

f prevent

g collect

h strangest

i memorabilia

j walking stick

Exercise A2

a dissuade

b explorer

c inhalation

d alternative

e irresponsible

f blizzard

g stumbled

h legible

i rations

j struggled

Exercise A3

a   62.71 kilograms
b   123
c   60 000
d   56.7 °C
e   5.78 seconds
f   14 410
g   23 410
h   33 333

Exercise A4

a   8 hours and 50 minutes
b   1 166 000 tonnes
c $21 787 000
d   86.2
e   150 million
f   8.1
g   157 348 000
h   162 minutes
i $150 000
j   56.3%

Exercise B1

a   That's the saddest film I've ever seen.
b   Is that the tallest building in the world?
c   It's the fastest animal in the world.
d   That's the furthest I've ever run before.
e   Which dress is the most expensive?
f   I think English breakfast tea is the tastiest.
g   Would you carry the heaviest bag, please?
h   I think that is the most beautiful painting.

Exercise B2

a   When she went out to the cinema, she had already done her homework.
b   The cat ate all the chicken that my mum had just cooked.
c   He hadn't been to the countryside before last year.
d   When she arrived at the theatre, the play had already started.
e   They had lived in Italy before they moved to France for good.
f   If you had listened to me, you would have got that job.
g   My brother had got home by the time I arrived.
h   She got really upset when she realised she'd left her laptop on the bus.
i   The children were really hungry because they hadn't eaten for ages.
j   The children hadn't forgotten their teacher's birthday and bought her flowers.

Exercise B3a

In the first part of the sentence the word *kilometre* is being used as an adjective before the word *races* – in other words, it is describing *races*. In the second part, the word is being used as a noun, which is why it is plural *kilometres* after the number 20.

Exercise B3b

i   The box of chocolates weighed 500 grams, but most of that was packaging. (noun)
ii   It was a one-thousand-year-old building. (adjective)
iii The watch cost more than 500 dollars, and it's made of platinum. (noun)
iv   That's a 50-gram piece of gold, but I have no idea of its value. (adjective)
v   He's only 16 years old, but he's already got a place in the first team. (noun)
vi   It was only a 50-dollar ticket, but the service was excellent. (adjective)

Exercise C1

a   Jean-Francois Champollion – **ii** Linguist
b   Wolfgang Amadeus Mozart – **viii** Composed classical music
c   Nadia Comaneci – **v** Olympic gymnast
d   Malala Yousafzai – **i** Campaigns for girls' education
e   Mary Shelley – **iii** / **vii** Author
f   Louis Braille – **iv** Developed reading system for the blind
g   J.R.R. Tolkien – **vii** / **iii** Author
h   Florence Nightingale – **vi** Pioneer and nurse

Exercise C2 / C3 / C4 / C5

No set answers

Exercise C6

a   Louis Braille
b   J.R.R. Tolkien
c   Jean-Francois Champollion
d   Malala Yousafzai
e   Nadia Comaneci
f   Mozart
g   Louis Braille
h   Florence Nightingale
i   Mary Shelley
j   J.R.R. Tolkien

Exercise C7

I really think that Florence Nightingale made the greatest achievements out of all the people listed above. Without her, modern nursing would not be what it is today as she managed to pioneer the way nursing operates today and changed the professional nursing industry for women. Furthermore, in the year of 1860, Florence Nightingale established the first professional nursing school at St Thomas' Hospital in London. This nursing school was the first one of its kind worldwide and it is now part of King's College London. [86 words]

Unit 12: Organisations

Exercise A1

Exercise A2

a	hemisphere	g	Teenagers
b	continents	h	emergencies
c	adventure	i	location
d	expedition	j	environment
e	exploration	k	programme
f	destination	l	organisation

Exercise A3

a	location	d	destination
b	location	e	destination
c	destinations	f	location

Exercise A4

a	bean	e	quest	i	land
b	arch	f	organ	j	sphere
c	rate	g	now		
d	ant	h	act		

Exercise B1

Remember: A non-defining relative clause provides <u>extra information</u> about <u>someone</u> or something. If we <u>remove</u> the non-defining relative clause from a <u>sentence</u>, it will still make <u>sense</u>.

Exercise B2

a They had to feed the poor cat, <u>which stole the little boy's dinner</u>.

b Do you still go to that restaurant, <u>the one which we went to last year</u>?

c There is the woman, <u>who owns the bread shop</u>, but she's obviously not working today.

d <u>To get to Alberto's house</u>, take the road that has lots of tall trees along it.

e The lady who lives next door has offered to look after my house while I'm away.

f Nektarios, <u>who offered to lend me some money</u>, is a great friend.

g I'm looking for the person whose car is blocking mine.

h He received very bad grades for his essays, <u>which he finished quickly</u>.

Exercise B3

a Keeping fit, which should be done regularly, is a very important way to keep healthy.

b Michael went to university in London, where he studied English Literature.

c Michael, who was too poor to pay the fees, had to leave the university.

163

d My grandmother, who goes swimming every day in the lake, is 75.

e The car, which can reach speeds of up to 300 kph, costs $150 000.

f These trousers, which are a lovely dark blue colour, only cost me $15.

Exercise B4

a Incorrect – Neither Sara nor Emily does as they are told.

b Correct

c Incorrect – Either the dogs or the cat have to go.

d Incorrect – Hassan could find the key neither on nor under the mat. / Hassan couldn't find the key either on or under the mat.

e Correct

f Correct

Exercise B5

a either / or

b either / or

c neither / nor

d neither / nor

e either / or

f neither / nor

Exercise C1

a Oncilla – i

b Ocelot – iv

c Jaguar – iii

d Black panther – ii

Exercise C2

a Rescue – **iii** We aim to save many animals in need from sad circumstances, like circuses, captivity and pets.

b Raise awareness – **iv** To educate people worldwide about these animals and to learn to love and respect them and their environments.

c Mexican government – **i** To work with the authorities to keep changing laws in order to protect all species of animals.

d Endangered birds – **ii** As with our avian project, we aim to release the animals into the wild with the help of our supporters and the government.

Exercise C3

a To change people's attitudes and perceptions about animals.

b On a business trip in Mexico.

c Circuses, zoos and homes.

d Birds and dogs.

e Reproduce. Make people fall in love with them. Repopulate areas. Reintroduce the animals into the wild.

f To change laws to protect local species.

g They will be regained.

h If they can be released into the wild.

i They live together whatever the breed.

Exercise C4

No set answers

D Writing

Extended

Recently I had a two-day visit to the Black Jaguar – White Tiger™ Foundation, an organisation which is a leader in wildlife conservation and is passionate about wild animals and their long-term survival. The foundation also rescues animals from many different difficult situations, where they are in danger.

During my visit I learned that we should try to let animals live in places that are similar to their own natural environments, like jungles and forest, instead of keeping them in zoos and circuses where they will be unhappy. Also humans should not interfere too much in animals' lives because we can cause an imbalance in the way the animals live. They are animals not humans.

I think that I would enjoy telling my family and friends about my experience at the foundation and I am planning to do a presentation at my school so that my friends can learn more. Also I am going to write an article with photos for my school website. They need to understand about loving and respecting all living things, and not to treat them like toys. [182 words]

Unit 13: Famous people

Exercise A1

confidence	independence	ambition
dedication	selfishness	optimism
determination	skill	dominance
fearlessness	strength	sociability

Exercise A2

a self-assured – confidence
b loyal – dedication
c stubborn – determination
d cheerful – optimism
e courageous – fearlessness
f self-reliant – independence
g self-centred – selfishness
h controlling – dominance
i experienced – skill
j tough – strength
k determined (to succeed) – ambition
l friendly – sociability

Exercise A3

No set answer

Exercise A4

No set answer

Exercise A5

a ferocious – very fierce
b bewildering – confusing or overwhelming
c prolific – plentiful
d accessible – easily reached or understood
e renowned – well known

Exercise A6

a prolific
b bewildering
c accessible
d ferocious
e renowned

Exercise A7

No set answer

Exercise A8

a problem
b obstacle
c obstacles
d obstacles
e problem
f obstacle

Exercise B1

NOTE: The following are suggested answers but alternative answers are acceptable.

a It is a really expensive holiday; <u>nonetheless</u> they are going for a week.
b They were both invited to the exhibition <u>yet</u> only one of them is going.
c He was very careful with carrying the plates but <u>still</u> he broke five of them.
d The book was really difficult to read; <u>however</u>, she finished it in a week.
e She had just eaten her dinner; <u>nevertheless</u> she also managed to eat a cake.
f <u>Even though</u> she sat and revised for the exam all night, she failed.
g <u>Even though</u> she goes to the gym most days, she has put on so much weight.
h The price for local apples has fallen but <u>the fact</u> is that people are buying imported ones.
i She doesn't like cats very much; <u>however</u>, they've adopted two kittens.

Exercise B2

a aimlessly – adverb
b difficulty – noun
c comply – verb
d apply – verb
e architecturally – adverb
f lively – adjective
g supply – noun
h elderly – adjective
i nastily – adverb

Exercise C1

Felix Baumgartner

The sound barrier

Exercise C2

a Austrian

b skydiver

c sound barrier

d dangerous

e space

f extreme

g capsule

h helium balloon

Exercise C3

a sound barrier – **vii** A sudden increase in air resistance to something nearing the speed of sound.

b helium – **viii** A gas that is lighter than air.

c capsule – **ix** A small part of a spacecraft.

d daredevil – **iii** A reckless and very daring person.

e towed – **iv** Pulled.

f freefall – **x** A fast or continuing drop.

g launch – **vi** To send something into outer space or the air.

h weeping – **ii** Crying.

i famed – **xi** Famous, well known.

j incidents – **xii** Events or occurrences.

k coincidentally – **i** The occurrence of two or more unplanned things at the same time.

l feat – **v** An act or achievement that shows courage, strength or skill.

Exercise C4

a He fell from a height equivalent to almost four times <u>the height of a cruising passenger airliner</u>.

b During the fall, he travelled at an average speed of 1357.64 kilometres <u>per hour</u>.

c <u>He broke</u> the current freefall record.

d Attention was worldwide, with millions watching it <u>online</u>.

e It was the first time his parents had travelled outside <u>Europe</u>.

f He set <u>three</u> other world records.

Exercise C5

a A military parachutist.

b 'before leaping into the record books from a height of…'. He leapt physically from the capsule and in doing so broke the record, so he leapt figuratively into the record books.

c … four times the height of a cruising passenger airliner.

d Joe Kittinger, who set the previous freefall record in 1960.

e US test pilot Chuck Yeager became the first man to officially break the sound barrier aboard an aeroplane.

f He broke the record for the highest manned balloon flight.

g It ended in tragedy when one of the record-breakers drowned on landing.

h It means 'go' (as in a green light).

Exercise D1

Home and education

- born in Salzburg, Austria
- 43 years old
- former military parachutist

Achievements

- broke the world's freefall record
- broke the sound barrier
- during the fall, he managed to travel at an average speed of 1357.64 km/h

Family

- mother and father were with him in New Mexico
- parents have never travelled outside of Europe
- his mother was seen weeping

Core

The topic which today's article will discuss is about a man called Felix Baumgartner. Maybe one should not call him a 'man' but a 'superman'.

Felix Baumgartner is a 43-year-old Austrian, former military parachutist who managed to break the world record for freefall and break the barrier of sound. This incredible species of man who is described as a daredevil managed to reach a speed of 1357.64 kilometres per hour while falling.

While doing this amazing feat however he was not alone. Safe on the stable Earth beneath him were both his parents who travelled all the way to New Mexico with him in order to support him. His mother was seen crying as her son completed this amazing jump.

It is not every day that a human manages to break the barrier of sound and face up to other people's wildest fears. What an incredible man! [149 words]

Extended

Today's article will be all about amazing feats of achievement that humanity has managed to conquer. Take a moment to yourself and try to think of the most amazing thing you have ever done in your life. Whatever it is, I am sure that it cannot compare to the recent achievements of Felix Baumgartner!

Felix Baumgartner, an Austrian former military parachutist, has incredibly managed to break the world's freefall record and also managed to break the sound barrier. One might think that such achievements are only for the young and fearless but no, incredibly, Felix is 43 years old! During the fall, this daredevil man managed to reach speeds averaging around 1357.64 kilometres per hour. To put this speed into perspective, a car can usually reach about 180 kilometres per hour.

Achievements like these usually require a lot of support and Felix's family supported him throughout this extraordinary fall. They travelled with him to New Mexico, where the jump was taking place, even though they had never travelled outside of Europe before. His mother was also seen weeping with worry as this jump was considered a very dangerous one.

Do you think you could ever achieve something like this? I know I could not! [204 words]

Unit 14: Medical care

Exercise A1

Across

2	accident	9	injury
5	medication	10	treatment
7	ambulance		

Down

1	paramedic	6	emergency
3	patient	8	casualty
4	hospital		

Exercise A2

a	b	c	d	e	f	g	h	i	j	k	l	m	n	o
4	10	7	14	11	3	6	12	5	15	8	2	9	13	1

Exercise A3

a	waterborne	f	mature
b	Pedestrians	g	foundations
c	insecure	h	banning
d	academic	i	hygiene
e	priority	j	drought

Exercise A4

a	injuries	d	injured
b	wound	e	wound
c	wound	f	injuries

Exercise B1

The use of **would** as the past tense of **will** is often referred to as 'future in the past'. It is used to express the idea that in the **past** you thought that something else would happen in the **future**. It does not matter if you are correct or not. Both *was/were going to* and the past continuous can be used to express the **future** in the **past**.

167

Exercise B2

a When the doctors heard that Florence Nightingale <u>was going to work</u> (2) with them, they <u>felt threatened</u> (1).

b The doctors <u>felt threatened</u> (1) when they knew <u>she was soon coming</u> (2) to work with them.

Exercise B3

a	were about to	**e**	was planning
b	were going	**f**	send
c	would drive	**g**	would not ask
d	would go	**h**	would pass

Exercise B4

a	practise	**d**	practice
b	practice	**e**	practice
c	practise	**f**	practise

Exercise B5

a	advise	**d**	advised
b	advice	**e**	advise
c	advice	**f**	Advice

Exercise C1

a	i	**f**	i	**k**	ii		
b	iii	**g**	iii	**l**	iii		
c	iv	**h**	i	**m**	iv		
d	i	**i**	ii	**n**	iii		
e	ii	**j**	iii	**o**	iv		

Exercise D1

community nurse – nurse who works in a local area

cultural – to do with the ideas and traditions of a society

specialised in – to focus on a particular subject

experience – knowledge

rewarding – providing satisfaction

orthopaedic – to do with the bones and muscles

mental health – a person's emotional well-being

Exercise D2

a	specialised in	**e**	community nurse
b	mental health	**f**	orthopaedic
c	cultural	**g**	experience
d	rewarding		

Exercise D3

1	C	**4**	B	**7**	B
2	A	**5**	C	**8**	C
3	A	**6**	A		

Unit 15: Healthy living

Exercise A1

a	A <u>cluster</u> of flowers	**i**	honey and <u>ginger</u>
b	Nervous <u>system</u>	**j**	dietary <u>supplement</u>
c	<u>Egyptian</u> hieroglyphs	**k**	intense <u>aromatic</u> flavours
d	Couch <u>potatoes</u>		
e	<u>reduces</u> stress	**l**	perennial <u>plant</u>
f	no pain no <u>gain</u>	**m**	mineral <u>content</u>
g	aesthetic <u>appeal</u>	**n**	nature's <u>pharmacy</u>
h	high blood <u>pressure</u>	**o**	seventeenth <u>century</u>

Exercise A2

a	Perennial plants	**f**	reducing stress
b	dietary supplements	**g**	a cluster of flowers
c	no pain no gain	**h**	nature's pharmacy
d	Egyptian hieroglyphs	**i**	aesthetic appeal
e	couch potatoes	**j**	intense aromatic flavours

Exercise A3

a	correct		the body to allow movement.
b	correct		
c	correct	**e**	incorrect – The stomach is part of the abdomen.
d	incorrect – Joints attach two parts of		

f correct

g incorrect – Hoeing is where you use a garden tool called a hoe to move soil.

h correct

i correct

j incorrect – Leaves grow on the branches of a tree, not its trunk.

Exercise A4

a intensity

b intensity

c strength

d strength

e intensity

f strength

Exercise B1

a a variety of

b a little

c A number of

d a minority of

e a mix of

f a great deal

g A lot of

h a couple of

i plenty of

j a pair of

k several

l the majority of

Exercise B2

No set answers

Exercise B3

Speaker 1

a Admitting the fact that her lifestyle is not very healthy.

b She's not so sure that her lifestyle isn't healthy.

c Too busy – *I guess*.

d That her lifestyle is not so bad as she exercises.

Speaker 2

a Because she mentioned their various activities.

b *Furthermore* ...

Speaker 3

a a factual one

b not agreeing

c accepting

Speaker 4

a an opinion

b herself

Speaker 5

a *I believe / I think*

b *I'm afraid*

Exercise C1

a Asthma is a respiratory condition.

b *Triggers* means things that start or set off an illness or condition.

Exercise C2

a Asthma = 17

b Triggers = 16

Exercise C3

a They are breathing tubes in the lungs.

b No one knows.

c People have different triggers.

d One, two or a dozen.

e Talk to parent or doctor about getting allergy testing.

f Treatment in a hospital or clinic.

g Males 0–14.

h They can affect people who don't have allergies. [Examples will vary.]

i Switch to unscented or non-aerosol version.

j **i** Keep your room clean and dust free.

ii Wash sheets weekly.

iii Get rid of carpets and curtains.

iv Get rid of feather pillows and comforters.

Exercise D1

a Caroline

b Caroline

c George

d Both

e Caroline

f George

g Caroline

Unit 16: Social media

Exercise A1

a   send or <u>receive</u> text messages
b   <u>keep track</u> of appointments
c   <u>play</u> games
d   <u>send</u> emails
e   <u>store</u> contact information
f   <u>download</u> information from the internet
g   <u>watch</u> TV
h   <u>use</u> the built-in calculator
i   <u>take</u> pictures
j   <u>get</u> apps
k   <u>make</u> videos
l   <u>save</u> reminders

Exercise A2

No set answers

Exercise A3

a   abstained
b   compulsively
c   avid multitaskers
d   mind-boggling
e   self-esteem
f   suppressed
g   traits
h   sedentary
i   detrimental
j   profound
k   gauge
l   precursors

Exercise A4

a   sedentary
b   abstained
c   gauge
d   mind-boggling
e   compulsively
f   detrimental
g   precursors
h   multitaskers

Exercise A5

a   depending on
b   According to
c   while
d   while
e   according to
f   Depending on
g   depending on
h   while
i   Depending on

Exercise B1

chatting
texting
taking
using
shocking
spending
stopping

Exercise B2

chat, chatting
lie, lying
take, taking
stop, stopping
use, using

Exercise B3

a   As a verb after a preposition – **iii** After having a shower, I went to bed.
b   As sentence subject – **v** Cooking is one of her favourite hobbies.
c   To list activities – **i** Sewing, knitting, reading – they're all her hobbies.
d   To add information in a clause – **vi** She wandered off, speaking on her phone.
e   In continuous tenses – **iv** They are waiting for the bus in the rain.
f   After certain verbs – **ii** They like watching films at home together.

Exercise B4

No set answers

Exercise C1 / C2

No set answers

Exercise C3

a   It is currently the most successful. **A**
b   It does not appeal as much to young people. **B**
c   About twelve months ago it was most favoured by young people. **B**
d   Presently it is almost equal in popularity. **D**
e   Increased use by older people has made it less trendy. **B**

170

f An alternative and more recent social media. **C**

g It still hasn't reached the level of its main competitor. **A**

h It is connected to one of the main forms of social media. **D**

i This suits a specific market and is becoming popular. **C**

j It had never been the owner's intention for it to be hip. **B**

a true

b true

c true

d true

Exercise C4

a influential

b Not to be outdone

c garnered

d obsessed

e concur

f tool

Exercise C5

a 23 – the percentage of people who rated Facebook as the most influential social media site this year.

b 26 – the percentage of teens who rated Twitter as the 'most important' social media site.

c 23 (again) – the percentage of people who voted Instagram as the 'most important' social media site.

d 12 – the percentage increase in people voting for Instagram.

Unit 17: The environment

Exercise A1

a Beverage

b Biodegradable

c Discarded

d exotic

e Ecology

f bloc

g consensus

h have a glimpse

i curtailed

j vulnerable

k future prosperity

l Fertiliser

Exercise A2

a fertilisers

b exotic

c vulnerable

d discarded

e have a glimpse

f curtailed

g consensus

h biodegradable

Exercise A3

a effect

b affect

c affect

d effect

e affect

f effect

g effect

h affects

Exercise B1

a It seems as though

b seems

c It seems as if

d It seems like

e looks

f It looks as though

g It looks like

h It looks as if

i it looks like

Exercise B2

No set answers

Exercise B3

a hyponatraemia (literally 'low salt')

b a doctor

c the very young and the very old

d the very young and the very old

e people who run for a hobby

f people in nightclubs

g in the nightclubs

h the young woman

i the drinks

Exercise C1

No set answers

Exercise C2

No set answers

Exercise C3

a France – uses a French word / talks about the Seine, a river in Paris

b Peru – the Andean mountains / use of a Spanish word *huaico* / the city of Trujillo

c India – mentions Asia / the Western Ghats, a mountain range in India

d Rwanda – mentions Africa / mentions Kigali

Exercise C4

a true

b false – it's interesting that a lot of youngsters in … either in universities or doing art on the street, want to make a change, but feel stopped by the national government

c true – Africa is one of the most vulnerable continents to climate change

d true

Exercise C5

a That it is high.

b Industrialised nations should be setting an example.

c It used to be dry and hot.

d Because they're against the government.

e Number of rainy days.

f The world's largest and oldest democracies.

g Because Africa only makes a small impact.

h Pollution.

Exercise C6

Possible answers

Main environmental issues in my country

- pollution

- deforestation

How the environment has changed in my country

- many forests being used as land to build houses

- forests being destroyed by fires

What efforts (if any) are being made to improve the environment in my country?

- planting of trees

- preservation and protection of natural landscapes

- public is taking matters into their own hands as the government is not doing enough

- volunteers are cleaning up beaches and forests

Exercise D1

Pollution and *deforestation* in Cyprus are the two main environmental issues in my country.

Today many green areas are being destroyed in order to create land to build houses and many forests are being destroyed by fires.

Some efforts are being made to improve the environment, like planting trees and protecting natural landscapes, but it is not enough. So, people are beginning to take matters into their own hands. People are angry but now they are taking action and so they are planting trees, while volunteers offer to clean beaches and forests from all the rubbish. [96 words]

Unit 18: Hunger

Exercise A1

			c	o	n	**S**	u	m	p	t	i	o	n	
c	o	n	f	e	c	**T**	i	o	n	e	r	y		
	i	n	n	o	v	**A**	t	i	v	e				
	d	i	s	c	a	**R**	d							
		a	l	l	e	**V**	i	a	t	i	n	g		
			d	y	n	**A**	m	i	c					
			b	i	o	**T**	e	c	h	n	o	l	o	g	y
						I	n	v	e	n	t			
			d	i	s	p	**O**	s	e					
				m	a	**N**	i	p	u	l	a	t	e	d

Exercise A2

a alleviating

b discard

c manipulated

d invent

e consumption

f confectionery

g innovative

h dynamic

i biotechnology

j dispose

Exercise A3

inventive

starve

prepared

alleviate

innovative

preparation

concentrate

innovator

innovate

concentrated

starvation

invent

alleviation

alleviated

starving

inventor

prepare

concentration

Noun	Verb	Adjective
alleviation	*alleviate*	alleviated
starvation	starve	starving
preparation	prepare	prepared
Inventor	invent	inventive
concentration	concentrate	concentrated
innovator	innovate	innovative

Exercise A4

a prepared

b concentration

c alleviate

d starvation

e invent

f innovative

g preparation

h starving

Exercise A5

a breath

b breathe

c breathe

d breath

e breath

f breath, breathe

g breathe

h breath

Exercise B1

a iv

b ii

c i

d iii

e vi

f v

Exercise B2

a by way of contrast

b nevertheless

c Consequently

d in addition

e Similarly

f to begin with

g furthermore

Exercise B3

(left–right)

Row 1: c, b, a, e

Row 2: d, g, f

Exercise B4

Variations possible

To begin with, you weigh the ingredients, i.e. flour, yeast, water, etc. First you mix the ingredients well until they form a dough. Secondly, leave the dough to sit until it has doubled in size. Thirdly, work the dough again and put onto a baking tray. Next leave the bread for about 40 minutes for a second rise. After that, put the dough into a hot oven and bake for about 40 minutes and finally remove from the oven and cool.

Exercise C1

a getting it to our shops and kitchens

b 11

c tropical ecosystems near the equator

d agricultural chemicals and polluted waste water

e has an impact on air quality

f fish

g more than half the world's population

h irrigation

173

Exercise C2

No set answers

Exercise C3

a	in favour	d	not in favour
b	not in favour	e	in favour
c	not in favour	f	not in favour

Exercise C4

a	4	c	2	e	3
b	5	d	6	f	1

Exercise D1

Core

Dear Sir / Madam,

I have recently heard about your idea to start cookery lessons at school. I do not believe this is a good idea and it is one I disagree with. I feel this way because I come to school in order to learn things that I would not be able to learn at home.

If I wish to learn how to cook, I will ask my mother or my grandmother. My parents cannot teach me Maths or Physics or foreign languages. School is a place where I come to understand things that will allow me to later go to university or get a degree. I feel that cookery lessons would be wasting the little precious time I have in order to learn the many things I need and that cookery will not help me in any way.

Best wishes,

Marios Genakritos [143 words]

Extended

Dear Sir / Madam,

I recently heard about your idea to introduce cookery lessons to our weekly school schedule and I wish to express my opinion of this. I think it is an excellent idea and I will happily support you with this new lesson.

I believe school is a place where children come to gain knowledge. Knowledge does not only mean learning how to solve mathematical equations and learning a foreign language. Knowledge is also learning about social skills such as making friends and learning how to control your anger and disappointment in difficult situations. Knowledge also means knowing how to live independently from your parents and I believe cookery skills can offer us this.

Being able to cook a few meals is an excellent skill. Providing opportunities such as these also offer enjoyment to children who prefer practical lessons where they are able to use their hands as well as their brains. It is important not to forget that not all children wish to go to university to study an academic degree. What would the world be like without chefs? Once again, I think it is an excellent idea!

Best wishes,

Peter Petroviko [194 words]

Unit 19: Fashions

Exercise A1

a	weave	h	market
b	crop	i	current
c	platform	j	trainer
d	scratch	k	gear
e	shade	l	pet
f	leaves	m	uniform
g	orange		

Exercise A2

a	iv
b	vi
c	v
d	viii
e	i
f	ii
g	vii
h	x
i	ix
j	xi
k	iii
l	xii

Exercise A3

a an atmosphere of pride

b ethnic minority groups

c avoid ridicule

d academic results

e alternative styles

f ethical fashion

g design and engineering

h latest gear

i erase their individuality

j sweeping the nation

k designer fashions

l peer-pleasing designs

Exercise A4

a global   **c** world   **e** global

b global, world   **d** world   **f** world

Exercise B1

a domesticated   **g** global

b mandatory   **h** fermented

c alternative   **i** personal

d fashionable   **j** businesslike

e hand-spun   **k** traditional

f complex   **l** contemporary

Exercise B2

b a mandatory decision

c alternative choice

d fashionable clothes

e hand-spun textile

f a complex crossword

g a global problem

h fermented juice

i a personal issue

j businesslike approach

k traditional practices

l contemporary art

Exercise B3

Variations are possible

adjective + noun

a latest fashion

b exam-style questions

c second listening

verb + adjective

d The cake smells good.

e Your hair looks great.

f Your car is very nice.

Exercise B4

No set answers

Exercise C1

a fibre – a thread from which textile is formed

b spin – turn or whirl round quickly

c thread – a long, thin strand of fibre

d weave – form fabric by interlacing thread

e cloth – a fabric made from wool or cotton

Exercise C2

hood

collar

pocket flap

175

Exercise C3

Variations possible

a What has <u>changed</u> about <u>clothing</u> over the years? A description

b How many <u>basic stages</u> are there in the <u>clothes-making process</u>? List of stages

c What <u>roles</u> do the <u>three partners</u> have? Description

d <u>Where</u> in the new jackets will the <u>earphones</u> be? Location

e What will <u>happen</u> when the <u>phone rings</u>? Event

f <u>How</u> are the phone and the MP3 player <u>controlled</u>? Information about gadget

g <u>Where</u> does Conte <u>get the ideas</u> for his clothes from? Place or event details

h What <u>type of garments</u> form the majority of Conte's collection? Description

i <u>What</u> does Conte hope to include in his <u>future designs</u>? Description

j <u>What</u> would be the <u>two benefits</u> of face-recognition cameras? Information

k <u>Why</u> do you think the interviewer <u>asks</u> if Conte's designs will look fashionable? Reply

Exercise C4

a fibres

b four

c GHK Electrics produces the technology, Conte designs the jackets, the Jeane Company makes them

d built into the hood or collar

e the MP3 player automatically cuts out

f via a hidden keypad

g collected clothes

h military

i face-recognition camera

j information about a person and parents watch their children

k because of all the technology included

Exercise C5

Technology tomorrow – the clothes industry

a Clothes fibres have changed, but clothes-making process is same: spinning, weaving, <u>cutting</u> and <u>sewing</u>.

b Technical clothing to be produced by GHK Electrics and the Jeane Company, range of <u>jackets</u>, designed by Giovanni Conte, and soon available in shops.

c Jackets will have phones with <u>voice-recognition</u> technology, microphone and earphones in hood or <u>collar</u>.

d <u>A keypad</u> controls everything, hidden under pocket flap.

e If dirty, jacket can be washed in <u>machine</u>.

f Conte gets ideas from all over the world, has in excess of <u>50000</u> items in his Bologna studio, which inspire his designs.

g Future designs could include <u>cameras</u> for face-recognition with technology <u>submerged</u> in the fabric, and therefore <u>invisible</u>.

h Clothes will still be <u>fashionable</u> and will not look like clothes from space.

Unit 20: Technology

Exercise A1 / A2

a mobile phone – talking face to face (h)

b internet connectivity – instantaneous and untethered communication (c)

c global positioning system – you will never get lost again (j)

d personal computer – a 30-ton monster (a)

e computer mouse – tail-like cord and round body (g)

f digital camera – information dissemination and communication (b)

g remote control – wirelessly change the TV channel (i)

h microwave oven – modernised the way we eat (d)

i digital music – sound quality and sharing ability (f)

j video camera – news dissemination and recording history (e)

Exercise A3

self-lacing trainers	aerial wind turbines	smart fridges	airport control centres
tightens the shoe	*electricity*	connected food	latest radar technology
reduce slippage	clean solution	technology	highest level of connectivity
sharpen concentration	off shore and underwater	brightly coloured	operate on time
best fit	wind farms	recipes	

Exercise A4

a   a team of engineers = iv airport control centres

b   above the clouds = ii aerial wind turbines

c   battery that lasts for about two weeks = i self-lacing trainers

d   biometric data = i self-lacing trainers

e   correct cooking time = iii smart fridges

f   embedded wifi = iii smart fridges

g   floor-to-ceiling radar screen = iv airport control centres

h   plus and minus buttons on the side = i self-lacing trainers

i   six megawatts = ii aerial wind turbines

j   the supermarket aisle = iii smart fridges

k   underwater noise = ii aerial wind turbines

Exercise A5

Variations possible

Text i

I can't imagine how much it would cost to buy a pair of shoes like this. I wonder how long they would last compared to a normal pair of trainers, including the battery, which you have to buy every two weeks. I think shoes like this are unnecessary and how long will the buttons on the side last?

Text ii

These sound great as a clean solution but what really worries me, and I think we haven't been told the whole story, is the impact on the environment. These wind turbines are huge and stretch above the clouds and downwards, so animals are going to be affected by them in some way.

Exercise A6

a   internal

b   inside

c   inside

d   internal

e   internally

f   inside

g   inside

h   internal

Exercise B1

a   tightens

b   loosens

c   is building

d   tend

e   are

f   will tell

g   is

h   monitors

Exercise B2

Variations possible

a   Even the most advanced technology in the world <u>will have faults in it</u>.

b   Several hundred years in the distant past <u>people had simpler lives</u>.

c   Once you and your family members <u>used to live without any technology</u>.

d   In many different ways our lifestyles <u>are more complex now</u>.

e   Thanks to the great inventors of the past and present, <u>our lives have improved immensely</u>.

f   The whole concept of life on other planets <u>is an exciting one</u>.

Exercise B3

Variations possible

a   Both Chas and Audrey <u>will be coming tonight</u>.

b   Honey as well as ginger <u>are excellent for your health</u>.

c   Neither mobile phones nor digital cameras <u>will ever be that cheap</u>.

d   Either the manager or the team leader <u>will have to attend the meeting</u>.

e   Neither video conferencing nor internet connectivity <u>will replace human contact</u>.

f   Either mobile phones or tablets <u>will not exist in the future</u>.

Exercise B4

a   I don't have a problem if

b   I don't even think that

c   But I believe that

d   And the great thing is

e   What's not to like about

f   The point nowadays is that

g   I can't think of

Exercise C1

a   App 8

b   App 6

c   App 3

d   App 10

e   App 2

f   App 9

g   App 1

h   App 5

i   App 4

j   App 7

Exercise C2

a	3	e	10	i	2
b	5	f	9	j	1
c	8	g	4		
d	7	h	6		

Exercise D1

Hakan: App 4 and App 10

Gamze: App 3 and App 8

Exercise E1

No set answers

Exercise E2

Core

Hi Alexandra,

Last week my classmates and I went to Limassol for a school trip that was based around using new technology in order to get to know your city better.

The point of the trip was to use a new app called 'Find your city' which lets you visit all the places tourists wouldn't normally get to see. It was great!

The app works by letting people who already live in the city post places that you wouldn't necessarily find in guidebooks. They put up all their favourite restaurants and bars, as well as things like unknown museums and little parks that are hidden away in the backstreets.

Next time we go somewhere new together we have to make sure that we use it. It's such a great idea and I loved using it!

Hope to speak to you soon,

Alekka. [142 words]

Extended

Hi Michalis,

We recently visited a castle in the town where I went with the school. The castle was the biggest I've ever been to and I was so excited to go there. Because not many of us wanted to visit the castle, we were given some money where we could download an app at the castle in our language. This app spoke to us over our mobile phone on loudspeaker and took us all over the inside of the castle to the beautiful rooms and into the gardens explaining all the different things and places there. It was great and I learnt so much. The good thing was, we could take our time and go to the places that we wanted; so if there were a lot of people in one place, we went back there later and found a quieter place instead. Even when we had lunch we were told about the sort of food people ate in those days and how it was cooked. It was great and I would love to spend another day there going to the places I didn't have time to visit.

Want to come with me next time?

See you around.

Sanjit [200 words]

Acknowledgements

We are grateful to the CATS School, Cambridge and Cambridge International School for granting permission to film.

Terms and conditions of use

This is a legal agreement between 'You' (which means the individual customer or the Educational Institution and its authorised users) and Cambridge University Press ('the Licensor') *for Cambridge IGCSE English as a Second Language Teacher's Resource*. By placing this DVD in the DVD-ROM drive of your computer, You agree to the terms of this licence.

1 Limited licence

a   You are purchasing only the right to use the DVD-ROM and are acquiring no rights, express or implied, to it, other than those rights granted in this limited licence for notfor-profit educational use only.

b   The Licensor grants You the licence to use one copy of this DVD-ROM.

c   You shall not: **(i)** copy or authorise copying of the DVD-ROM, **(ii)** translate the DVD-ROM, **(iii)** reverse-engineer, alter, adapt, disassemble or decompile the DVD-ROM, **(iv)** transfer, sell, lease, lend, profit from, assign or otherwise convey all or any portion of the DVD-ROM or **(v)** operate the DVD-ROM from a mainframe system, except as provided in these terms and conditions.

d   Permission is explicitly granted for use of the DVD-ROM on a data projector, interactive whiteboard or other public display in the context of classroom teaching at a purchasing institution.

e   If You are an Educational Institution, once a teacher ceases to be a member of the Educational Institution, all copies of the material on the DVD-ROM stored on his/her personal computer must be destroyed and the DVD-ROM returned to the Educational Institution.

f   You are permitted to print reasonable copies of the printable resources on the DVD-ROM. These must be used solely for use within the context of classroom teaching at a purchasing institution.

2 Copyright

a   All original content is provided as part of the DVD-ROM (including text, images and ancillary material) and is the copyright of the Licensor or has been licensed to the Licensor for use in the DVD-ROM, protected by copyright and all other applicable intellectual-property laws and international treaties.

b   You may not copy the DVD-ROM except for making one copy of the DVD-ROM solely for backup or archival purposes. You may not alter, remove or destroy any copyright notice or other material placed on or with this DVD-ROM.

3 Liability and Indemnification

a   The DVD-ROM is supplied 'as is' with no express guarantee as to its suitability. To the extent permitted by applicable law, the Licensor is not liable for costs of procurement of substitute products, damages or losses of any kind whatsoever resulting from the use of this product, or errors or faults in the DVD-ROM, and in every case the Licensor's liability shall be limited to the suggested list price or the amount actually paid by You for the product, whichever is lower.

b   You accept that the Licensor is not responsible for the availability of any links within or outside the DVD-ROM and that the Licensor is not responsible or liable for any content available from sources outside the DVD-ROM to which such links are made.

c   Where, through use of the original material, You infringe the copyright of the Licensor, You undertake to indemnify and keep indemnified the Licensor from and against any loss, cost, damage or expense (including without limitation damages paid to a third party and any reasonable legal costs) incurred by the Licensor as a result of such infringement.

4 Termination

Without prejudice to any other rights, the Licensor may terminate this licence if You fail to comply with the terms and conditions of the licence. In such an event, You must destroy all copies of the DVD-ROM.

5 Governing law

This agreement is governed by the laws of England, without regard to its 'conflict of laws' provision, and each party irrevocably submits to the exclusive jurisdiction of the English courts. The parties disclaim the application of the United Nations Convention of the International Sale of Goods.